LEPAM

# HOW SOCIAL SECURITY WORKS

## An introduction to benefits in Britain

Paul Spicker

This edition published in Great Britain in 2011 by

The Policy Press
University of Bristol
Fourth Floor
Beacon House
Queen's Road
Bristol BS8 1QU
UK

t: +44 (0)117 331 4054
f: +44 (0)117 331 4093
tpp-info@bristol.ac.uk
www.policypress.co.uk

North American office:
The Policy Press
c/o International Specialized Books Services
920 NE 58th Avenue, Suite 300
Portland, OR 97213-3786, USA
t: +1 503 287 3093 • f: +1 503 280 8832 • info@isbs.com

British Library Cataloguing in Publication Data
A catalogue record for this book is available from the British Library.

Library of Congress Cataloging-in-Publication Data
A catalog record for this book has been requested.

ISBN 978 1 84742 810 3 paperback
ISBN 978 1 84742 811 0 hardcover

Cover design by Qube Design Associates, Bristol
Front cover: image kindly supplied by Paul Green
Printed and bound in Great Britain by Hobbs, Southampton
The Policy Press uses environmentally responsible print partners

# Contents

# List of tables and figures

## Tables

## Figures

# About the author

Paul Spicker holds the Grampian Chair of Public Policy at the Robert Gordon University, Aberdeen. His research includes studies of poverty, need, disadvantage and service delivery; he has worked as a consultant for a range of agencies in social welfare provision. In 2007 he was a special adviser to the House of Commons Work and Pensions Committee for their report on benefits simplification. His books include:

*Stigma and social welfare* (Croom Helm, 1984)
*Principles of social welfare* (Routledge, 1988)
*Social housing and the social services* (Longmans, 1989)
*Poverty and social security: Concepts and principles* (Routledge, 1993)
*Planning for the needs of people with dementia* (with D S Gordon, Avebury, 1997)
*Social protection: A bilingual glossary* (co-editor with J P Révauger, Mission-Recherche, 1998)
*Social policy in a changing society* (with Maurice Mullard, Routledge, 1998)
*The welfare state: A general theory* (Sage Publications, 2000)
*Policy analysis for practice: Applying social policy* (The Policy Press, 2006)
*Liberty, equality, fraternity* (The Policy Press, 2006)
*Poverty: An international glossary* (co-editor with S Alvarez Leguizamon and D Gordon, Zed, 2007)
*The idea of poverty* (The Policy Press, 2007)
*Social policy: Themes and approaches* (The Policy Press, 2008)
*The origins of modern welfare* (Peter Lang, 2010).

# Preface

*How social security works* is concerned with how the system of benefits is put together, what it does and how it does it. The book tries to explain the shape of the social security system, to explain how benefits are provided and to give readers an understanding of the key issues. The approach is founded in Social Policy and Administration. The subject was developed for the purposes of training people who would work in the social services. People who are doing that sort of training could be following a variety of different courses. Some will be taking professional qualifications, like social work, housing management and health studies; some will be doing other courses in further education, like certificates in Health and Social Care; and some will be studying the subject as part of a degree in Social Policy, Public Policy, Social Work or Law.

The book offers an outline of benefits, rather than a detailed analysis. Before it is possible to understand the system in greater depth, students need to put together a mental map of the field. This should make it possible to go on to read other texts in the subject with enough background to make sense of them. It also implies, necessarily, that some substantial topics have to be dealt with briefly. If you are looking at a map of Europe, London will be little more than a blob, and if you are looking at a map of benefits, the Social Fund is not going to loom as large as it often seems to welfare rights officers.

I have not attempted to summarise research in the field, because it would divert from the purpose of the book. Much of the empirical research currently being done reflects the agenda of governments, focusing on issues like transitions to work. Academic studies have tended to focus on issues that cast light on social science: sociologists are particularly interested in work, gender and inequalities, economists in distributive issues and incentives. Few writers seem to be interested in social security in its own right: there is precious little being produced on the design, management, operation and delivery of benefits. Currently, there are two main types of basic text in the field. On one side, there are some useful texts in this field that discuss social security policy, such as those edited by John Ditch or Jane Millar.[1] This book is more concerned with basic information than either of them, and it should be helpful as an introduction. On the other, there are books that explain the law and rules by which benefits operate, of which the best is the Child Poverty Action Group's *Welfare benefits*

---

[1]  J Ditch (ed) (1999) *Introduction to social security*, London: Routledge; J. Millar (ed) (2008) *Understanding social security*, Bristol: The Policy Press.

*and tax credits handbook.*[2] This can be difficult to get to grips with; an outline like this should help to give some shape for an understanding of the material.

The book's aims are modest, then, but they are not easy to meet. The first problem is that the system is, frankly, baffling. You might as well try to make sense of the telephone book – the main legal text on *Social security legislation* has nearly 6,000 pages,[3] and even the CPAG guide has started to list the classes of benefit in alphabetical order. I have tried to get around the problems partly by trying to structure the material thematically, and partly by dealing with the material very selectively. To cover the range of topics, I have written the book in 27 short chapters. The selection is based on what is needed to support that structure, but I have also tried to include material that will help to make sense of the system in practice. There is a limit to how clear it is possible to make things – the structure of benefits does not make sense, some of the areas covered are not well supported by the literature and any book that made it all seem coherent and rational would not be doing justice to the topic.

The second problem is that the things which are important in principle are not always the things which matter in practice (and vice versa). The book is practically oriented – as you might expect from a book with the title *How social security works* – but that phrase is interpreted in fairly general terms. It is intended to give an understanding of what social security benefits do, how they do it and how they fit together, rather than the more specific questions that need to be addressed for welfare rights. If you want to make sense of the system, you need to understand concepts like residual and institutional welfare, the structure of National Insurance, and means testing. All of those are covered in this book. If you are advising or working with claimants, or if you are a claimant yourself, you need to know quite different information. For example, the rules on backdating are complex and thorny, despite the government's attempt to wipe them away,[4] and many if not most advisers will have had a problem relating to late claims at some point. In this book, I only have one sentence on late claims (apart from the last one). The book offers some foundations for later learning; I think it will be interesting for welfare rights workers, and I hope for some claimants; but it is not a book about welfare rights in practice.

Third, social security changes with alarming rapidity. Even recent figures refer to a clutch of benefits that no longer exist in the same form – benefits like Family Credit, Working Families Tax Credit, Severe Disablement Allowance and the Minimum Income Guarantee. Any discussion of policy in this field has

---

[2]   Child Poverty Action Group (2010) *Welfare benefits and tax credits handbook 2010/2011*, London: CPAG.

[3]   D Bonner (ed) (2009) *Social security legislation 2009/10*, London: Sweet and Maxwell.

[4]   M Rowland and R White (2009) *Social security legislation 2009/10, volume III: Administration, adjudication and the European dimension*, London: Sweet and Maxwell, p 418.

to refer to measures that do not exist any more; descriptions are like a ride on a ghost train, where long dead spectres keep jumping out at you. In the hope that it will be helpful, I have put the names of old and obsolete provisions in a grey font like this. It should be fairly obvious, in the sections about the ancient history of the subject, that I am referring to obsolete provisions (even if it does seem at times that politicians need to be reminded that the Poor Law is no longer in force). It is not so obvious when I get on to discussions of more recent benefits, and the labelling should help. That still leaves scope for confusion about some important developments. Incapacity Benefit is being replaced by Employment and Support Allowance, but the change is taking place gradually. Severe Disablement Allowance was closed to new claims in 2001, but there are still a quarter of a million recipients. The abolition of Income Support, which used to be one of the most important benefits in the system, is going to be done partly through transferring its functions to other benefits, and partly through transitional arrangements that have yet to be determined. The spectral wraith may be haunting us for years to come.

A lot of the knowledge in the field is disposable. People who work in this field for any length of time find that their knowledge becomes not just outdated, but dangerous. My head is cluttered with old rules and regulations dating back through the last thirty-five years, which helps to give me some perspective on policy but also makes me disturbingly unreliable about welfare rights. Referring to older rules increases the depth of the coverage, and it helps to explain what some rather complicated rules are about, but it also reduces its direct application. When that is combined with the rapidly changing rules, there is always a risk of error. Nothing in the book should be taken as a statement of current law.

The book has some features that I hope will help to make it more useful as a student text. There are brief outlines of the content at the beginning of each chapter. There are several boxes containing short outlines of the workings of some of the more complex benefits. For those who relate better to graphics, I have drawn a few timelines, laid out in 'swim lanes', to show how benefits have developed in certain areas. At the end of each chapter, there are questions for discussion, of a kind that might be helpful in university seminars. The questions are simply put, but they are difficult to resolve: there is no 'right answer'. I have, however, held the use of current statistics to a minimum; they change so rapidly that, in a very short time, they would make the book less useful rather than more. A guide to sources at the end of the book gives readers a guide as to where current information can be found. A companion website, accessible via www.policypress.co.uk, provides regular updates to the material in this book and is suitable for lecturers and students.

Some small parts of this book are based on material I have previously published in different places:

- Chapter 13, 'Understanding complexity', is taken from 'Five types of complexity', *Benefits*, February 2005
- Chapters 15, 'Benefits for people with disabilities', and 16, 'Incapacity', both include material taken from 'Distinguishing disability and incapacity', *International Social Security Review*, 2003, vol 56, no 2, pp 31-43
- Chapter 24, 'Responding to poverty', is drawn from *Poverty and the welfare state*, London: Catalyst, 2002

I owe thanks for comments to Geraldine Wooley, Peter McLaverty, Nicola Livingston, Jane Fong, Rebecca Mair, John MacKendrick and Maggie Kelly. I want to make special mention too of Kim Eberst, a welfare rights officer from Dundee, who was an enthusiastic supporter of the book from the outset and read it in draft at two stages. Kim sadly died in an accident just as the book was being prepared for typesetting, and I'd like to dedicate the book to her memory.

*Paul Spicker*
*October 2010*

# Part I

## Introduction:
## social security benefits in principle

# Chapter 1

# What is social security?

Social security is often written about as if it was only concerned with the relief of poverty; many of the key debates are about how to do that more effectively. However, social security is provided for many other reasons: they include prevention, social protection, redistribution and economic policy, as well as economic and social measures intended to benefit society as a whole. Further aims include compensation, income smoothing and the promotion of solidarity. There is much more to benefits than providing a safety net, or getting people back to work.

## The idea of social security

In Britain, the term 'social security' is a term used for income maintenance provided by the state. 'Income maintenance' is the provision of financial resources when personal income is interrupted or insufficient. The social security system is mainly made up of benefits administered by the Department for Work and Pensions – such as Retirement Pension and Jobseeker's Allowance, and a suite of benefits run by Her Majesty's Revenue and Customs (the UK tax authority), including Child Benefit, Child Tax Credit and Working Tax Credit. Other benefits, including Housing Benefit and Council Tax Benefit, are administered by local authorities.

This description of the social security system is fairly conventional, and like many conventional classifications it does not really stand up to close examination. The first question is: what are financial resources? Does a benefit cease to be social security if people get the goods rather than the money? In many other countries, social security includes a range of activities well beyond financial support, including health care; but few people in Britain would think of the National Health Service as a form of income maintenance, because that is not how the health care system works here. Payments for social care, which have not been included in this book, are not currently classified as social security benefits. At the same time, several benefits which provide goods, rather than money, are treated as social security: examples are milk supplements and vitamins for expectant mothers, free school meals and school clothing vouchers. These are referred to as benefits 'in kind',[1] but it is very unclear why they are classified differently from the provision of services such as medical care or nursing.

---

[1] See, for example, M Rein (1983) 'The design of in-kind benefits', in M Rein, *From policy to practice*, London: Macmillan

Is every form of income maintenance a form of social security? In Britain, the payment of rent is treated as social security, but it has been treated as part of the housing budget in the past, and the payment for support from housing management may be treated as social care. Legal aid is provided for people who cannot afford to take legal action, but that is not generally thought of as a social security benefit. Fiscal welfare provisions – tax reliefs and allowances – are a form of financial support, but usually they are left out of the assessment. Agricultural subsidies are not usually thought of as social security in the UK, though they might be in other places – arrangements in Finland and Greece have put agricultural compensation together with social insurance for farmers.[2] The leading legal textbook on social security in Britain states confidently that Child Tax Credit is a social security benefit, while Working Tax Credit is not; but the two benefits are administered in tandem, and it is very difficult to tell the difference between them.[3]

Is it essential that social security benefits should be provided by the state? In continental Europe, similar arrangements are used to provide benefits by non-state organisations: the system of pensions in France is administered in large part by a complex network of autonomous funds, while unemployment benefit is the responsibility of a convention agreed between employers and workers. Few people in the UK would think of insurance for mortgage protection or funerals as social security, but it takes very little to see privately funded arrangements in that light; several countries have built their national systems on the basis of voluntary contributions. Conversely, transferring the operation of benefits from the state to private organisations does not mean that social security has ceased to exist. Before 1983, the National Insurance system offered Sickness Benefit to workers whose work was interrupted by sickness. Sickness Benefit was largely replaced by Statutory Sick Pay, which is paid by the employer. One way to explain this is to say that SSP has been taken out of the remit of the social security scheme; another, that employers have been co-opted into the scheme. This sort of co-option is commonplace in other fields - for example, the administration of tax by employers - and it is questionable whether a different method of service delivery implies any major difference in principle.

Much of the way we think about social security comes from our particular history, not from any obvious reasoning about the subject. For a British reader, social security is a national system, part of the welfare state set up after the Second World War. If it was part of that system, like Retirement Pension, Industrial Injuries Benefit or Unemployment Benefit, it was social

---

[2] European Commission (2006) *Agricultural insurance schemes*, annexes 8 and 12 (http://ec.europa.eu/agriculture/analysis/external/insurance/).

[3] N Wikeley, D Williams, I Hooker (2009) *Social security legislation 2009/10, volume IV: Tax credits and HMRC-administered social security benefits*, London: Sweet and Maxwell, pp 110-11.

security. If it was not part of the system, like occupational pensions, life insurance or compensation in the courts, it was not social security. People from different countries understand the basic concepts differently. In the United States, social security usually means the social insurance system introduced in the 1930s by the Roosevelt administration, which covers old age, survivors, disability and sickness; other forms of income maintenance are 'welfare'. In Mexico, social security for families includes day care for pre-school children. In France, *la Sécu* means health insurance to most people, and unemployment benefits are outside the government's social security system altogether. The definition of social security seems to reflect the administrative arrangements, rather than any common understanding of what social security is meant to do.

## Reasons for providing social security

Social security is provided for many reasons. The system of government has been central to the development of social security in Britain, so most of those reasons reflect in some sense the policies of governments past and present, but the provision of social security also reflects the influence of other groups, like employers, the labour movement and the friendly societies. This section looks at the aims most commonly attributed to social security benefits.

The first is *the relief of poverty*. For many people in Britain, this seems to be the most basic function of the social security system, though as I shall explain, it is not necessarily the main one. The relief of poverty is important partly because it has been highly influential in the development of benefits, but also because people from all shades of the political spectrum think that benefits ought to be about the relief of poverty. People who support the benefits system are critical when benefits fail to relieve people's poverty. People who oppose the benefits system tend to be critical when benefits are wasted, as they see it, by spending money on others who are not poor. Both these positions depend on the assumption that the relief of poverty is what benefits are supposed to do. That may be true, and it may not. Income Support was specifically geared to people who are on low incomes, which is not quite the same thing as poverty; others, like the State Pension or Jobseeker's Allowance, are not only available to people who are poor, but cover circumstances in which people might otherwise be likely to be poor; and some, like War Pensions or the universal pension for people over 80, do not have much to do with poverty at all. (There are some relatively marginal benefits which I think can be argued to be directed towards 'the poor', like parts of the Social Fund and discretionary payments in social work. I discuss these in Chapter 21.)

In historical terms, the benefits system was not intended principally to relieve poverty. On the contrary, it was based in an attempt to break away from the relief of poverty, the principle which had dominated the provision of welfare for 350 years.[4] This is part of a much broader set of issues, and I will deal with it the course of this book. For the moment, all that it is necessary to say is that the reasons which follow are different types of reason for social security, and that if they apply, they imply other kinds of provision than the relief of poverty alone.

A second reason for providing benefits is the *prevention of poverty*. Poor relief is supposed to mean that poor people have resources despite their poverty; 'relief' implies that their resources will be brought up to a minimum level. Preventing poverty calls for more than a minimal safety net. If people become sick or unemployed, they should not, the argument goes, have to lose their possessions or sell their homes as a result. One sometimes hears the comment that 'people on benefit have cars and television sets', as if this was somehow reprehensible. The question is whether they should be forced to sell their car or television before they can receive benefit. If the intention is to avoid people becoming poor, they should not.

This shades into a third reason, which is at least as important as the first two. Benefits are basic to *social protection*. The very idea of 'social security' implies that people ought to be able to feel secure. Security involves not just being protected against poverty, but also being protected or insured against the eventualities that are likely to arise through a sudden change in circumstances. Social protection is the most important principle in much of continental Europe: there may be holes in their safety nets, but most workers will be protected in the event of old age, sickness and unemployment. For the United Nations, 'Social protection refers to policies designed to reduce people's exposure to risks, enhancing their capacity to protect themselves against hazards and loss of income.'[5] The World Bank similarly explains: 'Social Protection interventions assist individual, households, and communities to better manage the risks that leave people vulnerable.'[6]

Social protection includes provision against poverty, and it can be seen as a way of helping to prevent people from becoming poor, but it is a much broader principle than either of those. Insecurity can produce hardship and need, but it is not just poorer people who can benefit from sharing risks. Social protection is supposed to mitigate the effects of drastic changes in people's incomes. It follows that benefits may need to redistribute resources from people in work on low wages to others who may have higher incomes out of work; the cap on household benefits recently introduced by the British government runs directly agains that principle. Benefits may have to pay more to people with more to lose; many

---

[4]  A Briggs (1961) 'The welfare state in historical perspective', *European Journal of Sociology*, vol 2, pp 221-58.

[5]  I Ortiz (2007) *Social policy*, New York: United Nations Department for Economic and Social Affairs (http://esa.un.org/techcoop/documents/PN_SocialPolicyNote.pdf).

[6]  World Bank (2001) *Social protection sector strategy*, Washington, DC: World Bank.

benefit schemes in Europe take contributions according to earnings, and pay earnings-related benefits. If this means that richer people take more out, that is not necessarily a problem; they also have to put more in.

A fourth set of aims relates to *compensation*. People receive compensation – from courts, from employers, from insurers – in many kinds of circumstances, and some of these are reflected in social security systems. Some compensation is for special expenses – the cost of disability or sickness. Some is for personal loss, like industrial injury or war pensions. Some is for the loss of earnings capacity, like the former allowance for reduced earnings in the industrial disablement scheme.[7] The principle of compensation leads to some puzzlingly unequal results: people faced with exactly the same issues and needs will be treated differently if their disability results from an industrial accident, a traffic accident, a domestic accident or a medical intervention. But compensation is still, nevertheless, one of the most firmly established principles in social security across the world, and compensation for industrial injuries was among the earliest provisions to be generally established.

The fifth reason for benefits is *redistribution*, taking money from some people to move to others. Social security might be thought of, not as a form of public spending, but as a 'transfer payment' – moving money from one person to another. This can be done for many reasons, not just to make people richer or poorer, and although it can be seen as an end in itself, attempting to make the distribution of income more just, it can also happen simply because that is what social security has to do. At the simplest level, redistribution is necessary because large numbers of people have very little income, and roughly speaking, the people in the bottom fifth of the income distribution could not live without it.

Redistribution is much more complex than this implies, however. There is vertical redistribution, which goes between rich and poor; it is called 'progressive' if it goes from rich to poor, and 'regressive' if it goes from poor to rich. There is also horizontal redistribution, which goes from people in some kinds of circumstances to others in different circumstances. Jobseeker's Allowance, which goes to people who are not working and on inadequate incomes at the expense of people who are working and paying tax, is progressive. Child Benefit, by contrast, is largely a form of horizontal redistribution, going from people without children to people with children, and from men and single women to others. Chapter 26 considers the distributive effects of the benefits system.

Sixth, there is a process described by Barr as '*income smoothing*', where resources are effectively moved from the times when people are able to earn to those times when they are not.[8] One way of understanding social security is as a form of compulsory saving, which happens most clearly in the operation of

---

[7]   Child Poverty Action Group (2010) *Welfare benefits and tax credits handbook 2010/2011*, London: CPAG, pp 340-4.

[8]   N Barr (1991) 'The objectives of old age pensions', in T Wilson and D Wilson (eds) *The state and social welfare*, London: Longman.

pensions schemes. Another way of understanding the same process is as a form of redistribution across the life cycle.[9] The mechanisms which are used to bring this about are confused, and confusing. Sometimes contributions are paid into a fund, and kept until they are required; that has been the system in relation to occupational and personal pensions, but not state pensions. Sometimes there is a nominal fund, but the accounts are never balanced. Sometimes there is no fund, and benefits are actually paid for by people currently in work. The 'National Insurance Fund' is not really a fund; it is an annual account, more or less equivalent to taxation.

What most of the reasons mentioned have in common that they are concerned with the circumstances of people who receive the benefits. The last of these understandings of social security points in another direction. The level of savings and the management of resources over time are not just matters for the individual; they are also issues in economic management. The seventh principle that guides social security, then, is *economic policy*. There is a naive view in some quarters that spending on social security is bad for the economy. There is no evidence to suppose that this is true; nor is there much evidence to support the contrary argument. Social security spending tends to be higher in richer countries, but that is because they have more money to spend. Within the industrialised countries, however, there is no clear association between social security spending and economic performance.[10] What is true is that social security provision, in every industrial country, is very substantial. It affects the economy, for good or for ill. Saving, investment and wage rates are crucial elements in economic management, and social security regulates the way in which these occur. One view of pensions, for example, is that they are a form of compulsory saving (and occupational pension schemes, which invest the capital funds, are the largest bloc of investors on the stock market). Governments cannot ignore the economic impact of social security, and considerations of economic management cannot sensibly be divorced from decisions about benefits.

Economic management is an example of using social security, not just for the benefit of the recipient, but to achieve social objectives. The eighth reason for developing social security is that it is used *to shape people's behaviour*. This is often dressed up as an economic argument, in the form of a discussion about 'incentives'. This is a complex subject, which I will return to, but 'incentives' are not just about how people respond economically. Incentives are used to change the way

---

[9] J Falkingham, J Hills and C Lessof (1995) *William Beveridge versus Robin Hood: Social security and redistribution over the lifecycle*, London: London School of Economics Welfare State Programme.

[10] A B Atkinson (1995) 'The welfare state and economic performance', in A B Atkinson, *Incomes and the welfare state*, Cambridge: Cambridge University Press.

that people behave, by rewarding some behaviours and discouraging others.[11] If we want people to stay on at school, to leave the labour market, to look after children, to work for more or less of their lives, social security provisions are used to guide and steer the pattern of behaviour. It may not work – France has been trying, without success, to use social security benefits to encourage women to have more children for much of the last eighty years[12] – but social security does, at least, play a part in such attempts. The principle of affecting behaviour extends further, because sometimes rewards and punishments are thought of as desirable in themselves, as a moral judgement on people's actions. An example is the Child Support, Pensions and Social Security Act 2000, which made social security for offenders conditional on compliance with the terms of a community sentence.[13]

All of the aims and approaches considered so far have been about government. They are the kinds of reasons why governments should be involved in social security provision, and they give a sense of the kind of things that they want to achieve by doing it. But social security is not only made by governments; indeed, in much of Europe, governments came to the issue rather late in the day. Social security grew from traditions of mutual support, based partly in a desire for social protection and partly out of a sense of mutual responsibility.[14] The ninth reason given for providing social security is usually referred to as the principle of *solidarity*. This term is rarely used in Britain, but it is frequently found in texts on social security throughout Europe.[15] Social security is seen not as charity, nor as government intervention, but as a form of mutual cooperation. For some, solidarity refers to mutual aid and pooled resources: people put their funds together in order to protect themselves and others from socially recognised risks. This is the principle behind private insurance, and it applies no less to social insurance (which in many countries began through the development of mutual aid).

The idea of solidarity is used not just to refer to mutual aid, but to think about social organisation. A society can be seen as a system of networks of solidarity: people who are part of those networks are said to be included, while those who are not part of them are excluded. The tenth reason for developing social security is, then, *promoting social cohesion*. The provision of social security

---

[11] P Spicker (2006) 'Understanding incentives', annexure 1 in M Steele (ed) *Report on incentive structures of social assistance grants in South Africa*, South Africa: Republic of South Africa Department of Social Development.

[12] R Lenoir (1991) 'Family policy in France since 1938', in J Ambler (ed) *The French welfare state*, New York: New York University Press ; L King (1998) 'France needs children', *Sociological Quarterly*, vol 39, no 1, pp 33-52.

[13] G McKeever (2004) 'Social security as a criminal sanction', *Journal of Social Welfare and Family Law*, vol 26, no 1, pp 1-16.

[14] P Baldwin (1990) *The politics of social solidarity*, Cambridge: Cambridge University Press.

[15] P Spicker (2006) *Liberty, equality, fraternity*, Bristol: The Policy Press, part 3.

is represented as part of the glue that brings a society together. In Catholic social teaching, solidarity is seen as a central principle governing the relationship of people to others in society.[16] Solidarity is not, simply self-interested: it extends to redistribution because of moral obligations. This principle is extended to the rest of the welfare state.

These ten principles are probably the most important, but this is not a complete list. Others will be considered in the course of the book, especially when we get to more complex issues like provision for disability. There is much more to social security than the relief of poverty. It has been common for books about social security to focus on the issue of poverty, but poverty is not the only test of social security – or even the most appropriate one. Equally, the suggestion in the Freud review that benefits are basically about providing a safety net, or getting people back to work,[17] seems very superficial. Benefits are about much more than that.

## QUESTIONS FOR DISCUSSION

What are the other reasons, besides those in this chapter, why social security is offered? What is the difference between social security and economic support for other activities, like farming or industrial subsidies?

---

[16] N Coote (1989) 'Catholic social teaching', *Social Policy and Administration*, vol 23, no 2, pp 150-60.

[17] D Freud (2007) *Reducing dependency, increasing opportunity*, London: Department for Work and Pensions.

---

# Chapter 2

# Social security and the welfare state

The idea of the 'welfare state' is used to represent a model in which the state accepts responsibility for the welfare of its citizens. The core debate lies between an 'institutional' model, which offers welfare to everyone as a right, and a 'residual' model, which provides welfare only when other means fail. This is often translated into a debate between 'universal' benefits, which go to broad categories of people, and 'selective' ones, which are reserved for poorer people or people in need. The general sense that benefits should be provided as of right has eroded, and there is an increasing emphasis on the responsibilities, as well as the rights, of citizenship.

The idea of the 'welfare state' is used in different senses. It can mean, simply enough, the provision of welfare by a government; this is the sense in which the term is mainly used in the United States.[1] It can refer, as it does in most of Europe, to a collection of services delivered not just by the state but by a range of independent and voluntary providers. The term is also used, though, to refer to an ideal model of welfare, in which the state accepts responsibility for the welfare of its citizens. Asa Briggs, in a classic essay on the British welfare state, founded after the Second World War, identified three core elements. These were:

- a guarantee of minimum standards, including a minimum income,
- the offer of social protection for a range of contingencies;
- the provision of welfare at the best level possible.[2]

This contrasted sharply with the system which came before it, a system which was based on a minimal commitment, reserved for those who were unable to cope in any other way.

## Residual and institutional models of welfare

The distinction between the welfare state and the Poor Law, the system that came before it, is basic to understanding contemporary approaches to welfare. The concepts were formalised by Wilensky and Lebeaux as 'residual' and 'institutional'

---

[1]  For example, T Marmor, J Mashaw and P Harvey (1990) *America's misunderstood welfare state*, New York: Basic Books.

[2]  A Briggs (1961) 'The welfare state in historical perspective', *European Journal of Sociology*, vol 2, pp 221-58.

models of welfare.[3] Residual welfare sees welfare as a safety net, which is only for those people who need it. This is often linked with the idea of 'dependency' and the 'dependency culture',[4] ideas that condemn income maintenance as something which undermines individual responsibility and competence. Certainly, the kind of residual welfare practised under the Poor Law was extremely restrictive, and its legacy is still evident in many of the approaches and arguments current nowadays. But residualism can be seen in a different, less prejudicial light.

The process of economic development has led, in most European countries, to the development of strong individual rights, based in contributions over a lifetime. This has often been done, though, at the expense of inadequate and incomplete coverage for those who have not been able to contribute. Residual welfare is based in the argument that people should not fall below a basic minimum standard. This identifies residual welfare with the idea of a safety net, or a guarantee of protection, and such guarantees are usually applied generally and comprehensively. If people have a general right to welfare, there must either be a comprehensive service (that is, a service to all), or a guarantee of service when necessary. If there is a guarantee, and there is not general coverage, there is a residual system. Many writers condemn residualism,[5] but from the point of view of welfare it represents a major advance over the fragmentary, incomplete coverage that has tended to precede it.

Institutional welfare rests on the view that everyone has needs at some time (everyone is at some time a child, sick, old, possibly unemployed), and that this is a social responsibility. Needs are 'institutionalised' in society. This is largely a matter of attitude. People who receive social security are often described as being 'dependent'; the same is not said about people who use public services, like roads or libraries. The welfare state was intended, in principle, to put the receipt of services like health and social security on the same footing as public services. In the case of health, it may have succeeded; in the case of social security benefits, the picture is much less clear. Some benefits, like insurance-based pensions, are generally accepted. Some, like means-tested Jobseeker's Allowance or the 'dole', tend to be rejected, and recipients are likely to be classed as 'dependent'. Some, like the minimum income guarantee for pensioners, are in a more ambiguous position; they are broadly accepted, but subject to the rules of means-tested, conditional benefits, which are associated with residualism.

---

[3] H Wilensky and C Lebeaux (1958) *Industrial society and social welfare*, New York: Free Press.

[4] D Green (1999) *Benefit dependency*, London: Institute of Economic Affairs; A Blair (1999) 'Beveridge revisited', in R Walker (ed) *Ending child poverty*, Bristol: The Policy Press; Cm 7913 (2010) *21st century welfare*, London: Department for Work and Pensions.

[5] For example, R Titmuss (1974) *Social policy: An introduction*, London: Allen & Unwin; R Mishra (1981) *Society and social policy* (2nd edn), London: Macmillan.

## Universality and selectivity

The difference between types of benefits is sometimes referred to on the basis of 'universality' and 'selectivity'. These terms are used inconsistently. Selectivity is where people receive benefits according to need. This is sometimes read as if it only meant means testing,[6] but this is not what selectivists argue;[7] selectivity implies a test of means or need. Some writers, then, would see benefits like Disability Living Allowance, for which the tests are whether a person is able to walk or in need of care, as selective; others would not.

Universality implies benefits that are given to all as of right. A social policy textbook from the 1970s stated that 'A universal social service is ... one to which all citizens contribute equally, and from which all are entitled to draw equal benefits.'[8] This is not the way that we use the idea nowadays, but it was arguably the view of the Beveridge report.[9] Beveridge wanted his scheme to be comprehensive, and expected the same flat-rate contribution from everyone who could pay it – he believed rights had to be earned, not given by the state. However, no benefit has ever been universalist in these terms, and this is not how the idea of 'universality' is understood by most writers. The test of universality is that everyone is covered and has a right to benefit, not that everyone contributes. The best examples of universal provision are education, Child Benefit – everyone is a child at some time – and the National Health Service.

Universality is linked with institutional welfare because the idea that everyone is in need at some time is linked with the idea that everyone should benefit. Selectivity is linked with residual welfare because the idea of a 'safety net' implies a concentration on those in need. For Rothstein, selective social services are characterised by limited services and minimal intervention.[10] Townsend argues that selectivity

> fosters hierarchical relationships of superiority and inferiority in society, diminishes rather than enhances the status of the poor, and has the effect of widening rather than reducing social inequalities. Far from sensitively discriminating different kinds of need it

---

[6]  M Reddin (1970) 'Universality versus selectivity', in W A Robson and B Crick (eds) *The future of the social services*, Harmondsworth: Penguin;  D Mitchell, A Harding and F Gruen (1994) 'Targeting welfare', *The Economic Record*, vol 70, no 210, pp 315-40; B Rothstein (1998) *Just institutions matter*, Cambridge: Cambridge University Press, p 20.

[7]  For example, A Seldon and H Gray (1967) *Universal or selective social benefits*, London: Institute for Economic Affairs.

[8]  K Jones, J Brown and J Bradshaw (1978) *Issues in social policy*, London: RKP, p 44.

[9]  W Beveridge, (1942) *Social insurance and allied services*, Cmd 6404, London: HMSO.

[10]  B Rothstein (1998) *Just institutions matter*, Cambridge: Cambridge University Press, p 146.

lumps the unemployed, sick, widowed, aged and others into one undifferentiated and inevitably stigmatised category.[11]

But universality and selectivity are methods, or ways to achieve different aims; institutional and residual models represent principles. One could argue for combining institutional welfare and selectivity - like Marx's 'to each according to his needs' – or residual welfare and universality, on the basis that universal benefits like Child Benefit may be a better way than selective benefits to provide a safety net against poverty.

It has become common to hear in the broadcast media the complaint that universal benefits simply don't make sense. Why, the argument runs, should someone who is wealthy get any benefit at all? The answer to that question is fairly straightforward. Universal benefits are meant to be for everyone, in that same way that hospitals, roads and schools are for everyone. They are simple, practical, effective and popular. If wealthy people don't get benefits, there has to be some way of excluding them, and then the problems start.

The arguments for universality are:

- *Basic rights* Universal benefits offer all citizens a guarantee of resources, without stigma, as a matter of right. Universal benefits are seen as minimally intrusive and in consequence are less likely to infringe liberty than benefits to which conditions are attached.[12]
- *Simplicity* Universal benefits can be simpler than selective benefits, with the attendant advantages in comprehensibility and administrative cost.
- *Effectiveness* Proponents claim a virtually full take-up of benefit.

The central criticism of universal benefits is that they are costly. Arguments for a more extensive use of universality, offering a Citizen's Income, have also been criticised on three further grounds:

- *Limited flexibility* Universal benefits cannot be adapted to individual need without ceasing to be universal; they are limited in their scope. This does not matter when universal benefits constitute only a small part of a benefits system; in relation to the argument that they can supplant other systems, the argument becomes increasingly important.
- *Incentives to work* The delivery of benefit unconditionally would make it possible in theory for someone to live without having to earn a wage, or agree to take part-time work in place of full-time work. Incentives depend

---

[11] P Townsend (1976) *Sociology and social policy*, Harmondsworth: Penguin, p 126.
[12] R E Goodin (1992) 'Towards a minimally presumptuous social welfare policy', in P van Parijs (ed) *Arguing for basic income*, London: Verso.

necessarily on the structure of alternatives, including the marginal rewards of labour; this makes the argument difficult to judge in isolation.[13]

- *Equity* Benefits are distributed on a range of different principles, including not only financial need and rights, but also compensation and reward for merit; attempts to develop benefits based on one principle alter the balance relative to others.

'Selectivity' refers to a process in which people are identified and selected in order to receive benefits and services. This is sometimes confused with 'targeting',[14] a subject which we will return to in Chapter 23, but selectivity is much more specific – it is concerned not just with getting benefits to some people, but with stopping benefits going to others. Selectivity comes down to means testing if needs can be met through financial provision – a person who can employ a housekeeper does not have the same need for domestic help as someone who cannot, even if their functional capacities are the same. But where needs cannot simply be described in financial terms – which may be the case in benefits for old people and people with physical disabilities – selective benefits might not be means tested.

The basic argument for selectivity is that it is an efficient means of poor relief, offering maximum benefit at least cost. Offering benefits to people who are not poor is seen as wasteful. The other main argument is that it is a limited approach, in a context in which state intervention is held in some distrust. Selectivity makes it possible to hold social security to the necessary minimum for the relief of extremes of deprivation, which links the approach with a general ideological attempt to hold state intervention to a residual level.

There are five main arguments against selectivity:

- *Boundary problems* Selectivity relies on a distinction being made between those who are entitled and those who are not. There are problems of equity and in dealing with the boundaries between those who are entitled to benefit and those who are not. When circumstances change, so must entitlement to benefits, and the loss of benefits limits the potential of individuals to improve their circumstances. The problem is most clearly associated with means testing, where it is called the 'poverty trap',[15] but also applies in relation to other benefits (for example, return to work after sickness, or rehabilitation of people with disabilities).

---

[13] See J Pechman and M Timpane (1975) *Work incentives and income guarantees*, New York: Brookings.

[14] For example, in D Mitchell, A Harding and F Gruen (1994) 'Targeting welfare', *The Economic Record*, vol 70, no 210, pp 315-40 or P Whiteford (1997) 'Targeting welfare: a comment', *The Economic Record*, vol 73, no 220, pp 45-50.

[15] D Piachaud (1973) 'Taxation and poverty', in W Robson and B Crick (eds) *Taxation policy*, Harmondsworth: Penguin.

- *Incentives* Means testing penalises people who have made private or independent provision, and those who have been thrifty – behaviour that many advocates of means testing would wish to encourage. Even if that behaviour is not really affected by the incentives (there is some argument about whether it is), the idea that desirable activity should be penalised seems unfair, and sometimes perverse.

  There are special problems, too, for members of the same household. The effects of the 'household means test' in the 1930s were reputed to break up families because the effect of one person earning was to reduce the income of other family members.[16] (The test was abolished in 1941.) The earnings of adult children or parents are no longer taken into account, but there are controversies concerning the effects of benefit receipt on partners – Clasen et al suggest that strict means-tested benefits may discourage the wives of unemployed men from employment.[17]

- *Administration* Selectivity is administratively costly, which calls into question its efficiency. The process of testing claimants is liable to be cumbersome and complex; in the context of developing countries, the World Bank has argued that the most efficient means of distribution is not to target individuals, but to target whole sectors of a population.[18]

- *Stigma* The problems of stigma arise both because the benefits are dealing with stigmatised groups, like the poor or lone parents, and because the operation of benefits is often humiliating or degrading.[19]

- *Take-up* Despite the claims made for it, selectivity is not effective in directing resources to the poor. Many potential recipients fail to receive benefits to which they are entitled.[20] The central problems are ignorance about benefits – both about their existence and the terms on which they are available; the complexity of the benefits system, which acts as a deterrent to claiming; and the problem of stigma. The argument is most usually made in relation to means testing, although arguments about ignorance of entitlement, administrative complexity and degrading treatment can be applied equally to other benefits.

Richard Titmuss argued that any comprehensive system of social security would need in practice to combine aspects of universal benefits with selective systems designed to complement the basic measures and to meet individual needs.[21]

---

[16] G Orwell (1937) *The road to Wigan Pier*, London: Folio Society, 1998 edition, pp 70-1.

[17] J Clasen, J Davidon, H Ganssmann and A Mauer (2006) 'Non employment and the welfare state', *Journal of European Social Policy*, vol 16, no 2, pp 134-54.

[18] World Bank (1990) *World development report*, Oxford: Oxford University Press.

[19] P Spicker (1984) *Stigma and social welfare*, Beckenham: Croom Helm.

[20] See W van Oorschot (1995) *Realizing rights*, Aldershot: Avebury.

[21] R Titmuss (1968) *Commitment to welfare*, London: Allen & Unwin.

## Rights and citizenship

The idea of the welfare state is characterised not only by a commitment to the provision of welfare, but a sense that welfare is provided as of right. The idea of rights is complex, and detailed discussion would take us into deeper water than we need for an outline of the benefits system; for the purposes of this introductory section, it should be enough to distinguish moral rights from legal ones. Moral rights are based in a sense that people are entitled to receive support, and that they can legitimately demand it. In the thirty years or so after the benefits system was introduced, there was some puzzlement and disappointment that claimants seemed not to feel that benefits were a right, and that many of them failed to claim the benefits they were entitled to.[22] Subsequently, the atmosphere changed. Critics expressed fears that welfare had generated a 'dependency culture', a term that implies that benefits were not to be seen as a right. Arguments have grown about 'conditionality', limiting rights, emphasising responsibilities and imposing sanctions.[23] As a result of that shift, far less research has been done in recent years about promoting claimants' rights.[24]

Legal rights are rules that allow people to bring them into force on the issues that affect them. They have been one of the main means through which people with little power are able to bring about change, both for themselves and, where they lead to the establishment of general rules, for others.[25] The idea of legal rights is tied up with the idea of 'citizenship', which T H Marshall saw as one of the cornerstones of the welfare state.[26] Citizenship has been described as 'the right to have rights'.[27] People who received benefits in the time of the Poor Law were treated as 'paupers', and denied the rights available to others. One of the most important developments associated with the welfare state was the idea that the people who received benefit would be full citizens. Over time, the force of the idea of citizenship seems to have weakened, and contemporary debates are more concerned with 'inclusion' – the idea that people who are likely to be left out or rejected by society need to be brought into networks of

---

[22] See, for example, A B Atkinson (1969) *Poverty in Britain and the reform of social security*, Oxford: Oxford University Press.

[23] P Gregg (2008) *Realising potential*, London: Department for Work and Pensions.

[24] But see G Craig, P Dornan, J Bradshaw, R Garbutt, S Mumtaz, A Syed and A Ward (2003) 'Underwriting citizenship for older people', *Benefits*, vol 11, no 3, pp 187-92.

[25] See T Campbell (1983) *The left and rights*, London: Routledge and Kegan Paul; P Spicker (2001) 'The rights of the poor', in P Robson and A Kjonstad (eds) *Poverty and the law*, Oxford: Hart, pp 1-14.

[26] T H Marshall (1963) 'Citizenship and social class', in T H Marshall, *Sociology at the crossroads*, London: Heinemann

[27] Earl Warren, cited in R Goodin (1982) *Political theory and public policy*, Chicago, IL: University of Chicago Press.

social relationships.[28] This process requires adjustments by the excluded person as well as by society, and contemporary criticisms of the idea of citizenship have emphasised the inter-relationship of rights and social responsibilities.[29]

## Public and private

Social security works mainly by making money available. People are given a basic allowance, and left to choose what they want to buy. Essentials like food, fuel and clothing are paid for from their benefits. This sounds obvious, but it is not what happens in every case. A range of goods and services are given directly to people, and they do not have to pay for them. In some cases, like the National Health Service, the services are delivered directly. In other cases, people receive services that they have to pay for, but some people may be exempt from the charges. Examples are free prescriptions, which are given to all pensioners, young people, people on low incomes and people with particular illnesses such as diabetes and AIDS. The residents of old people's homes, under the rules governing community care, have to pay charges if their income or capital comes above certain levels, while others are exempt. In some cases, people receive a formal 'benefit' to pay the charge which is being levied for the provision of a public service; this is what happens with Housing Benefit for local authority tenants, or when children are allowed free school meals.

Social security makes it possible to use the market for the distribution of goods while protecting the position of people who cannot afford them. There are often non-market alternatives to social security. Housing Benefit came into existence because housing subsidies were largely removed.[30] Free prescriptions are treated in this book as part of the social security system only because prescription charges were introduced into the health service; formerly, all prescriptions were free. They have been made free again in Wales, and Scotland is on course to follow; if we return to free prescriptions throughout Britain, it is unlikely that they will be discussed in this context again.

There are arguments for and against public or private provision. They are not what this book is about, because the discussion of public provision would pull us away from thinking about 'social security' provision as such. At the same time, it is important to recognise that social security distributed in the form of money implicitly assumes that there is a private economic market in operation.

---

[28] See, for example, P Askonas and A Stewart (2000) *Social inclusion: Possibilities and tensions*, Basingstoke: Macmillan.

[29] L Mead (1997) 'Citizenship and social policy: T H Marshall and poverty', in E Paul, F Miller and J Paul (eds) *The welfare state*, Cambridge: Cambridge University Press; See also H Dean (2001) 'Welfare rights and the "workfare" state', *Benefits*, vol 30, pp 1-4.

[30] W Beckerman and S Clark (1982) *Poverty and social security in Britain since 1961*, Oxford: Oxford University Press.

If the distribution of goods falls outside the market, like much of education or health, the topic ceases to be a matter for social security at all.

## QUESTIONS FOR DISCUSSION

Should social security be confined to the poor?
Is the National Health Service the same kind of thing as social security?

# Chapter 3

# Social security and society

The provision of social security is also guided by a series of assumptions and values. The conventional academic focus on class, gender and 'race' does not quite capture what is happening, but there is a powerful emphasis on the related values of work, family and nation. There is an expectation that claimants will fit into expected patterns of behaviour, and those who do not – those whose work is marginal or temporary, whose family is unusual, or who come from outside the country – can experience problems as a result.

If we are trying to improve people's welfare, it is helpful to try to understand something about the way that people are, and how welfare policies relate to their situation. Some writers have gone further, arguing that because welfare takes place in a social context, it can only be understood in that context. This has been particularly important for 'critical social policy', which begins from a view of social policy as underpinned by structured social inequality – primarily the inequalities of class, gender and 'race'. It is possible to find practical examples of all of these inequalities in discussions of social security, but a strong word of caution is merited. This kind of overview gives us, at best, an indistinct and contradictory picture of the way that social security works. Class, gender and 'race' are important, but their influence is oblique; if we want to understand how the benefits system works, they are not the best place to start.

The concept of class tends to assume that there is a long-term pattern and structure of opportunities, describable in terms of social stratification.[1] Social security is often predicated on similar assumptions, and policy outcomes are presented in terms of vertical redistribution from rich to poor (though some policies, of course, work in the opposite direction). However, the assumption that people fall neatly into definable, predictable categories does not square closely with experience;[2] one of the core problems of social security has been its failure to adjust to the unpredictable, unstable nature of the contemporary labour market.

---

[1]  G Mooney (2000) 'Class and social policy', in G Lewis, S Gewirtz and J Clarke (eds) *Rethinking social policy*, London: Sage Publications.

[2]  A Bryson and D Kasparova (2003) *Profiling benefit claimants in Britain: a feasibility study*, DWP Research Report 196, London: Department for Work and Pensions.

In relation to gender, the system is not pro- or anti-women; it may be riddled with assumptions about the role of women, or 'gendered',[3] but that is not the same thing. There are some blatant examples of gender discrimination in social security policy – one of the most remarkable was the attempt to bar housewives from claiming certain disability benefits in the 1970s,[4] which is discussed later in Chapter 16. But there are also examples of favourable treatment for women, in the provision of pensions at earlier ages, or giving people in different circumstances a choice of types of provision, which was done for married women paying reduced contributions after 1977.

In relation to 'race', there is little in the system that touches on it directly. Gary Craig thinks this is a reason to criticise,[5] but others might see the omission in much more positive terms, because an explicitly racialised system could hardly avoid being a racist one. The stereotyped view that minority ethnic groups are poor and dependent on benefits is both inaccurate and stigmatising to those groups. There is a huge variety of experience.

None of these three concepts has the power to explain issues directly. Many people will feel, however, that there is something here which helps to explain how benefits are designed and delivered, and that is almost true. Each of these ideas comes close, but none of them quite captures the way that the issues are constructed. Social security policy depends not on class, gender or 'race', but on the imposition of core values in three discrete but closely related areas: work rather than class, family rather than gender and nation rather than race.[6]

## Work

The workplace is at the root of many understandings of social organisation, including concepts of class, status and the economic structure of society. An understanding of social policy in continental Europe often begins from discussions of industrial relations and the relative role of the 'social partners' – government, employers and unions. The same is not true in the UK, but the importance of the economy and the labour market is nevertheless taken for granted as the framework within which social security policies have to be constructed. The relationship of social security to work, particularly in dealing with the 'able-bodied' poor, was central to the historical development of policy.

---

[3]  C Pateman (2000) 'The patriarchal welfare state', in C Pierson and F Castles (eds) *The welfare state reader*, Brighton: Polity Press.

[4]  R Lister and T Emmet (1978) *Second class disabled*, London: Equal Rights for Disabled Women Campaign.

[5]  G Craig (1999) '"Race", social security and poverty', in J Ditch (ed) *Introduction to social security*, London: Routledge.

[6]  F Williams (1989) *Social policy*, Brighton: Polity Press.

Work is still a dominant theme in the organisation of social security, both as an organising principle and as a value in itself. As an organising principle, many benefits begin from the assumption that most people will normally be in full-time work for an employer for most of the time. The administration of taxation and contributions in the UK depends largely on people working for employers: the employers do the calculation, rather than the individual taxpayer. (This is not necessarily true in other countries.) Social security works by filling the gaps – dealing with situations where the normal pattern of work is interrupted. Equally, where someone is long-term unemployed, the emphasis has shifted to moving people into work. The contingencies that benefits primarily deal with – retirement, disability, long-term incapacity and child care – are contingencies that interrupt a person's work record. Things could, of course, be arranged differently. Benefits could be arranged without reference to work status: Child Benefit is an example. If this does not seem to happen much in practice, it is a testimony to the power of these norms.

As a value in itself, work represents a model of what people ought to be doing. Work is seen as the norm for an adult. Saying that work is 'normal' does not mean that most people do it, or that the average person does: it means that people are expected to do it, and they are penalised for not doing so. A 'norm' is an expectation, coupled with a sanction. Work is desirable, and not working is undesirable. Work should be full time, and people who work part time may be disadvantaged by different rules. Voluntary unemployment is disapproved of, and even an action that might improve someone's position in the labour market, such as taking unpaid work experience, is not sufficient to remove the obligation to be available for work. The rules of social security benefits make it difficult for people who do not conform to the norm of employability and employment; some recent reports seem to suggest that they have not done so enough, and argue for greater 'conditionality' in benefits to make the emphasis on work clearer and stronger.[7] In the United States, 'workfare' programmes have required claimants to work as a condition of receiving benefits; the 2009 Welfare Reform Act made provision for similar rules in Britain.

Recent reforms have been driven by the concern to ensure that people without work are able to move into work. Often this is understood as a change of state (from unemployed to employed); sometimes it is represented as a progression (from non-work, to initial work, to stable work). There is a myth in some circles that 'active labour market policy', emphasising the responsibility on claimants to look for work, is a recent development.[8] It is not; there have been penalties for not working through much of the last century.

---

[7] D Freud (2007) *Reducing dependency, increasing opportunity*, London: Department for Work and Pensions; P Gregg (2008) *Realising potential*, London: Department for Work and Pensions.

[8] Freud (2007).

The emphasis on work may all seem glaringly obvious, but it rests on a series of barely explicit assumptions, and it tends to prevent people from developing other choices and patterns of life. Lifelong learning, or personal development through extended leave, are not approved objectives. Withdrawing from the labour market to look after children or people with disabilities is accepted only half-heartedly; a key recent change has been the insistence that lone parents with children in primary school must now be actively seeking work.[9] Early retirement does not seem to be encouraged, but the level of early retirement reflects favourable terms offered by some pensions.[10] There is some ambivalence about the desirability of unemployment through redundancy, which is partly supported because of its importance for economic organisation and the functioning of the labour market.

Current strategies for benefits rely heavily on the development of employment as an alternative to benefit receipt. Before the crisis beginning in 2008, the British economy created relatively high levels of employment: compared to many other developed countries, Britain's labour force is a higher proportion of its population, and within the labour force its standardised unemployment rate has been relatively low. There are three fundamental problems in trying to respond to poverty through improving employment prospects. The first is that it can only ever be a partial response. Even when we had supposedly 'full employment' in the 1950s and 1960s, there were still people moving out of the job market or marginalised within it. There will never be enough jobs for everyone to work, and wherever there is competition for jobs, some people will not be chosen for work by employers. Second, employment is not enough to secure an adequate income. The figures for *Households below average income* show that 59% of poor children − defined as those who live in households below 60% of the median income − have parents in work.[11] Third, some patterns of work, even if income appears to be adequate in the short term, do not guarantee adequate security or opportunities. In many circumstances people are only partly integrated into the labour market. Their situation is variously characterised as:

- a 'dual labour market', a term distinguishing the social position of secure employees on adequate pay from a class whose conditions of employment are consistently worse;[12]

[9]  HM Treasury (2010) *Budget 2010*, HC 61, London: The Stationery Office, p 33.

[10]  J Gruber and D.A Wise, cited in N Barr (2004) *The economics of the welfare state* (4th edn), Oxford: Oxford University Press, p 205; and see S Arkani and O Gough (2007) 'The impact of occupational pensions on retirement age', *Journal of Social Policy*, vol 36, no 2, pp 297-318.

[11]  Department for Work and Pensions (2010) *Households below average income: an analysis of the income distribution 1994/95-2008/09*, London: DWP, table 4.3.

[12]  N Bosanquet and P Doeringer (1973) 'Is there a dual labour market in Great Britain?', *Economic Journal*, vol 83, no 330, pp 421-35.

- a distinction between 'core' and 'peripheral' workers: peripheral workers are those whose role in the economy is more marginal, and who are liable to displacement during economic cycles;[13] and
- a situation of 'precariousness', describing the role of marginal workers who move between casual and part-time work and joblessness.[14]

Unstable economic conditions lead to social instability – for example, marginal employment is associated with family breakdown. Economic instability also reduces the level of social protection available.

Benefit rules tend to be built around the assumption that people's circumstances are identifiable, stable and conform to conventional patterns of employment. The provisions that the Beveridge scheme made to cover casual and daily labour were removed in the 1990s; the records that were maintained by the Benefits Agency of 'Repeated Short Term Claims' no longer seem to be made. The norm applying now takes it that:

- where work is done, it can be assumed to be directly remunerative unless there is clear evidence to the contrary;
- the work that people do will provide a regular wage;
- people know how much they are earning; and
- the flow of income will be regular over time.

Casualised, informal and indeterminate patterns of remuneration are often taken to be fraudulent. This seems remote from the experience of people in an insecure, shifting labour market. The problem with work-focused models is not just that some people are not directly engaged in the labour market, but that they do not necessarily fit the patterns that benefit structures expect them to fit.

## Family

Jane Lewis has suggested that, although the dominant models of welfare all assume that women are dependent on a male breadwinner, there are important variations:

- A *strong* male breadwinner model supposes that women's incomes are secondary to men's. This is the model in the UK and Ireland.
- A *modified* male breadwinner model gives women a special status in relation to motherhood. This is the model in France.
- A *weak* male breadwinner model allows for women to act as breadwinners in the same way as men. This is the pattern in Sweden, where there have been attempts to introduce a 'dual breadwinner' pattern.

---

[13] J Payne and C Payne (1994) 'Unemployment and peripheral work', *Work, Employment and Society*, vol 7, no 4, pp 513-34.

[14] S Paugam (1995) 'The spiral of precariousness', in G Room (ed) *Beyond the threshold*, Bristol: The Policy Press

The idea of the 'family wage' has been an important one in European social policy;[15] it assumes that resources in the household are aggregated, that men support women and that women's wages are supplementary. All of those assumptions seem increasingly questionable in view of the changing nature of families, and in particular the very high rates of separation and divorce.

An illustration of the strength of the idea can be seen in survivors' benefits. People who lose their breadwinner receive these benefits because of the assumption that survivors were dependent on the insured person – other people who are bereaved by losing a child or partner are not insured. The National Insurance benefits for widows introduced in 1948 were based on the system introduced in 1925, and included three main benefits:

- Widow's Allowance (from 1988, a lump sum Widows's Payment), covering the early period of widowhood for all widows;
- Widow's Pension, for dependent women under pension age but over the age of 50, later 45 (the assumption was that younger women could be expected to work); and
- Widowed Mother's Allowance, for widows with dependent children.

The system was largely (but not completely) replaced in 2001 with a gender-neutral system, including Bereavement Payments and a Widowed Parents Allowance. A Guardian's Allowance, for orphaned children, has been maintained, but a Child's Special Allowance, introduced in 1959 for the orphaned children of divorced parents, has not. The hangovers from the old system were the cause of a legal action, which went to the House of Lords; they decided that as it had been legitimate to provide protection for widows in the first place, it was not possible to overturn the decision solely on the basis of gender discrimination. Lord Hoffman commented:

> there has never been any social or economic justification for extending WP [Widow's Pension] to men under pensionable age. The argument for WP was that in the social conditions which prevailed for most of the last century, it was unusual for married women to work and that it was unreasonable to expect them to be equipped to earn their own living if they were widowed in middle age. This argument self-evidently did not apply to men.[16]

The passing of these conditions was not, however, taken as a reason to end the payments altogether. In theory, it is possible for survivors simply to receive the

---

[15] I Montari (2000) 'From family wage to marriage subsidy and child benefits', *Journal of European Social Policy*, vol 10, no 4, pp 307-33.

[16] *R v Secretary of State for Work and Pensions, ex parte Hooper and others, 2005 UKHL 29* (www.publications.parliament.uk/pa/ld200405/ldjudgmt/jd050505/hoop-1.htm).

same benefits as other people, and in practice there has always been a contingent of formerly dependent widows receiving the basic means-tested benefit. The fact that survivors' benefits have largely been preserved as a distinctive category of benefit suggests that the principle of insuring families against the loss of the breadwinner is still generally accepted.

The idea of the 'breadwinner' has attracted particular attention, but the dominant model of the family applied in social security seems to me even more restrictive. Benefits tend to work around a concept of a 'normal' family. 'Normal', as in the case of work and employment, does not mean 'average' – it means 'conforming to social norms'. The normal family consists of two parents with one or more children, but it is increasingly untypical in developed countries. Several factors have contributed to this trend:

- ageing populations, which mean that increasing numbers of households consist of elderly people without children;
- the delay in undertaking childbirth, which means that more households consist of single women or couples without children;
- the growth of one-parent families; and
- household fission, the tendency for households to split because of divorce and earlier independence for children.

Social policies sometimes seek to reinforce the normal family, by rewarding normal conduct or penalising 'deviant' (non-normal) circumstances. Rewards include subsidies for married dependents and children; penalties include requirements to support one's family and legal and financial deterrents to divorce. Because of the assumption that normal families include two adults, there has to be a rule for other couples – the 'cohabitation rule' – to make sure that they are not dealt with differently. This will be returned to later, in Chapter 19.

It is more difficult to suggest an alternative to these assumptions than it is to suggest alternatives to work-based benefits. Family benefits reflect social norms, but they also reflect a variety of practical arrangements, particularly as they affect children. Feminists have criticised benefits that make this sort of assumption, but they have also criticised benefits which fail to take into account the realities of domestic arrangements, and consequently which fail to redress the disadvantage of women.[17] This is a double bind; each approach is criticised for not doing what the other one does. It is not possible to offer universal, individually based benefits regardless of gender, and simultaneously to redress the disadvantage of women in the family. We have either to choose between these approaches, or to offer some compromise between them.

---

[17] For example, G Pascall (1994) *Social policy: a feminist analysis*, London: Routledge.

## Nation

Historically, social welfare became important shortly after the rise of 'nation states' — David Miller argues that the nation is the principal community on which welfare provision depends.[18] National identity is often used, however, to exclude people from welfare as to promote inclusion, and the influence of nationalism on welfare has tended to be negative. Titmuss criticised the idea of the 'welfare state' in part because it seemed to limit the scope of welfare to a particular locality.[19] Universalists have promoted an inclusive concept of welfare; in principle, this concept is inclusive, but in practice, it tends to be confined to citizens, or members, of the political community.

Immigrants, by definition, come from outside a community; wherever social protection depends on a principle of contribution to the collective welfare, immigrants are liable to be excluded. Residual income support may be available in some countries, but it is unusual for non-contributory benefits to be available directly to immigrants. (Britain is not unusual in this — many countries have some kind of minimum residential qualification.) Since 1971, immigrants from outside the European Union have commonly been admitted on condition that they do not take up 'public funds'. This includes Child Benefit, means-tested Jobseeker's Allowance or Employment and Support Allowance, Housing Benefit, Tax Credits and some disability benefits. People who try to claim are reported to the UK Border Agency and liable to deportation. Technically, this is not part of the rules of the benefits system, but it does mean that immigrants cannot claim.

There are also restrictive rules within the benefits system. For example, there is a test of 'habitual residence', justified in Parliament because otherwise 'You arrive in London, sign up at an employment office and suddenly money and rebates fall at your feet.'[20] Press reporting of these issues in the UK verges at times on the hysterical. For thirty years there have been recurrent exposés of 'benefit tourism' by rapacious Europeans intent on despoiling Britain's insanely generous welfare state. Here are a few clips from the British media: most of them are recent, but the last one was just too lurid to leave out.

> Immigrants 'defrauding benefits to pay for houses back home'.
>
> Some Poles 'claim benefit twice'.

---

[18] D Miller (1989) *Market, state and community*, Oxford: Oxford University Press.

[19] R Titmuss (1987) 'Welfare state and welfare society', in R Titmuss, *The philosophy of welfare*, London: Allen & Unwin.

[20] A Thomson (1995) 'Benefit test for foreign claimants defended', *The Times*, 1 March, p 8.

Nothing would more swiftly check the immigration tide than calling time on newcomers' automatic claims to benefit and housing.

BRITAIN'S benefits system is being MILKED of thousands of pounds by immigrant families − flooding in because they know their dodgy claims won't get properly checked.

Foreign spongers scandal, by judge: 'hundreds of thousands abuse benefits'.

Britain is becoming a mecca for foreign drug addicts. Thousands are flocking here to take advantage of generous social security benefits and free treatment on the NHS.[21]

The European Union has done nothing to correct the misconceptions: a publicity campaign about social securty rights in 2010 announced that 'Europe is your playground'.[22] European Union citizens do have rights to benefit as workers, and the government is not permitted to discriminate between its own nationals and other EU nationals.[23] It is however possible to reject claims from EU nationals who do not have a right to reside, [24] and a series of legal cases have consequently been based on the argument that 'national governments are entitled to restrict the right of residence of EU nationals and to restrict any social assistance to them.'[25] This means in practice that claims have to be negotiated through a labyrinth of complex rules about status and residence. The position of non-European immigrants is even more heavily restricted. There is no 'automatic' right to benefits or housing; on the contrary, the effect of restrictions may be to make some people liable to deportation if they claim. However, migrants who have to pay tax also get the right to tax-based benefits; those who contribute to National Insurance earn rights within that system; and many of the rights are based on

---

[21] Sources: J Merrick (2006) 'Immigrants defrauding benefits to pay for houses back home', *Daily Mail,* 3 July; A Goldberg (2007) 'Some Poles claim benefit twice', *BBC 5 live,* 23 September; M Hastings (2009) 'So is David Cameron ruthless enough to save Britain?', *Daily Mail,* 3 October; G Basnett and D Wight (2009) 'Greedy fakers', *News of the World,* 18 January; C Riches (2009) 'Foreign spongers scandal by judge', *Daily Express,* 29 July; J Burke (1996) 'Addicts flock to Britain', *Sunday Times,* 19 May.

[22] European Commission (2010) New campaign on social security coordination: Europe is your playground, http://ec.europa.eu/social/main.jsp?langId=en&catId=89&newsId=931&furtherNews=yes

[23] Child Poverty Action Group (2010) *Welfare benefits and tax credits handbook 2010/2011,* London: CPAG, pp 1436-7.

[24] M Rowland and R White (2009) *Social security legislation 2009/10, volume III: Administration, adjudication and the European dimension,* London: Sweet and Maxwell, pp 846-54.

[25] Tribunal of Commissioners in CIS/3573/2005, cited by Rowland and White (2009) p 849.

reciprocal arrangements with other countries, providing protection for millions of British expatriates. Claiming benefits in those circumstances is not 'abuse'.

Understanding the pattern of support for migrants depends on a much more complex set of issues than social security alone – it demands consideration of rules relating to residence and the labour market as well as entitlements to benefits. Much immigration consists of movements of people from poorer countries to richer ones; immigrants tend to come with relatively limited resources. Few countries offer immigrants a full range of social protection or benefits, and in the short term this is likely to lead to disadvantage. At the same time, migrants tend to be younger and more mobile than host populations. In the longer term, much depends on the economic niche occupied by immigrant groups, and their relative status and resources. Immigrant experiences are highly differentiated. Groups that came from the West Indies in the 1950s entered on very different terms from people from the Indian sub-continent; the difference in immigration rules led to significant differences in benefit entitlement and housing support. Research by the Policy Studies Institute shows that Chinese and East African immigrants are in a similar position financially to the rest of the population; people from Caribbean communities and from India are disadvantaged relative to the majority of the population; but it is Pakistanis and Bangladeshis who are most poor.[26] More recent evidence suggests that migrants from sub-Saharan Africa may be catching them up.[27]

In later years, people have come from more disparate areas, and there has consequently been a greater diversity of minority ethnic groups, with less community support: asylum seekers and economic migrants come from a wide variety of backgrounds. They have in common that their ability to draw on systems of support in the UK is extremely limited. In the case of asylum seekers this is coupled with restrictions on entering the labour market, which mean that they cannot act to support themselves or gain entitlements. The Immigration and Asylum Act 1999 led to full separation of provision for asylum seekers from other forms of immigration. The system of support is limited and sometimes punitive, extending to the restriction of personal liberty. Strict conditionality in benefits for migrants has been a consistent theme in benefits administration for the best part of a century. It is difficult to imagine the conditions under which a government would liberalise benefit rules to permit immigrants to claim more extensively, but there is little indication that the current rules reflect a response to any real, rather than potential, problem.

---

[26] T Modood and R Berthoud (1997) *Ethnic minorities in Britain*, London: Policy Studies Institute.

[27] G Palmer and P Kenway (2007) *Poverty among ethnic groups*, York: Joseph Rowntree Foundation.

## Social security and social structure

None of the issues outlined here is straightforward. If we are looking for examples to support any point of view, we can probably find them somewhere in the bowels of the social security system, but we can probably find as many counter-examples. It does not really work if we begin an interest in class, gender and 'race', and then try to find direct examples from social security. It makes more sense to come at this issue the other way about: the importance of class, gender and 'race' is not direct, but implied by the emphasis on work, family and nation. Social security is guided by norms and assumptions about the way society is organised. Those assumptions explain where some rules come from – though the norms are so strongly entrenched that it may be difficult to apply the insights sufficiently to allow benefits to be operated differently.

---

### QUESTIONS FOR DISCUSSION

What is wrong with making assumptions about people's role in work or the family?
Is there an alternative?
Should social security be offered to non-citizens?

---

# Part II

The development of the system

# Chapter 4

# The origins of social security in Britain

Social security developed through three main strands: the Poor Law, the growth of measures intended to avoid the problems of the Poor Law, and the tradition of mutual insurance. The Poor Law was a deterrent system, intended to restrict the dependency of the poor and to make a clear distinction between paupers and workers. The system that replaced it was intended to work on different principles: it was not to be confined to the poor, it would offer benefits as of right and it would apply to everyone.

Before the foundation of the welfare state, social security developed through three main strands. The first was the Poor Law. This was a national system of poor relief – the first in the world; it lasted, in various forms, from 1598 until 1948. Second, there were schemes developed in reaction to the Poor Law – alternative ways of protecting people's income without subjecting them to the 'stigma of pauperism'. The third strand was the development of cooperative and mutual assistance schemes, mainly represented in Britain by the friendly societies, and in the United States by fraternal societies. Relatively few histories in Britain make much of this,[1] which reflects the influence of the Poor Law. By contrast, schemes of this type are seen in much of continental Europe as central to development,[2] and they played an important part in Beveridge's understanding of social security.

## The Poor Law

The Poor Law cast a giant shadow, and much of the British social security system developed under it. Introduced in 1598 and consolidated in 1601,[3] the Elizabethan Poor Law was not an original idea. Many of the policies in England had been punitive, including whipping, branding and execution of able-bodied beggars.[4] The solidaristic schemes of European cities offered a different approach; a

---

[1] But see H E Raynes (1960) *Social security in Britain*, London: Pitman; D Green (1999) 'The friendly societies and Adam Smith liberalism', in D Gladstone (ed) *Before Beveridge*, London: Institute for Economic Affairs.

[2] P Baldwin (1990) *The politics of social solidarity*, Cambridge: Cambridge University Press.

[3] D Fraser (1973) *The evolution of the British welfare state*, London: Macmillan, p 30.

[4] S Webb and B Webb (1927) *English local government: The old Poor Law*, London: Cass.

description of one of the first, the poor relief system of Ypres, was first translated into English in 1531,[5] and it influenced early Tudor legislation.[6] The Elizabethan Acts were based in the idea that the organisation and control of poor relief was the responsibility of government.

The old Poor Law had three main elements: a compulsory poor rate, the creation of 'overseers' of relief to administer the system and provision for 'setting the poor on work'. Despite the national scope of the law, it was far from national in its practice. It was introduced at a time when communications were poor, and enforcement was weak. There was no general mechanism through which it could be enforced, and the Poor Law's operation was inconsistent between areas. The parish was the basic unit of administration, and different parishes acted differently, according to the lights of local worthies.[7] The civil war exacerbated the fragmentation; the Poor Law was a national system only in name.

It was from this fragmented, confused system that the first workhouses developed. The workhouse was a means of 'setting the poor on work', allowing overseers to establish systems in a cheap, effective way. There was a workhouse established in Abingdon in 1631,[8] but it is unclear whether the overseers had the legal authority right to do it: when, in 1696, the Bristol Corporation wanted to establish a workhouse, it required a private Act of Parliament. The Bristol scheme was influential, but expensive, and the establishment of workhouses was initially confined to only a few places. Knatchbull's Act, passed in 1722/23, allowed English and Welsh parishes to build workhouses without first taking out private Acts of Parliament, and the system spread more widely after that.[9]

The workhouses of the 18th century did not serve a single purpose. The problem was that even if they were intended to 'set the poor on work', many of the people who came into the workhouses were not able-bodied: they were elderly, sick or orphaned. Gilbert's Act, in 1782, allowed parishes to form Poor Law Unions in order to build poorhouses. No less important, it stated that workhouses should become poorhouses, relieving only those who were not able-bodied (a principle increasingly disregarded in later years). Like any law in Britain, this was not taken too literally. The first deterrent workhouse was established in 1819 in Bingham, Nottinghamshire, reviving the idea of 'setting the poor on work' in a disciplinary establishment. It was followed in 1825 by another at Southwell, also in Nottinghamshire; George Nicholls, the overseer, was to become a Poor Law commissioner on the strength of his work there. (The building is still there; it was used for homeless people until 1977, and

---

[5]  See P Spicker (ed) (2010) *The origins of modern welfare*, Bern: Peter Lang.
[6]  G Elton (1953) 'An early Tudor Poor Law', *Economic History Review*, vol 6, no 1, pp 55-67.
[7]  Fraser (1973), p 31; S Webb and B Webb (1927).
[8]  P Higginbotham (2008) *The workhouse* (www.workhouses.org.uk/).
[9]  Fraser (1973), p 32.

subsequently for elderly women. It is now in the ownership of the National Trust, and open to the public.)

If able-bodied poor people could not go into the workhouse, what help was available? Often there was none. Gilbert's Act made provision for them to receive 'out-relief', that is, relief outside the poorhouse, a measure which had been tested out in Glasgow a few years earlier. Another development, which was the subject of considerable criticism in the movement to reform the Poor Law, was the 'roundsman' system, hiring out paupers as cheap labour. It was used as a means of 'setting the poor on work', but it also had the effect of undercutting wages.[10]

Probably better remembered is a modification made to the system of out-relief by magistrates in Speenhamland, Berkshire, known as the Speenhamland system. Speenhamland made out-relief available not simply for the destitute, but for people in work who were not receiving enough wages to manage.[11] The Speenhamland system was widely criticised, like the roundsman system, for rewarding employers who employed people at inadequate wages. This was believed to undercut the wages of others in work, and Speenhamland became a symbol of the vices of the old Poor Law; the example is still trundled out whenever people want to object to benefits that subsidise wages. President Nixon's office in the US, for example, went back to study Speenhamland when he was considering a Family Assistance Plan.[12]

## The New Poor Law

The changes of the industrial revolution led to the development of the towns, rapid population growth and the first experience of modern unemployment and the trade cycle. All this caused increasing poor rates. The reform of the Poor Law followed the publication of the report of the Poor Law Commission in 1834.[13] This was a long time after the problems of industrialisation, unemployment and illegitimacy had come to the fore; the delay reflects the fragmented, uncoordinated nature of the response.

The reform movement centred on three main doctrines.[14] The first came from the ideas of Thomas Malthus on population. Malthus's *Essay on the principle of population*[15] was published in 1798. He argued that the population was increasing beyond the ability of the country to feed it: food production increases in an

---

[10] S Checkland and O Checkland (eds) (1974) *The Poor Law report of 1834*, Harmondsworth: Penguin, pp 102-3.

[11] M Neuman (1972) 'Speenhamland in Berkshire', in E Martin (ed) *Comparative development in social welfare*, London: Allen & Unwin.

[12] V J Burke and V Burke (1974) *Nixon's good deed*, New York: Columbia University Press.

[13] Checkland and Checkland (1974).

[14] J R Poynter (1969) *Society and pauperism*, London: Routledge and Kegan Paul.

[15] T Malthus (1798) *An essay on the principle of population*, London: Dent, 1973 edition.

arithmetic ratio, population in a 'geometric' or exponential one. (2, 4, 6, 8 is an arithmetic sequence; 2, 4, 8, 16 is 'geometric'.) Population had to be controlled, and it could only be done by war, famine, disease or 'vice' (by which he might have meant birth control). The Poor Law was seen as an incentive to indiscriminate breeding; indeed, one of the central issues of the 1834 report was a concern with 'bastardy', which would now be called illegitimacy. (Malthus's predictions were wildly wrong, but that has not stopped generations of eco-warriors from reiterating the same fallacies in decade after decade. Population does not increase exponentially, food production has generally increased at least in line with population and in many developed countries population levels have become static, or even started to shrink.[16])

The second key figure was David Ricardo. His 'iron law of wages' was believed to show that the Poor Law was undermining the wages of independent workers. Ricardo argued that wages would always tend to the level required for subsistence: if they were lower, workers would die off, creating a labour shortage. The effect of undercutting wages for some was to cut wage rates for everyone, and so to undermine the position of the independent labourer.

Third, there was Jeremy Bentham. He argued that people did what was pleasant and would not do what was unpleasant – so that if people were not to claim relief it had to be unpleasant. The Benthamite influence was central to the development of the deterrent workhouse, intended to be 'an object of wholesome horror'.[17] The Poor Law Commission of 1834 emphasised two principles. The first was the principle of *less eligibility*: the position of the pauper must be 'less eligible' (that is, less to be chosen) than that of the independent labourer. The second was the *workhouse test*. No relief was to be given outside the workhouse.

The logic of less eligibility was based partly in equity, but partly in Ricardo's 'iron law': a strong distinction was needed to protect the independent labourer, who would otherwise be driven to starvation. It may be difficult to understand in retrospect, but the authors of the Poor Law report certainly believed that they were helping and protecting the poor. For most, less eligibility was taken to mean that the position of the pauper must be made very bad. In 1828 Becher wrote that:

> the advantage resulting from a Workhouse must arise, not from keeping the Poor in the House, but from keeping them out of it; by constraining the inferior Classes to the Parish to silence the clamour, and to satisfy the cravings, of wilful and woeful indigence.[18]

---

16 See M Todaro and S Smith (2006) *Economic development*, Harlow: Pearson, ch 6.
17 Cited by S E Finer in D Gladstone (ed) (1997) *Edwin Chadwick*, London: Routledge, p 85.
18 J T Becher (1828) *The antipauper system*, London: W Simpkin and R Marshall.

---

The principle of less eligibility has been one of the recurring sores of British social policy. It recurs continually in suggestions that there is an 'unemployment trap', so that people are better off not working, that it is wrong for anyone to get as much in benefits as someone else gets in work, or that people are 'better off on the dole'. This is usually condemned as undermining the 'incentive to work'.[19] The arguments about social security and incentives will be looked at again in Chapter 20, but this example has very little to do with incentives. If the issue were one of incentives, the test should be whether each person is better or worse off – which is the test applied in much of continental Europe, where unemployment benefits are related to previous earnings. What is happening instead is that people on benefits everywhere are being compared to people in work anywhere – a direct reflection of less eligibility and the 'iron law of wages'. Practical men, Keynes once commented, are often the slaves of some defunct economist.

The rationale for the workhouse test was less clear. Partly, it was a means of ensuring less eligibility; partly, it was a means of restricting costs; and partly, it was a deterrent measure.

> The workhouse should be a place of hardship, of coarse fare, of degradation and humility; it should be administered with strictness – with severity; it should be as repulsive as is consistent with humanity.[20]

The Poor Law Commissioners suggested that the discipline of the workhouse would be a comfort to elderly people, and a deterrent to the idle. The logic of this was that workhouses should be unpleasant. Although it was not for want of trying, there was no way that the conditions of many people inside the workhouses – sometimes called 'pauper palaces'[21] – could be much worse than conditions outside. Where the Guardians of the Poor did introduce dreadful regimes, there could be a scandal – which happened in Andover, where the paupers were fed so little that they were found chewing the gristle of bones they were supposed to be crushing.[22] Where they did not, they were criticised for their generosity and incitement to dependency. Increasingly, Poor Law administrators came to rely on the 'stigma' of pauperism – a sense of shame – rather than the physical unpleasantness of the workhouse. When hospital provision attached to workhouses was expanded in the 1870s, Guardians were instructed to ensure

---

[19] For example Cm 7913 (2010) *21st century welfare,*, London: Department for Work and Pensions, p 10.

[20] Milman, cited in E Chadwick (1833) *Report from E Chadwick Esq on London and Berkshire*, Publisher unknown.

[21] A Digby (1978) *Pauper palaces*, London: Routledge and Kegan Paul.

[22] I Anstruther (1973) *The scandal of the Andover workhouse*, London: Geoffrey Bles.

that people using the hospitals came through the workhouse entrance, so that they would know where they were.[23]

## The reaction against the Poor Law

The foundations of the modern social security system came not from the Poor Law but from the reaction to it. As services were expanded, there was increasing pressure to provide services outside the scope of the Poor Law, to avoid the stigma of pauperism. The measures taken included labour exchanges, free school meals, the school medical service and, most importantly from the point of view of social security, systems of pensions and National Insurance, introduced in 1908 and 1911. (The 1911 National Insurance system was not the same as National Insurance today; the system was reconstructed after the Second World War.) The argument for old age pensions had been made by Charles Booth, whose research on poverty since 1889 had established him as the leading authority.[24] The 1908 Old Age Pensions Act offered an almost universal pension for people over 70 − nominally means tested, but with a level high enough to mean that most old people would qualify. The main exclusion was that people who had been paupers or criminals were not entitled.

The cost of the 1908 pensions proved greater than expected; it alarmed the government, and when three years later benefits for health and unemployment were introduced, they were tied to insurance contributions, primarily to ensure that there would be some means of recouping costs. The 1908 pensions were finally replaced in 1925 by insurance benefits, for reasons of economy.[25]

In the period after the First World War, services continued to be introduced outside the Poor Law. The increasing level of unemployment prompted a series of temporary measures intended to protect unemployed people without bringing them into the scope of the Poor Law: examples were out of work donations given to unemployed people after 1918, transitional payments introduced in 1927 and the system of Unemployment Assistance introduced in 1934. The dole and the means test were not, then, part of the Poor Law. On the contrary, they were introduced to avoid the problems of the Poor Law, in the belief they would be more acceptable.

## The mutualist tradition

There is a third strand in the development of social security, which is the role of mutual aid and the 'friendly societies'. The principle of social insurance was

---

[23] B Abel-Smith (1964) *The hospitals 1800-1948*, London: Heinemann.
[24] P Spicker (1990) 'Charles Booth: the examination of poverty', *Social Policy and Administration*, vol 24, no 1, pp 21–38.
[25] B B Gilbert (1970) *British social policy 1914-1939*, London: Batsford.

based on cooperative arrangements between people in related work. Mutual aid was initially associated with socialism: in much of Europe, there was a strong link between mutual aid and working-class movements. The system developed in Germany by Bismarck was directly based on the mutualist model – Bismarck saw it as stealing the socialists' thunder.[26]

Mutual aid provided the basis for a number of important social measures. The building societies were developed as mutualist, non-profit organisations, and a number of insurance companies began life in this way. Prior to the foundation of the National Health Service, much of the focus fell on health. According to a French observer, half of all the adult males in Britain in 1850 were members of friendly societies.[27] The National Insurance Act 1911 had a major effect in consolidating the work of the friendly societies, because it gave them a major role in the organisation of primary care: under the terms of that scheme, general practice in many places was commissioned by the friendly societies.

The Beveridge plan for social security was very much concerned to retain the role of mutual associations in the provision of social security. It failed to do so,. Part of the reason was the NHS, which took away one of the main reasons people had for contributing while in work. The establishment of a national scheme for retirement pensions equally undercut the role of friendly societies in the provision of pensions. Post-war, mutualist pensions dwindled away to a marginal role; for many years it was common for occupational pensions to be limited to £4 per week, the maximum level permitted before a pension might affect entitlement to National Assistance.

The subsequent growth in occupational and 'private' schemes will be dealt with in due course. The decline of mutualism in social security in the UK is, in important ways, untypical. The system of insurance in Germany supplanted the mutuals, but kept their methods of operation; the system in France built social security provision around them, enshrining the principle of solidarity at the heart of social protection.[28] Continental insurance schemes were often seen, in Britain, as failing to provide the comprehensive, consistent provision that state welfare was able to offer. Over time, however, their coverage has improved, and the level of benefits they have been able to offer has been substantially superior to benefits in the UK.

---

[26] See G A Ritter (1983) *Social welfare in Germany and Britain*, Leamington Spa: Berg.

[27] Laurent (1865), cited in B Gibaud (1994) 'La mutualité française entre État et marché, naissance d'une identité (1850-1914)', in B Palier (ed) *Comparer les systèmes de protection sociale en Europe vol 1: Rencontres d'Oxford*, Paris: Mire, p 192.

[28] J-J Dupeyroux (1989) *Droit de la sécurité sociale*, Paris: Dalloz.

## The Beveridge report

The Beveridge report, which was published in 1942, is widely considered to be the foundation of the British welfare state.[29] It begins with a wide-ranging rhetoric about the future of welfare. There were 'five giants' to slay: the giants of Want, Idleness, Ignorance, Squalor and Disease. The report was about social security, but Beveridge went much further: if social security was to work, there had to be full employment, family allowances and a national health service. Beveridge was proposing, in his own words, a 'British revolution'.

The Beveridge report is an odd document, and the passing of the years has not diminished its strangeness. It begins from a value base that is difficult for many people nowadays to relate to. Beveridge's critics point to his muddled combination of liberalism and social planning, his patrician assumption that he knew what was best, and particularly the assumption of a normal family in which the man was a wage earner and the woman was his dependant.

All this is true, but there was much more to it. Beveridge was an old-fashioned administrator – old fashioned even by the standards of the 1940s – who had been sidelined. He had worked with Winston Churchill before in the Liberal government, and he expected to be made responsible for munitions, in his view a better and more important job than social security – Jose Harris, his biographer, records that when he was told he was going to be responsible for social security, there were tears in his eyes. 'I didn't feel', he said, 'that welfare was up my street.'[30] But he took over the process, to such an extent that the committee he was chairing declined to sign the report, which came out in his name. Churchill did not want the report and was prepared to sit on it, but Beveridge leaked it to the press, and so Churchill reluctantly agreed to publication. The report was a best seller, with long queues forming to buy it. The Nazis were annoyed; they had thought of social security and welfare provision as among their strengths. The report became a symbol of what Britain was fighting for, and it proved to be such an effective propaganda tool that the Allies dropped copies of it by parachute into occupied territory.[31] When the war was over, reforms inspired by Beveridge were introduced not just in Britain, but in other continental countries, including Belgium and France – though their understanding of the report was so different that it might as well have been a different document. To the British, the Beveridge report created a system that was unified and universal, covering people 'from the cradle to the grave'. To the French, Beveridge's emphasis on the role of mutual action (the friendly societies) and voluntary effort tied the report to the idea of 'solidarity', and helped to justify their own, very much more diverse, approach to benefits.

---

[29] W Beveridge (1942) *Social insurance and allied services,* Cmd 6404, London: HMSO.

[30] J Harris (1977) *William Beveridge,* Oxford: Oxford University Press.

[31] J-J Dupeyroux (1989) *Droit de la sécurité sociale,* Paris: Dalloz, p 72n.

Social security in Britain has been dominated by the history of the Poor Law. The 'institutional' and 'residual' models used to explain the nature of social security benefits are drawn directly from a contrast between the Poor Law and the welfare state that came after it. The Poor Law was for the poor; the welfare state was for everyone. The Poor Law was stigmatising; the welfare state would treat people as of right. This may not have been strictly accurate – many earlier developments did offer services as of right, and some of the most contentious issues, such as means testing, were not part of the Poor Law – but it was near enough to be credible.

In many ways, Britain has never left behind the legacy of the Poor Law. The arguments that dominated discussion in the 19th century are still prominent today. The welfare state was not supposed to be reserved for the poor, but many of the arguments about its success or failure are based in the assumption that it is. The arguments about 'incentives' and being 'better off on the dole' are still around. The belief that welfare undermines people's sense of independence and responsibility, a recurrent theme of criticism of the Poor Law, was a popular refrain 200 years ago. One writer complained that 'It has been the experience of every country, that a liberal provision for the poor has been followed by sloth, prodigality, and neglect of their families.'[32] The belief that things were different a few years ago is another recurring theme. In 1818, thirty years before the previous quotation, Gascoigne wrote,

> A general feeling of self-dependence pervaded the labouring class; that parish relief was considered as disgraceful and disgusting; and that to apply for it, even in old age, was to admit either idleness, improvidence, or extreme misfortune.[33]

We can hear the same arguments today when people suggest that the welfare state has introduced a 'dependency culture'. The welfare state was supposed to institutionalise dependency, and make it accepted as a normal part of everyday life. If it was true that people were more ready to accept dependency as the result of the welfare state, that would not be a sign of the failure of the welfare state, but of its success. It may be true, but there is very little evidence either way.

## QUESTIONS FOR DISCUSSION

What is wrong with principles of the Poor Law?
Was it a mistake to move away from mutual and voluntary effort?

---

[32] D Porteous ('A citizen of Glasgow') (1783) *A letter to the citizens of Glasgow*, Glasgow: Robert Chapman and Alexander Duncan, p 1.

[33] H B Gascoigne (1818) *Pauperism*, London: Baldwin, Cradock and Joy.

# The politics of social security

Despite the apparent consensus on social security in political terms, there have always been differences between left and right wing views on social security. Broadly speaking, the left is seen as institutional, in favour of public provision and for universal benefits; the right is more likely to favour residual welfare, selectivity and retrenchment. These differences do not always emerge in practice, because the complexities of the benefit system make reform slow, difficult and inconsistent. The main political parties share a common discourse that has increasingly emphasised returning people to work and means testing benefits.

## Left and right wing views

Ideologies are interrelated sets of views and opinions. People do not often work out positions from scratch; they refer to general ideas, principles and discourses on policy. Broadly speaking, the 'right' wing is associated with residual welfare, selective benefits and private provision; the 'left' wing is associated with institutional welfare, universal benefits and public provision. However, the correspondence between these ideas and political groupings is far from perfect, and there are many people, from different places on the political spectrum, who do not fit the model. Taking money from the rich to give to the poor is selective, but it is usually thought of as 'left wing'. Giving people the money is supposed to be 'right wing', but there is a paternalistic argument for giving people food rather than money – the case for a soup kitchen – which is as likely to appeal as much to the right as the left. Offering them public provision is 'left wing', but the left does not argue for the state distribution of goods, like food or clothing. In Chapter 2, I made the point that social security is implicitly based in the private market. Identifying social security in those terms makes many people uncomfortable, because in the UK arguments for the economic market are associated with the political right wing, and right wingers are also likely to be opposed to state benefits. People on the right may dislike being identified with arguments for social security; people on the left may dislike being identified with arguments for the market.

The problem is that 'left' and 'right' stand for a wide range of different views, and sometimes those views pull in different directions. In many European countries, these links are desperately unpredictable. In Italy, public provision is sometimes seen as a way of propping up the supports of the political right, and opposed by the left. Support for the poorest in France is strongly linked, through social Catholicism, with the political right. The 'right wing' Juppé plan, which brought the unions out on the streets in protest, proposed the removal of special privileges in pensions for certain occupational groups, universal rights to health care and guaranteed access to treatment. Marc Blondel, for *Force Ouvrière*, a radical trades union, described the plan as 'the biggest rip-off in the history of the French Republic. It is the end of the *Sécurité Sociale*.'[1] In Belgium, proposals for a minimum state benefit in the 1980s were opposed with the comment that it would only benefit 'drunkards, whores and nuns'.[2] It is unwise to assume that there is any obvious, rational link between social security policy and familiar ideological positions.

## Labour and Conservative

Britain has been a two-party democracy for much of the last hundred years, and in the post-war period nearly all governments have been clearly identifiable as Labour or Conservative. The main exception is the Conservative-Liberal Democrat coalition of 2010, but even then the coalition committed itself substantially to the programme for welfare reform outlined in the Conservative party manifesto.[3] British politics is usually described in two dimensions, with Labour on the left and the Conservatives on the right; Liberal Democrats are sometimes thought of as centre-left, though following their coalition with the Conservatives that is open to question. The terms 'left' and 'right' wing are conventional, and they are not always helpful: all the political parties are broad coalitions of interest, with contradictory elements. Labour has mixed a general commitment to rights to welfare with a sometimes restrictive view of the 'undeserving' poor, and the rights of people out of work.[4] Conservatives have mixed liberal or 'laissez faire' views with an authoritarian emphasis on order;[5] in the course of the last thirty years they have been heavily influenced by American condemnations of welfare provision.[6]

The difficulty of placing people on the 'left' or 'right' is amplified because, over time, the dividing lines shift. In the 1940s, both Labour and Conservatives were

---

[1]  V M Blondel (1996), 'L'étatisation, antichambre de la privatisation', *Droit Sociale* no 3, March; and see P Spicker (1998) 'Le trou de la Sécu: social security in France', in E Brunsdon, H Dean and R Woods (eds) *Social Policy Review 10*, Kent: Social Policy Association.

[2]  J Vranken (1984) 'Anti-poverty policy in Belgium', in J C Brown (ed) *Anti-poverty policy in the European Community*, London: Policy Studies Institute.

[3]  Conservative Party (2010) *Invitation to join the government of Britain*, London: Conservative Party; HM Government (2010) *The coalition: our programme for government*, London: Cabinet Office.

[4]  N Dennis and A Halsey (1988) *English ethical socialism*, Oxford: Clarendon Press.

[5]  D King (1987) *The new right*, London: Macmillan.

[6]  See A Deacon (2002) *Perspectives on welfare,* Buckingham: Open University Press.

committed to the 'welfare state', including family allowances, National Insurance and the expansion of council housing; they were divided on nationalisation. In the 1960s, Conservatives and Labour shared views on health, social security benefits and higher education; they were divided on housing and secondary education. In the 1990s, both Labour and Conservatives accepted arguments for tax reductions, the privatisation of certain state activities and the reduction of benefits to certain 'undeserving' groups. 'Left' and 'right' wing are relative positions, and their meaning has changed over time.

At the time of the Beveridge report, there was a war on, and a national coalition government. Both parties were committed to the development of the social security system, and the first major reform (the introduction of Family Allowances in 1945) was introduced by the coalition government. Both political parties, in the post-war period, were committed to common aims: the extension of social protection and the prevention of unemployment by Keynesian methods. The 1944 White Paper on Social Security declared:

> The scheme as a whole will embrace, not certain occupation and income groups, but the entire population. Concrete expression is thus given to the solidarity and unity of the nation, which in war have been its bulwarks against aggression and in peace will be its guarantees of success in the fight against individual want and mischance.[7]

It is part of the accepted wisdom of social policy that war is a major influence on its development. The reference to national solidarity, and the commitment to a universal, uniform state scheme, show this very clearly. The war gave people a common purpose; it also led to the creation of a massive government machine, which made new kinds of policy possible.

The introduction of the new National Insurance system, and the abolition of the Poor Law, fell to a Labour government, in office from 1945 to 1951, and the foundation of the welfare state has irresistibly been identified with Labour. The scope of their actions was limited by economic stringency; Beveridge's proposals were pared down, with only a limited commitment to Family Allowances (which were not given for the first child), a limited contribution from the Treasury (just over a third of the level Beveridge had proposed) and a restrictive view of the minimum income guaranteed by National Assistance.

That was largely how the situation remained until the 1960s. Labour's radical proposal for an earnings-related pension in the 1950s was watered down, and 'graduated pensions' were introduced in 1959, with limited finance and very limited benefits. There were other changes at the same time: for example, concern about the failure of the National Insurance scheme to protect the bereaved children of divorced parents led to the introduction of a new benefit, the Child's Special

---

[7]    Cmd 6550, (1944) *Social insurance part 1*, London: HMSO, p 6.

Allowance. (Very few people qualified, and fewer ever claimed it – the main effect of the leaflets seemed to be to confuse people who had intended to get information on Child Benefit. It was closed to new business in 1987, and no child is now eligible.)

This period has been described as a period of 'welfare consensus'.[8] That term fails to describe the reality, for three reasons. First, it suggests that the parties were agreed about policy. They were not, as their actions in other areas – such as nationalisation or private rented housing – confirmed. Social security was not a legislative priority by comparison, but there were material differences between the parties. The Beveridge scheme was introduced in the 1946 National Insurance Act, and implemented in 1948. It was only eight years before Labour, in opposition, called for a fundamental reappraisal of pensions.[9] Second, it suggests that a failure to introduce change indicates consensus. What both Labour and Conservative governments were to find was that the social security system was very much more difficult to reform than they might have wished. Often the changes that took place, notably reforms in 1966, 1975, 1980 and 1984, were heralded as fundamental alterations to the system – each was presented (as the reforms announced in 2010 are being presented) as the most significant reform since Beveridge. Somehow, the system seemed to glide inexorably onward. The analogy has been drawn with turning around an ocean liner – it takes a long time before a change in direction becomes visible.

The third problem is the suggestion that this period was somehow anomalous, that the parties later came to disagree on fundamentals and to engage in radical reform. The truth is very different. The social security system is a massive, shapeless monster, and at any one time, most of it is untouched by reform. Despite many substantial, often radical reforms, most benefits have an inordinately long shelf life. Even One Parent Benefit lasted 20 years, from the early days of Child Benefit Increase in 1977 until 1997 – which was surprising, in view of the Conservative government's long-standing concern with the dependency of lone parents. Some benefits simply undergo repeated changes of name: National Assistance became Supplementary Benefit in 1966, then Income Support in 1988. The rules have changed continually, but they are all recognisably the same benefit. The insurance benefits have lasted longest. Sickness Benefit lasted from 1948 till 1983, though a stump lasted until 1995; Invalidity Benefit from 1971 to 1995; Unemployment Benefit from 1948 to 1996.

Every reform has drawn on the pattern of services that existed before it. The Beveridge scheme drew heavily on the 1911 National Insurance scheme. When Labour introduced National Assistance in 1948, it did not scrap everything that had existed before; many of the rules and regulations were drawn directly from the 1934 Unemployment Assistance Board. When the Conservatives introduced

Rent Rebate and Rent Allowance (later combined in Housing Benefit), they based the design on Labour's incomprehensible 1967 scheme for Rate Rebate.

## The end of 'consensus'?

After 1970, the 'consensus' seemed to break down. The Conservative government, under Edward Heath (1970-74), experimented with many of the ideas later associated with 'Thatcherism'. The policies did not all tend in one direction. Often attracted by radical and experimental schemes, the Heath government proposed some major reforms (notably floating the idea of a scheme to unify aspects of social security and taxation[10]) as well as a bundle of lesser schemes. Probably their main legacy was a major increase in the use of means testing, with the introduction of Family Income Supplement as a benefit for people on low wages, and the introduction of Rent Rebate and Rent Allowance in place of general subsidies to council housing. The Labour government that followed had aspirations to promote greater equality, in enhanced pensions, rights for women and for people with disabilities. However, the depth of the country's financial crisis in the mid-1970s compromised these policies, and later introductions were focused on containing the cost of benefits. The introduction of Child Benefit in 1977 was set to be postponed, but the government was embarrassed publicly into implementing it.[11] The review of Supplementary Benefit in 1978 proposed an acceptance of the scheme's 'mass role' − effectively, an acknowledgement that means testing was fundamental − in a set of reforms to be taken at no extra cost.[12]

The Conservative government returned under Margaret Thatcher seemed, and still seems in retrospect, the model of an ideologically committed political movement, determined not to be 'blown off course' by mass unemployment or the collapse of manufacturing industry. The policies the Thatcher government introduced, such as the Social Security Act 1980 and the Fowler Reviews, were often presented as major structural reforms. In practice, however, the changes in social security over this period were characterised much more by progressive, incremental attempts to reduce the cost of benefits. Their task was made exceptionally difficult by the staggering rise in unemployment generated by the government's restructuring of the British economy. (Unemployment rose, officially, threefold, despite numerous downward revisions of the count. Long-term unemployment rose sixteenfold.) The economies included, among many others, the abolition of certain benefits, like Death Grant and Maternity Grant; reductions in entitlement, including the abolition of earnings-related supplements for Unemployment and Sickness Benefit and the extension of qualifying periods for Unemployment Benefit; the transfer of costs to other

---

[10]  Cmnd 5116 (1972) *Proposals for a tax credit system*, London: HMSO.
[11]  F Field (1976) 'Killing a commitment', *New Society*, 17 June.
[12]  Department of Health and Social Security (1978) *Social assistance*, London: DHSS.

budgets, like Housing Benefit and the introduction of Statutory Sick Pay and Statutory Maternity Pay; and the attempt to curb demand for extra benefits, through reforms of the system of discretionary grants in 1980 and the abolition of the new system in 1988 when it proved too costly. The same pattern of continuing economy was maintained under the Major government, which introduced Incapacity Benefit in an attempt to curb the cost of long-term sickness.

The Labour government elected in 1997 emphasised the role of benefits as either a response to poverty, or as a route to the labour market. A wide-ranging review of the principles behind many benefits was limited in part by the commitment to maintain Conservative spending plans in the early years, which led in particular to a cut in benefit for lone parents, and the strict control of expenditure maintained by the Treasury. Labour's most important reforms were probably the introduction of various Tax Credits, which extended means testing across a wide range of incomes, and the reform of allowances for dependents, so that Child Benefit is no longer deducted from the income of the poorest families. However, the government came to be increasingly driven by a commitment to 'personalisation' – mainly interpreted as individualistic employment support – and conditionality, understood in terms of the imposition of moral sanctions for non-compliance.[13] Labour's 2008 White Paper rethought the organisation of benefits for working-age claimants, distinguishing those who are 'work ready' from those who are 'progressing' to work.[14] The Conservative manifesto similarly spoke of penalties for people who refused to work and a 'single Work Programme for everyone who is unemployed', including claimants of Incapacity Benefit.[15] Like the Labour government's programme, that would be done by commissioning private sector and independent services to offer personalised training for employability. The policy of the Conservatives was largely adopted by the Conservative-Liberal Democrat coalition, though there was one significant amendment: the Work Programme is now aimed not at all unemployed people, but at vulnerable groups and the long-term unemployed.[16]

## Party and principle

Can any identification be made between party and principle? In general, the left wing is supposed to be associated with universal views and a preference for non-means-tested benefits; the right wing has tended to favour a residual model

---

[13] P Gregg (2008) *Realising potential*, London: Department for Work and Pensions.

[14] Department for Work and Pensions (2008) *Raising expectations and increasing support*, Cm 7506, London: The Stationery Office.

[15] Conservative Party (2010) *Invitation to join the government of Britain*, London: Conservative Party, p 15.

[16] HM Government (2010) *The coalition: Our programme for government*, London: Cabinet Office.

with means tests that 'target' resources on those who are poorest. Consistently with this, since 1970 Conservative governments have been responsible for Family Income Supplement, Housing Benefit and the 1988 reforms; Labour, for non-contributory benefits for disabled people and Child Benefit. At the same time, there are measures that do not fit the convenient political stereotype. The Conservative Tax Credit scheme of the 1970s was based in an institutional model of welfare; Labour's Tax Credits, introduced in the late 1990s, were a form of means testing. The 1975 pensions scheme, in which Labour replaced a Conservative plan with its own, greatly increased subsidies to (private) occupational pensions schemes. The reform of Supplementary Benefit began life under a Labour government (in 1978), but was introduced by the Conservatives. 'Active labour market' policies, stressing the responsibility of each individual claimant to return to work, replaced job creation and training programmes during the Conservative administration of the 1980s. They were pursued vigorously by Labour[17] and have been continued into the Conservative-Liberal Democrat administration. Lord Freud, whose review for the Labour government promoted that policy, subsequently became a Conservative junior minister for Work and Pensions. Perhaps the parties are more flexible than they seem; perhaps their steps are guided by a path they have been set on by their predecessors. All the parties share a common way of approaching and thinking about the issues – a 'discourse', a vocabulary and framework of understanding – that limits and shapes the options they will ultimately follow.

## QUESTIONS FOR DISCUSSION

What should a party that favours the private sector be arguing for?
What do the political parties agree on?

---

[17]  A Bryson and J Jacobs (1992) *Policing the workshy*, Aldershot: Avebury; S Wright (2002) 'Activating the unemployed: the street-level implementation of UK policy', in J Clasen (ed) *What future for social security?*, Bristol: The Policy Press.

# Chapter 6

# A unified system?

The Beveridge system has been represented as universal, uniform and based in a unified administration. None of these is strictly true. The system was limited and hemmed in by conditions. It was deliberately designed to be bureaucratic and centralised, but the model of service delivery has greatly changed over the years. The scale of the administrative operation implies rather more diversity than is at first apparent, and responsibilities are shared across a range of agencies. Schemes for unification do not necessarily simplify the administration.

Describing social security as a 'system' tends to imply that the parts have some kind of structural relationship to the whole. That was certainly what the Beveridge report was intended to achieve. Beveridge provided the blueprint for social security in Britain, and the scheme of social insurance dominated policy for at least forty years. The details of the Beveridge report are principally concerned with National Insurance, which Beveridge planned to cover people 'from cradle to grave'. Insurance could not do that; the coverage has never been comprehensive, and other benefits have grown to fill in the gaps. The limitations, and then the progressive erosion of the insurance base led over time to a different kind of scheme: a multiplicity of benefits, covering a range of contingencies through a variety of methods. The post-war British system has been characterised, in continental literature, as having three elements: universality, uniformity and unified administration.[1] None of these is true, but understanding why they are not true offers a useful starting point for the analysis of a complex, diverse field of activity.

## The limits of universality

The coverage of the social security system was intended, in principle, to be comprehensive. In so far as universality offers a 'right to welfare', benefits should be available to everyone in need. However, the situation is not so simple. Despite wide-ranging coverage, there are several important restrictions. Benefits are often conditional on meeting special requirements, such as residence or good behaviour, that have nothing to do with need. There are commonly exclusions on the basis of age, nationality (notoriously, the exclusion of asylum seekers) and

---

[1]  J J Dupeyroux (1989) *Droit de la sécurité sociale*, Paris: Dalloz.

personal situation: young people who have left school are assumed for a period to be dependent on their parents, while students are excluded from a number of benefits (such as Housing Benefit). In the jargon of the field this is referred to as 'conditionality'.

Conditionality is a muddled topic, which lumps together three different kinds of issue. The first set relates to the administration of the benefit or service. The requirements to fill in specified forms, to sign claims or to provide supportive evidence as a condition of receiving benefit are intended to facilitate service delivery. Some of these procedures have been shown to be unnecessary in practice,[2] and some seem to represent a punitive distrust of claimants, but the general rationale for their inclusion is clear enough: they shift the burden of managing data from the service administrator to the user. In principle, this should not affect eligibility, but in practice it has important effects for specific groups – for example, although the practice is in decline, homeless people have sometimes had to claim on a daily basis in circumstances where other people claim fortnightly. (If banks are given the Universal Service Obligation announced in the last budget of the outgoing Labour government in 2010, homeless people will be able to manage their money through bank accounts, as they do in France.)

Second, there are conditions used as a form of rationing; limiting eligibility is a way of limiting costs. Governments make considered decisions about where they want resources to go. Examples include limiting the value of housing that benefits will pay for, lowering the rate of benefits for younger claimants, or the reduced coverage available to married women in the Beveridge scheme.

Third, some conditions are imposed for moral reasons. Residence tests are widely used to deter newcomers from claiming non-contributory benefits; limitations on the rights of people in prison can be seen as part of the punishment. Making people sign off benefit if they have previously committed fraud can be seen as an administrative precaution, but equally it has the taste of moral intervention. Possibly the best-known restrictions are the denial of benefits to people who are on strike, or the six-month suspension for those who have become unemployed through 'misconduct'. In the same vein, extra conditions for people with drug or alcohol dependency were introduced from autumn 2010.

Any of these conditions can be seen as a way of regulating the conduct or position of people who use social services. The conditions, taken together, can be identified with 'discipline' in the sense in which it is used by Foucault or Donzelot.[3] For Foucault, power is made up of 'a multiplicity of relationships of

---

[2]    Alabama Social Welfare (1965) 'A simplified method of establishing continuing eligibility in the adult categories', vol 30, Jan-Feb, pp 13-14;  M Phillips (1972) *The impact of the declaration procedure upon the perceptions and attitudes of mothers receiving Aid to Families with Dependent Children*, unpublished DSW: Columbia University.

[3]    H Dean (1991) *Social security and social control*, London: Routledge; C Jones and T Novak (1999) *Poverty, welfare and the disciplinary state*, London: Routledge.

force which are inherent in the domain in which they are exercised, and which make up their organisation'.[4] Regulation has, necessarily, the effect of ordering the conduct of recipients.

There are, however, many motives for the imposition of conditions besides a concern with social control. One is the desire to administer services effectively and by clearly defined rules, which can be explained just as persuasively in terms of the protection of users' rights as it can in any desire to regulate users. A second motive is the desire to provide services equitably. 'Less eligibility' was plausibly presented in its day as a way of preserving equity between workers and non-workers – primarily by protecting the position of the independent labourer from the starvation otherwise implied by Ricardo's 'iron law of wages'. The central rationale of a cohabitation rule, similarly, is to avoid an invidious distinction between the status of married and unmarried couples. A third motive is to manage the financial aspects of benefits. One effect of linking benefits to contributions is to require people to have a work record in order to qualify, but this was never the primary intention; insurance schemes, initially developed by mutual aid, were largely self-financing, and they opened up to governments the opportunity to offer social protection without the major financial commitment that would have been required to support an equivalent extension of social assistance.[5] These examples suggest that discipline and regulation are as likely to be a by-product of conditionality as they are to be the primary motivation. Taken together, they point to a key limitation on the idea of universality. Benefits have never been intended to go to everyone.

## Uniformity

Social security in Britain is centralised to an extraordinary degree. The system was designed to be run from the top down: rules were made at the centre (generally in the Department of Social Security) and given to local offices as tablets of stone (or more accurately, in a very lengthy series of instructions held in loose-leaf binders). This stands in striking contrast to many of the systems in continental Europe, where benefit administration has differed in three main ways:

- benefit rules in much of Europe were usually established not by a central ministry, but by a range of independent or quasi-independent funds;
- the administration of many benefits is decentralised, often at the level of a local authority;
- many benefits, particularly related to health and public assistance, are discretionary, and depend on the judgement of an official or social worker.

---

[4]   M Foucault (1976) *Histoire de la sexualité: la volonté de savoir*, Paris: Gallimard, pp 121-2.
[5]   B B Gilbert (1966) *The evolution of national insurance in Great Britain*, London: Joseph.

The differences in the British system were deliberate. We had had a decentralised, discretionary system under the Poor Law, and politicians and officials after the Second World War were determined that the new system should not be like that. A central element of the new structure was that people should not be subject to official discretion: discretion drives out rights, and if people were dependent on the judgement of officials, they would not be genuinely entitled. That was the reason, too, for the strict division between social work and social security — if social workers handled money, they would become like Poor Law officials.

The system introduced in 1948 was administered by two bodies: the Ministry of Pensions and National Insurance and the National Assistance Board. Benefit officers were civil servants, and as such they were bound by the codes of the civil service: every action they took was taken in the name of the minister, and they were entitled (and required) to be anonymous, because it was not their decision to make. This structure survived the combination of these bodies into the Ministry of Social Security (1966) and the Department of Health and Social Security (1968); local offices of the DHSS generally had an administrative split between long-term (insurance) and short-term (assistance) benefits.

The DHSS, later to be the Department of Social Security, was one of the most complete 'bureaucracies' ever to function in Britain. Weber's ideal type of bureaucracy contains a number of elements:

- the system is governed by rules, that are framed in abstract terms and can then be applied to specific cases;
- there is a hierarchy of authority, with a chain of command stretching from the top to the bottom;
- people have specified tasks: 'the regular activities required for the purposes of the organisation are distributed in a fixed way as official duties';[6]
- the system is impersonal; outcomes are decided according to the rules, rather than personal relationships.

The DHSS was built around these principles, and the local office of the DHSS passed cases up a 'stream', working as if it was a Fordist production line. This system was phenomenally effective: most claims, in a time prior to computerisation, were turned round well within two weeks, and complex National Insurance calculations were often processed within four or five days. Despite the record, it was easy to be critical of the DHSS. In cases that went wrong, the wheels could grind exceeding slow — the effect of appealing against a decision was to take a case out of the stream, adding weeks to the processing of basic queries. One of the most frequent complaints heard from members of the public was that 'They can't find my file'. The system was not designed to find

---

[6]   H H Gerth and C Wright Mills (1948) *From Max Weber*, London: RKP.

files, which could be at any one of fifteen or more places in the office at any one time; it was designed to put the files through at maximum speed.

The creation of the Benefits Agency in the 1990s coincided with the introduction of computerisation, in place of the production line. The Department of Social Security (now the Department for Work and Pensions) made a major investment in the largest computer system of its type in Europe, hoping for an all-singing, all-dancing system that would respond to all its administrative needs at a stroke. Most of the problems of computerisation were predictable: bugs that had to be ironed out and unexpected downtime, with some spectacular crashes. Less predictable, perhaps, was the sweeping effect that the computers had on the administrative process. Computers have many virtues. They can perform repeated calculations rapidly and accurately; they allow cross-referencing and sharing of information; and they have improved the presentation of documents immeasurably (even if they cannot translate letters into plain English). But they also have vices. Centralised systems are vulnerable to crashes: before the system moved to internet-based access, the system was regularly and frequently down. Computers do not handle correspondence well, and basing the file on computer made it necessary to hold files in more than one place. Benefits Agency staff were instructed to put the unnecessary correspondence in long-term stores, and then BA offices were charged for retrieving them – which meant, in practice, that BA officials had to sit illicitly with a pile of bootleg files cluttered around their sleek new workstations, to avoid being without the essential information. (The DWP still relies on central storage: in the call centres that are being used in place of the old benefits offices, officials have few opportunities to vary the rules, which means that the files are stored after a few weeks, and become either difficult to retrieve or irretrievable.) And computers are inflexible. One of the most unfortunate side-effects of using external contractors to manage computer systems is that every change and every refinement costs money. Bringing together payment dates across a range of benefits, for example, required the DWP to commission new programmes for every benefit affected. If these systems worked, some inflexibility might have to be tolerated. Often, unfortunately, they do not. Purpose-written programmes have to be debugged point by point: staff complain that there are still problems in the system that have not been sorted after more than ten years. 'We're still doing work-rounds,' an officer told me.

A second major change was in management style. The Benefits Agency, as successor to local offices of the DHSS, moved away from the civil service model. The managers of offices have been given a degree of financial autonomy, allowing them to vary the physical structure and pattern of service delivery. Benefit recipients became 'customers'. Staff were issued with uniforms and name tags (though, for security reasons, the name tags may not be in the official's real name). Several other parts of the Department of Social Security were split off into 'agencies', or nominally autonomous management units. These include:

- the Fraud Investigation Service (formerly the Benefit Fraud Inspectorate)

- the Contributions Agency
- the Information Technology Services Agency, and
- the Veterans Agency (the renamed War Pensions Agency)
- the Child Maintenance and Enforcement Commission (the replacement for the Child Support Agency), whose abolition was announced in October 2010.

Two agencies that have not survived further reforms are the Benefits Agency itself, and the Resettlement Agency (for people without a settled way of life), which was absorbed back into the DSS in 1996 and then transferred to the Social Exclusion Unit before being parcelled out to Communities and Local Government. The Benefits Agency has been split between Jobcentre Plus and (after a brief interregnum as two agencies) the Pensions, Disability and Carers Service. The Department for Work and Pensions reports that 40% of current contacts – that is, of over 150 million telephone calls every year – are from people who are currently trying to deal with more than one agency within the DWP (and not including, therefore, those dealing with Tax Credit, Child Benefit or Housing Benefit).[7]

A third, more radical, change has been the shifting of work from local offices to other administrative units. This was prompted partly for reasons of economy (it had become impossible to hire staff in London at national rates), partly because of changes in the administration (particularly the shift to payment through bank accounts) and partly because of general changes in the benefit system, with specific benefits being administered by other bodies. The break-up of the Benefits Agency has reinforced a general trend towards dealing with long-term claimants at arm's length. For practical purposes the Pensions, Disability and Carers Service mainly deals with its clients through call centres. Jobcentre Plus is administered in three main types of office. The First Contact call centres take new claims, entirely by telephony – there is a 'virtual network' operating nationally, so that calls from any part of the country can be diverted to any office that has the capacity to take the call. (It has recently become possible to make the initial claim for Jobseeker's Allowance over the internet. At the time of writing, this covers only about one claim in six, but the DWP believes the online system will account for most new and repeat claims within a very short time.) After the initial claim, the application is passed to the second branch, a local Jobcentre, where claimants will be expected to attend for a 'work-focused interview'. Then the claim goes to another office that is not open to the public, a Benefit Delivery Centre, which deals with assessment, review and payments – functions that previously would have been administered at the level of a local office.

There are some variations in practice between areas; the differences have been encouraged through a series of 'pilots' and experiments, particularly in relation to employment. However, the fundamental structure of benefits remains highly

---

[7]  S Holt (DWP Change Manager) (2009) DWP Scottish Forum, Glasgow, 25 November.

centralised, and bureaucratic in form. Most of the work is done by people working at clerical and executive grades. The task of benefit officers is to operate a huge, complex system as efficiently as possible.

The computerisation of most claims has changed the process, so that there are fewer functional divisions within the offices than used to be the case. Computerisation increasingly means that a benefits adviser should be able to view the essential details on the computer file, but the process for managing information still needs to be rationalised. The Pensions, Disability and Carers Service does have a system of 'one touch' processing – the same officer can see a case through from the initial telephone call to authorisation of payment – but this is a rarity (and it is not always considered desirable from the point of view of security). There will still be a series of people working sequentially on each case, and depending on what needs to be done about the case it will be passed to different parts of the office for processing. That leads to problems in the management of information: it has been typical for changes in address to have to be reported three times, while deaths have had to be reported on average five times.[8] Both are the subject of new procedures to allow people to 'tell us once'. There are also problems with handling of correspondence: it is difficult to include relevant correspondence in the electronic file. (The PDCS has recently introduced a system for scanning letters into the files. The pilot was a formidable enterprise – the office operating it received 10,000-15,000 items of correspondence every working day. Envelopes still have to be opened, papers laid flat and key documents acknowledged and protected; before the pilot they had sub-contracted the massive task of opening and sorting the morning's mail.)

The shift to telephony in place of local offices has also had a significant impact on services. The DWP estimate that half the 150 million calls they receive are of no value either to the user or to the DWP. For example, six and a half million go through to the wrong office, seven and a half million calls are from people asking where their money is and over five million more are progress chasing – 'what is happening to my application?'[9] Research for the Joseph Rowntree Foundation comments:

> The majority of those interviewed had experience of telephone services. A few had had difficulty knowing which number to call, particularly for JCP [Jobcentre Plus], for which there appears to have been 'a long list of phone numbers'. Almost all had had difficulty getting through to the right service on a number of occasions, either finding a number engaged or being put on hold for long periods of time. ... Interviewees complained also that when they had reacted angrily towards being put on hold for long periods, they had been

---

8   Holt, 2009.
9   Holt, 2009.

refused help, had their call terminated, or been threatened with a note on their file warning other advisers of their aggression. Service users feel that staff should be more sympathetic to the fact that users had often been waiting for long periods to get through.[10]

To put this in perspective, relationships were no less problematic when people were being dealt with in local offices – and the exposure of staff to the risk of violence was greater.

In the days of local offices, a typical office dealt with several thousand cases every week. The call centres have very different kinds of caseload: currently in Scotland the Benefit Delivery Centres in Jobcentre Plus have loads varying from 60,000 to 160,000, while the Pensions Service call centres may deal with over a million. It would be naive to suppose that, under this pressure, things do not go wrong extensively; many clients report problems, and despite computerisation, claims are still often wrongly calculated. Offices have performance targets, and comparisons are made between offices. Jobcentre Plus has a range of targets, scoring responsiveness to claimants on timeliness, professionalism and the quality of information given.[11] Splitting up Jobcentre Plus administratively has come at a cost: claimants and advisers can be confused about which office to refer to, and which number to call; the procedures for passing claimants between different branches are not of the best (often they depend on the claimants to make further phone calls); and there can be some to-ing and fro-ing.

The most astonishing thing about the social security system, however, is not how many cases go wrong, but how many are processed successfully and promptly. When Housing Benefit was introduced, the administration in several local authorities virtually collapsed under the strain (a Housing Association I was a member of had to deal with one authority that had still failed after eight years to process some applications from frail, elderly claimants in stable circumstances). *The Times* called Housing Benefit 'the greatest administrative fiasco in the history of the welfare state'[12] (though that, of course, was in the days before the Child Support Agency). Some continental systems can take months, or even years, to sort out a claim. Jobcentre Plus, by comparison, is staggeringly effective. It works in the main to a target of 14 days, and in most cases it exceeds it comfortably. Where individual offices are overburdened, there is the capacity and the processes in place to redistribute the work to others which are less burdened. New claims

[10] D Finn, D Mason, N Rahim and J Casebourne (2008) *Delivering benefits, tax credits and employment services*, York: Joseph Rowntree Foundation, p 40.

[11] Department for Work and Pensions (2010) *Jobcentre Plus targets 2010-11* (www.dwp. gov.uk/about-dwp/customer-delivery/jobcentre-plus/targets-and-performance/).

[12] *The Times*, cited in R Walker (1986) 'Aspects of administration', in P Kemp (ed) *The future of housing benefits*, Glasgow: Centre for Housing Research, p 39.

for Jobseeker's Allowance are generally done in less than 10 days, and changes in circumstances are routinely processed in a couple of days.

## Unified administration

Despite the level of centralisation, the regimentation and the uniformity, social security has never really had a unified administration. Rather, it has been characterised by parallel administrations, often with incompatible rules. Although Income Support, Retirement Pensions and Incapacity Benefit were administered by local offices, many benefits were not, and the establishment of the Pensions, Disability and Carers Service has now split off another large tranche of services. For several benefits – notably benefits for people with disabilities – the administration has been located in national centres; the contact centre forwards claims, rather than dealing with them directly. Other functions are held by local authority education offices (which administer school meals and school uniform grants) and local authority housing or treasurer's departments, which administer Housing Benefit and Council Tax Benefit. Child Benefit and Tax Credits (including the administration of low-income benefits for working people) have been given to Her Majesty's Revenue and Customs, formerly the Inland Revenue. HMRC has had to adjust to a process dealing with millions of people who need to have their applications processed in days rather than months.

It is certainly true that benefits could be improved by greater integration between systems. The different agencies work to different rules and different time periods. One change, introduced in 2009, is to give a number of benefits a common pay day, so that benefits which start on one day of the week do not have to be recalculated when a new benefit starts up two days later. This apparently simple measure has taken six years to introduce and will take two years to be implemented in full. At the same time, moves to simplification have often been illusory: the 'unified' Housing Benefit scheme, which replaced Rent Rebate, Rent Allowance and Rate Rebate, became one of the most complicated benefits in the canon, with different rules applying – as the component benefits had applied different rules – to people claiming for private rented accommodation, rented social housing and supported accommodation.

The 'welfare reform' pursued by the Labour government initially seemed designed to change the administration of welfare towards a client-based system, breaking up the Benefits Agency, separating out provision for pensioners, unemployed people and people with sickness and disability and creating generic benefits for each of these groups. This pattern has subsequently been reconsidered, not only because of increasing emphasis on 'personalisation', but also reflecting the desire to move everyone – whether unemployed, disabled, sick, responsible for child care or in early retirement – into work. Both the main parties have expressed some interest in the argument for a 'single working-age benefit', subsequently crystallised in proposals for a 'Universal Credit'.[13]

The idea of a single benefit harks back to a former time, and seems to ignore the reasons why monolithic, unified benefits like Supplementary Benefit were abandoned. Witnesses to the House of Commons Work and Pensions Committee from pressure groups working with employment, disability and one-parent families were sceptical about its advantages:

> It really worries me as to whether a Single Working Age Benefit would actually be that simple .... Within one benefit there seem to be all these different rates and complexity, depending on what work activity you get involved in, then possibly further sanctions .... Often they start off by looking simple but end up being relatively complex.

> If you took our families as an example, a single working age benefit would need a disabled child premium, the disabled child premium would probably have to be differentiated, perhaps into a higher, middle and lower rate, and then you have basically replicated Disability Living Allowance ... so you might spend an awful lot of time and money replicating the existing system when it came down to brass tacks and to delivery.

> A lot of the attempts to simplify are someone sitting down, looking at a piece of paper and saying 'Gosh, this looks terribly complicated. Let's just make it simpler' without thinking through the implications.[14]

If, as a clutch of recent reports seem to imply, a single benefit was to entail a radical simplification of objectives and a common treatment of people in different circumstances,[15] it would imply substantial injustice and hardship, forcing people to fit inappropriate categories. If, on the other hand, it was to provide different benefits for people who are working, disabled, incapacitated or have responsibilities as carers, it would not be unified. It would have to be a portmanteau benefit, like Supplementary Benefit used to be, with different rules for different circumstances. That seems to be the direction the plan for the

---

[13] R Sainsbury (2006) 'Long term benefits reform', *Disability Rights Bulletin*; K Stanley (2007) 'One benefit rules all', *House Magazine*, 22 September; Cm 7957 (2010) *Universal credit: Welfare that works*, London: DWP.

[14] Select Committee on Work and Pensions (2007) *Seventh report*, London: House of Commons, annex A.

[15] D Freud (2007) *Reducing dependency, increasing opportunity*, London: Department for Work and Pensions; P Gregg (2008) *Realising potential*, London: Department for Work and Pensions; Cm 7913 (2010) *21st Century Welfare*, London: DWP.

Universal Credit is heading in: the proposed benefit would combine a personal allowance with additional elements to cover housing costs and children.[16]

## QUESTIONS FOR DISCUSSION

Should benefits be more democratically organised?
Should the administration be decentralised?

---

[16] Cm 7957 (2010) p 18.

# Part III

## Benefits

The National Insurance system introduced in 1948 failed to cover all the contingencies, and over time other benefits were developed to fill in the gaps. The system has grown progressively more complex. There are five main types of social security benefit. (Government leaflets used to describe three, but this meant that some very different kinds of benefit were lumped together.) The five are:

1.  National Insurance (for example, Retirement Pension). These are benefits paid for by contributions.
2.  Means-tested benefits (for example, Income Support or Housing Benefit). These are for people on low incomes.
3.  Non-contributory benefits (for example, Disability Living Allowance). There is no test of contribution or of means, but there may be a test of need.
4.  Universal benefits (for example, Child Benefit or the non-contributory over-80s pension). These benefits are based on broad categories of people, with no tests of means or needs.
5.  Discretionary benefits. The most important is the Social Fund.

The chapters in this part look in more detail at how these benefits developed, and how they operate.

# Chapter 7

# National Insurance

The National Insurance scheme was designed to be the backbone of the social security system, though its role has been eroded. It provides a range of benefits, principally now the State Pension and benefits for people who are bereaved. Despite the large numbers of people who are covered, the scheme has important deficiencies: people are not necessarily able to contribute, and insurance tends to exclude people in need, requiring different benefits to fill the gap. The range of National Insurance benefits has shrunk, and other benefits have been developed to meet the needs.

*Commission*

## Bismarck or Beveridge?

Social insurance developed historically through two main routes: the development of systems of mutual aid by trades unions, guilds and professional groups, and the action of governments.[1] There are still countries where the provision of insurance benefits is within the province of independent mutual associations, rather than government. Bismarck's social insurance scheme in Germany, which was the first national scheme, was based on a system of independent funds under national tutelage.[2] Contributions and benefits were geared to income and occupational status. This became the dominant pattern in central Europe. The British national system, first introduced in 1911 to cover health care and unemployment, aimed for more comprehensive coverage, using levels of contribution and benefit based on what was economically and politically feasible rather than any actuarial foundation; this was continued in the Beveridge scheme of 1942.

The primary distinction in patterns of social insurance is still commonly represented in terms of 'Bismarckian' and 'Beveridgean' schemes.[3] Bismarckian systems are supposed to offer individualised, earnings-related benefits based on

---

1   P Baldwin (1990) *The politics of social solidarity*, Cambridge: Cambridge University Press.
2   W J Mommsen (1981) *The emergence of the welfare state in Britain and Germany*, Beckenham: Croom Helm;  E Rosenhaft (1994) 'The historical development of German social policy', in J Clasen and R Freeman (ed) *Social policy in Germany*, Hemel Hempstead: Harvester Wheatsheaf.
3   For example, B Palier and G Bonoli (1995) 'Entre Bismarck et Beveridge', *Revue Française de Science Politique*, vol 45, no 4, pp 539-44; H Cremer and P Pestiau (2003) 'Social insurance competition between Bismarck and Beveridge', *Journal of Urban Economics*, vol 54, no 1, pp 181-96.

occupational status, and administered by independent (or quasi–autonomous) funds. The Beveridgean model is often represented as comprehensive and general, offering uniform benefits from a unified administration (though a detailed examination of the scheme would raise doubts about all these points). A French text presents the distinction in the terms outlined in Table 7.1.[4]

**Table 7.1: Beveridge or Bismarck**

| Beveridgean system | Bismarckian system |
| --- | --- |
| 1. Social protection for all | 1. Socio-professional social insurance |
| 2. State administration | 2. Decentralised administration |
| 3. Financed from taxation | 3. Financed by social contributions on salary subject to a ceiling |
| 4. Flat-rate social benefits | 4. Proportionate social benefits subject to a ceiling |
| 5. Obligatory for all | 5. Obligatory only for insured people whose salary is below a ceiling |

Taken too literally, this is probably as misleading about social insurance in Germany[5] as it is about the detail of social insurance in the UK – there are far too many exceptions in both systems for the generalisation to hold water. As a shorthand, however, it helps to point to a key difference in approach. The German system was geared to occupational status and provided benefits that were proportionate to people's contributions. The Beveridge scheme aimed to provide low-level benefits to everyone, rather than better benefits to those who could contribute more. Nick Barr points to four central principles.

- The Beveridge scheme was *strategic*: it tried to present a plan, considering the interrelationships between benefits, not simply a collection of proposals.
- It was *universal*.
- It was *actuarial*: it linked contributions to benefits after the fashion of private insurance. (At the same time, Beveridge's determination to introduce elements that reflected needs, rather than insurable risks, was a departure from actuarial principles.[6])

---

[4]  D Lenoir (1994) *L'Europe sociale*, Paris: Editions la Découverte.
[5]  J Clasen (1997) 'Germany', J Clasen, *Social insurance in Europe*, Bristol: The Policy Press.
[6]  M Evans and H Glennerster (1993) *Squaring the circle? The inconsistencies and constraints of Beveridge's plan*, London: Suntory-Toyota International Centre for Economics and Related Disciplines, p 5.

- Lastly, it was *parsimonious*, or mean.[7] Many of the problems of the system arose because the benefits were not good enough to avoid problems, and the system had to be supplemented.

In the years that followed the introduction of the Beveridge plan, there were growing doubts about the effectiveness of its approach. The benefits offered in continental Europe, especially their earnings-related pensions schemes, seemed to be substantially more generous. This led the Labour Party, as early as the 1950s, to ask whether some movement in the direction of earnings relation might be better.[8] After numerous attempts to reform pensions, the principle of earnings relation was finally implemented in the 1970s. On the same basis, earnings-related supplements were introduced for Unemployment Benefit in 1966 (they were abolished in 1982). At the same time as some were arguing for something more like the continental schemes, however, others had reservations. The emphasis in the Bismarckian countries on contributions and work record tended to exclude those who were unable to contribute. Some argued that we should go 'Back to Beveridge',[9] emphasising the universality of the scheme.

## The insurance principle

The principle behind National Insurance is that people earn benefits by contributions, paid while they are at work. The first advantage of insurance is that contributions are used to raise money for benefits. National Insurance has not been wholly self-financing, but it has not been expensive either. When pensions were introduced in Britain in 1908, they were not based on insurance, and for practical purposes they were fairly universal.[10] By 1925, the government had decided that this cost too much, and introduced insurance-based pensions instead.[11] Although Beveridge wanted a substantial (50%) subsidy from the Treasury, the contribution from the Exchequer (that is, from government funds) was set at a much lower level, around 18%.[12] For most of the history of the Beveridge scheme, the National Insurance Fund has delivered a surplus, with no Treasury contribution. (The Fund is really an accounting fiction, however; the appearance of sound finance has largely been maintained by increasing the contributions, while reducing the Fund's liabilities in areas like unemployment and sickness.)

---

7   N Barr (2004) *Economics of the welfare state* (4th edn), Oxford: Oxford University Press, p 31

8   Labour Party (1958) *National superannuation*, London: Labour Party.

9   See A B Atkinson (1969) *Poverty in Britain and the reform of social security*, Cambridge: Department of Applied Economics, ch 7.

10   P Thane (1978) 'Non-contributory v insurance pensions 1878-1908', in P Thane (ed) *The origins of British social policy*, Beckenham: Croom Helm.

11   B Gilbert (1970) *British social policy 1914-1939*, London: Batsford.

12   J Veit Wilson (1992) 'Muddle or mendacity? The Beveridge Committee and the poverty line', *Journal of Social Policy*, vol 21, no 3, pp 269-302.

The second advantage of National Insurance is that, because people pay for their benefits, they should feel entitled to them. Beveridge wrote that 'benefit in return for contributions, rather than free allowances from the State, is what the people of Britain desire.'[13] There is no evidence to show that the public have ever held this view; people seem to treat pensions as paid for, and they treat unemployment benefits as a form of dependency, whether or not they are based on insurance. Equally, it was widely believed, for many years, that if people had paid for benefits, the government could not abolish them − this was one of the justifications offered by Franklin Roosevelt in the United States.

> We put those payroll contributions there so as to give the contributors a legal, moral, and political right to collect their pensions and unemployment benefits. With those taxes in there, no damn politician can ever scrap my social security program.[14]

The argument is built on sand. There is no reason to believe that insurance benefits are protected politically in any special sense. A series of insurance-based benefits, which people have paid for, have been abolished; it began with earnings-related supplements to unemployment and sickness benefits, then moved on to benefits that were substantially replaced by other systems (Sickness Benefit and Maternity Allowance), and the abolition of smaller benefits (Death Grant). Other insurance benefits, such as Unemployment Benefit and Incapacity Benefit, have been combined with others that are not insurance based, which also raises questions as to whether the insurance components are safer than any other part.

Insurance has other disadvantages. One is that people must work to qualify. This leaves out large numbers of people − unemployed school leavers who have never worked, women who have been looking after children, or chronically sick and disabled people. This is the problem of 'exclusion'.[15] Insurance systems in continental Europe have gradually expanded in order to include people who have been excluded, but it is difficult to include them without suspending the principle of insurance altogether. This means that, in almost every system where there is insurance, there has to be a two-tier system: insurance benefits for the better-off, and some kind of special provision to cover the worse-off who have been unable to pay contributions. There is a risk, then, that the system will distinguish the 'deserving' and the 'undeserving' poor.

---

[13] W Beveridge (1942) *Social insurance and allied services*, Cmd 6404, London: HMSO, para 21.

[14] L Gulick (1941) Memorandum on conference with Franklin D Roosevelt concerning social security taxation (www.ssa.gov/history/Gulick.html).

[15] R Lenoir (1974) *Les exclus*, Paris: Editions du Seuil.

It is also a problem that poor people are less able than others to afford contributions. This leads to a dilemma. If contributions are set low, benefits have to be low – unless the state pays, in which case the point of having contributions at all is somewhat vitiated. Either benefits will be earnings related, so that poor people pay less and receive less, or they will be flat rate, so that everyone pays a limited amount and gets a limited benefit. Contributions in Britain:

> are not fixed on any rational basis but on the basis that you want a reasonable test and do not want to make it too hard for people to get the benefits because, after all, the contingencies are there and you do not want to resort to means-tested benefits. ... None of us has ever paid, or will ever pay, the full value of our benefits.[16]

## Beveridge and after

The Beveridge scheme was based on six 'principles' of insurance; all of them have been departed from since.

- *Comprehensiveness* No insurance scheme can be fully comprehensive, because some people cannot pay enough contributions. Beveridge wrote: 'However comprehensive an insurance scheme, some, through physical infirmity, can never contribute at all and some will fall through the meshes of any insurance.'[17] The people who are left out tend to be those unable to work. It is not necessary to exclude all of them from insurance cover: anyone who has worked and contributed might have qualified, and there are systems (like health insurance in continental Europe) that operate on that basis. This still leaves a problem for those who never work.

  The problems of exclusion were compounded by further deficiencies in the Beveridge scheme itself. Beveridge did not take proper account of the position of women – he assumed they were likely to be dependent on male breadwinners – and failed to anticipate trends in divorce and lone parenthood.
- *Classes* Beveridge's 'classes' of insurance included pensioners and children, to emphasise comprehensiveness. These were dropped in 1975, though children continued to receive 'credited' (make-believe) contributions. The special class of contributions for married women was phased out gradually from 1977 onwards.

---

[16] Evidence of a civil servant, cited in A W Dilnot, J Kay and C N Morris (1984) *The reform of social security*, Oxford: Clarendon Press, p 34.

[17] Beveridge (1942) para 23.

• *Flat-rate benefits, and flat-rate contributions* There are two assumptions here: benefits or contributions could be flat-rate or earnings related. Beveridge felt that they must be tied to each other if his scheme was going to be genuinely a form of insurance, and he plumped for flat-rate benefits even though the contributions created problems for low-paid workers. This tied the National Insurance system to low levels of benefit, by contrast with schemes in continental Europe, where earnings relation made a much more generous level of benefit possible. The Phillips Committee, which considered the problems in the early 1950s, wrote:

> At present the contribution ... is the same for all ... and in practice it cannot be set higher than the poorest can pay. This is a serious limitation and we should have liked to suggest some way of escaping from it. On consideration, however, we do not feel able to recommend a system of contributions varying according to income. We were assured that any proposal to vary the rate of contribution would meet with wide-spread opposition unless the rate of benefit were also varied according to the contribution.[18]

Following Labour's 1957 pensions plan, the Conservatives introduced a limited degree of earnings relation in 1959. In 1966, earnings relation was extended to Unemployment, Widow's and Sickness Benefit, but it was removed from Unemployment and Sickness Benefit in 1983 as an economy measure. Earnings-related contributions have remained.

• *Adequacy* The scheme introduced in 1948 had lower benefits than Beveridge recommended – the government said this was because people were getting free school meals, but in reality it was necessary because the Exchequer contribution was much less than Beveridge had recommended. However, Beveridge's scheme would have been inadequate anyway, because the rates he proposed were very low, and because he failed to consider the issue of housing costs, which he thought were too difficult. Both of these issues will be considered in greater detail in later chapters.

• *Unified administration* A national scheme was set up, but the inadequacy and poor coverage of the benefits meant that other benefits had to fill in the gaps.

For many years the Child Poverty Action Group, as the principal pressure group dealing with social security issues, argued that the benefit system should go 'Back to Beveridge'. As time went on, this position became less and less tenable, and it was dropped in 1980.[19]

---

[18] Cmd 9333 (1954) *Report of the Committee on the economic and financial problems of the provision for old age*, London: HMSO, p 45.

[19] G Fimister and R Lister (1980) *Social security: The case against contribution tests*, London: Child Poverty Action Group.

## National Insurance now

The main remaining National Insurance benefits are:

- *Retirement Pension* This is the most important part of the state pension, available for men over 65 and women over 60; the retirement age for women will go up gradually in the years 2010-20. Claimants must have contributed for a number of years to qualify.
- *Survivors' benefits* These include bereavement payments, Guardian's Allowance and some elements of the State Pension.
  - *Bereavement payments* All widows and widowers get an initial lump sum payment. People with children receive the Widowed Parent's Allowance, and those over 45 receive a Bereavement Allowance for a year. Before 2001, there were Widows' Pensions, which, unlike Bereavement Allowance, continued longer than a year, and a Widowed Mothers' Allowance; these benefits still exist, but they have been closed for people bereaved since April 2001.
  - *Guardian's Allowance* These are for people looking after children whose parents have died.
  - *Retirement pensions* Category B retirement pensions are available to widows and widowers on the basis of the contributions of a spouse or partner.
- *Industrial injuries benefits* Provision for industrial injuries was one of the earliest developments in social security, beginning with Workmen's Compensation in 1897. The principles were incorporated into the National Insurance scheme, although in fact workers did not have to establish a contributory record to be entitled. Entitlements have been reduced, particularly for lesser injuries, but the scheme continues to play a limited role.

There are two other benefits that in their time constituted a major part of the National Insurance scheme, but which are now being dealt with differently:

- *Jobseeker's Allowance* is the main provision for unemployment. Unemployment Benefit was insurance based, but the return of mass unemployment in the late 1970s and 1980s meant that large numbers of unemployed people either had not contributed to the scheme or were long-term unemployed. JSA continues, however, to have a contributory element, reflecting the former scheme.
- *Employment and Support Allowance* Invalidity Benefit was replaced by Incapacity Benefit in 1995, and Employment and Support Allowance started to replace Incapacity Benefit in 2008, as well as Income Support for new claimants with long-term illnesses. In 2001 Incapacity Benefit absorbed the non-contributory Severe Disablement Allowance, which was intended for people who were unable to make contributions. Like

Jobseeker's Allowance, ESA has retained a contributory element; unlike JSA, there are many people who are still entitled on a contributory basis. However, now that there are insurance, non-contributory and income-tested elements in the same benefit, it is debatable whether ESA can still be thought of as an insurance benefit.

National Insurance still accounts for over half of the expenditure on social security. It has grown steadily since its establishment. Although the figures in Table 7.2 are unreliable (the same statistical series produced inconsistent figures year by year) they give at least a sense of the direction of movement.

Initially, National Insurance was also intended to cover unemployment, and the insurance-based Unemployment Benefit played a major role until the 1990s. Subsequently, however, that role was eroded, partly through limitations on entitlement, but also because long-term unemployed people were unable to gain entitlements through contributions. Although the Jobseeker's Allowance has an insurance element for the first six months of unemployment, by the time of its introduction the National Insurance elements had already substantially been overtaken by non-insurance benefits.

**Table 7.2: Recipients of the principal National Insurance benefits (UK: 000s)[20]**

|  | 1951 | 1961 | 1971 | 1981 | 1991 | 2001 | 2010 |
|---|---|---|---|---|---|---|---|
| Retirement Pension/ State Pension | 4,224 | 5,941 | 7,982 | 9,015 | 9,920 | 11,036 | 12,417 |
| Sickness/Invalidity/ Incapacity Benefit/ Employment and Support Allowance (*not including related non-insurance benefits*) | 941 | 964 | 999 | 1,105 | 1,485 | 1,511 | 1,038 |
| Widows | 467 | 460 | 460 | 460 | 345 | 232 | 103 |
| Industrial injuries | 146 | 266 | 296 | 260 | 295 | 285 | 262 |

[20] Sources: Central Statistical Office, *Social Trends 1975*, table 5.23 for 1951-71; *Social Trends 1994*, table 5.10 for 1981-91; Department for Work and Pensions (2010) *Benefit expenditure tables*, table C1, for 2001-10 (http://statistics.dwp.gov.uk/asd/asd4/alltables_budget2010.xls).

## Box 7.1: How National Insurance benefits work

Entitlement to National Insurance benefits depends on contributions. Contributions are mainly made as part of employment, and are generally deducted from wages in the same way as taxes, through 'pay as you earn' (PAYE). There are different systems for self-employed people, and for attributed or voluntary contributions to make up gaps in the pension record, but only the contributions from employment count for important benefits like Jobseeker's Allowance and Employment and Support Allowance.

Contributions are made over the course of a tax year, running from April to March. It does not take a full year's payment to make up a full set of contributions – many people will have paid enough to be entitled to later benefits within about three months. The contributions count towards benefits claimed in the following calendar year, January to December. That means that someone who makes a claim in October may have to rely on contributions made after April two and a half years beforehand. In the case of Jobseeker's Allowance, it takes two years' contributions, so the relevant contributions begin a year earlier.

This means that for most people the direct relationship between the work they have previously done and their current entitlement is tenuous. What happens in practice is that a claimant's record is checked against their National Insurance number, and in almost every case that record is then taken on trust – a problem if (as sometimes happens) employers have failed to return the correct payments at the appropriate time.

There is nothing obvious or commonsensical about these calculations. In France, for example, contributions are calculated quarterly rather than annually, which makes it much easier to relate benefits to contributions in the recent past. The system in Britain became fixed in its path at first because it was difficult to change or even to adjust it in practice, and later because the eclipse of National Insurance meant it was no longer thought of as a pressing issue.

## Timeline: National Insurance benefits

| | 1944 | 1950 | 1956 | 1962 | 1968 | 1974 | 1980 | 1986 | 1992 | 1998 | 2004 | 2010 |
|---|---|---|---|---|---|---|---|---|---|---|---|---|
| Pensions | 1948 Retirement Pension | | | | | | | | | | | |
| | | | | 1959 Graduated Pension | | | 1975/78 State Earnings Related Pension Scheme (SERPS) | | | | 2002 State Second Pension | |
| Sickness and incapacity | 1948 Sickness Benefit | | | | | | (1982 Statutory Sick Pay) | | | | | |
| | | | | | | 1971 Invalidity Benefit | | | 1995 Incapacity Benefit | | | |
| | | | | | | | | | | | 2008 Employment and Support Allowance | |
| | | | | | 1966-82 Earnings Related Supplements | | | | | | | |
| Unemployment | | | | | | | | | | | | |
| | 1948-95 Unemployment Benefit | | | | | | | | 1995 Jobseeker's Allowance | | | |
| Maternity | 1948-82 Maternity Allowance | | | | | | (1982 Statutory Maternity Pay) | | | | | |
| | 1948-87 Maternity Grant | | | | | | | | | | | |
| Survivors | 1948-87 Death Grant | | | | | | | | | | | |
| | 1948 Guardians Allowance | | | | | | | | | | | |
| | 1948 Widows Pension; Widowed Mothers Allowance | | | | | | | | 2001 Bereavement Allowance; Widowed Parents Allowance | | | |

## The failure of National Insurance

It may seem strange in these circumstances to write about the failure of the National Insurance scheme. Most of the claimants of social security benefits, and most of the money that is distributed, are dealt with under the National Insurance rules. The system still provides benefits to over twelve and a half million people.

The central problem is that, in each area where the National Insurance scheme operated, it has proved to be deficient. These issues will be reviewed in more detail in the dedicated chapters on each subject, but briefly:

- In relation to pensions, National Insurance provides support that is only equal to, or less than, minimum income standards for about two and a half million pensioners. (Minimum income standards have been represented by a series of means-tested benefits, including National Assistance, Supplementary Benefit, Income Support and the Minimum Income Guarantee; currently the minimum standard is represented by the Guarantee Credit within Pension Credit.) The National Insurance scheme makes a difference for over nine million pensioners, which is a significant achievement, but its failure to cover the rest adequately has been persistent.
- In relation to short-term sickness, the benefits provided were inadequate to provide income protection. The National Insurance scheme no longer offers effective cover; short-term sickness and maternity are dealt with through the wages scheme.
- Long-term sickness was not part of the Beveridge scheme; Invalidity Benefit was introduced in 1971. This was subsequently replaced by Incapacity Benefit, which was based as much on a test of need as on the test of contributions. The integration of Severe Disablement Allowance with Incapacity Benefit in 2001 meant that IB was no longer solely reliant on the contributory system.
- Death benefits were eroded by inflation to the point where they were virtually worthless. The Death Grant was for many years limited to £25, and reducible for those who died too early.
- In the cases of unemployment, maternity and death, the National Insurance system has largely ceased to operate.

The Beveridge scheme did seem to work, more or less, for thirty to fifty years. Beveridge's assumptions were not met, but other countries have managed to provide adequate benefit systems without full employment or universal health services. The needs of the population were greater than Beveridge imagined, but that again is reflected in the conditions faced by other countries. This seems to imply that the problems must lie in the kind of scheme Beveridge was proposing. Two interrelated issues present themselves.

The central problem has been the assumption that National Insurance has to follow the pattern of private or mutual insurance. There is nothing in the concept of National Insurance which says that contributions have to be set with benefits in mind, or on an actuarial basis. (Beveridge's request for funding of 50% from the Exchequer emphasises the point.) There is no obvious reason to limit the duration of entitlement. It is not necessary to exclude people on the basis of their individual circumstances: when Beveridge wrote that divorce was not an insurable risk, he had lost sight of the principle of social protection. The choice of low-level contributions to provide low-level benefits has proved fatal to the scheme; it meant that basic protection for retirement, sickness and maternity was inadequate, and that the scheme had to be supplemented through other means.

The other main problem has been the legacy of the Poor Law. Debates on social security have been bedevilled by the assumption that the appropriate test of a benefits system was the effect it had on poverty. Benefits were effective if they went primarily to people who would otherwise fall below the poverty line, however defined. When benefits were squeezed, particularly during the 1980s, the benefits protecting the poor proved to be most robust politically; and, as benefits have been eroded or abolished, it is the benefits for people on lower incomes that have best survived.[21]

## QUESTIONS FOR DISCUSSION

Has the National Insurance system failed?
Should we go back to Beveridge?

---

[21] Compare M Andries (1996) 'The politics of targeting: the Belgian case', *Journal of European Social Policy*, vol 6, no 3, pp 209-23.

# Chapter 8

# Means-tested benefits: the basic minimum

Means-tested benefits are aimed at people on low incomes. The most important benefits are those that offer a basic minimum income, such as Income Support, Jobseeker's Allowance and Pension Credit. These benefits are widely criticised. Some of the criticisms are misplaced – non-means-tested benefits are also liable to be complex and stigmatising – but there are distinctive practical problems: the means-tested benefits are often inequitable, and they sometimes fail to reach people they are intended for. At the same time, the benefits provide essential income to many of the poorest people in Britain.

A 'means test' involves a test of low resources as a condition of receiving benefit. A test of 'means' is supposed to establish whether or not people who claim benefit are able to manage from their own resources. In principle, this could mean that they manage from capital resources, and there are some benefits that take capital into account; in practice, however, many claimants come to claim benefit with little or no capital resources, and the tests tend to focus on income. In some of the literature, 'means testing' is called 'income testing'. This is a simplification, because there are often tests of capital and assets as well, but some writers think it helps to make the effect of the tests clearer.

Some of the means tests are intended either to provide a minimum income, or to offer services for people who fall below a threshold. These are the most important means-tested benefits in Britain. They include:

- *Income Support* Income Support is a benefit for people who are not working and on very low incomes. It works as a supplement to other income, making up the difference between income and a set level, which is taken to be a person's 'requirements'. If other income increases, Income Support goes down. IS used to cover nearly five million claimants, but now that unemployed people are dealt with through a different system, pensioners have been switched to Pension Credit and people with incapacities are being transferred to Employment and Support Allowance, the numbers have come down to about a million, and the abolition of the benefit was anticipated in the Welfare Reform Act 2009. It will take some time to dismantle the benefit altogether, and understanding the principles is still important for understanding other means-tested benefits.

- *Pension Credit*  Pension Credit is basically a new name for the Minimum Income Guarantee, which replaced Income Support for pensioners. The first part of Pension Credit is the Guarantee Credit, which is based on Income Support; it guarantees people with no income a basic minimum. The second part, which is considered in the next chapter, is the Savings Credit, an addition that attempts to reduce disincentives to save by rewarding people for having modest additional incomes. Roughly half of all pensioners should have some kind of entitlement. It is administered by the Department for Work and Pensions, by contrast with most other 'credits', which are treated as part of the tax system.
- *Jobseeker's Allowance*  This has replaced both Income Support for unemployed people and Unemployment Benefit. The income rules are similar to Income Support, but for a limited number of claimants the benefit is insurance-based, and the rules are different.
- *Employment and Support Allowance*  This is for people who have long-term incapacities. ESA makes an extra payment, not available to JSA recipients, depending on whether claimants are in the 'work activity' group or the 'support group'. Although part of this benefit is governed under the contributory system, it also has an important means-tested component, applying to new claimants who would otherwise have claimed Income Support.

There are more means-tested benefits. Some supplement people over a range of income; they are considered in the next chapter. There are also benefits that extend the minimum coverage in special circumstances. Free school meals, free prescriptions, NHS benefits and Healthy Start food vouchers are all different benefits. There is some 'passporting', which means that people who have claimed some other benefits (like Income Support) can get these without a new test, but for the NHS benefits there is a separate means test for those who do not automatically qualify.

## The safety net

For most of the last sixty years there has been one 'safety net' benefit intended to ensure that people who had no other source of income would have a basic minimum. This benefit was called National Assistance in 1948; it became Supplementary Benefit in 1966 and Income Support in 1988. Several benefits have gradually replaced Income Support – Jobseeker's Allowance, Employment and Support Allowance and Guarantee Credit (for pensioners) – but they all work to similar principles. The idea behind these benefits is picked up in one of the old names, 'Supplementary Benefit'. The benefits are designed as a supplement; they work in principle by topping up other income, bringing income up to a set level. If the threshold increases, more people become entitled; if it is cut, fewer people are entitled. The extra amounts means testing may deliver are sometimes small, especially for pensioners, but they make a major difference for people on very low levels of income. The effect of topping up also means that any other benefits people receive – such as State Pension – are much less important than their cash value suggests: claimants end up with the same amount of income, regardless of the proportion of money that has come from different sources.

The benefits do not, however, offer a minimum for everyone. Some people get less than the minimum, because of deductions. And although the coverage is wide, it is not true to say that there is a comprehensive safety net in Britain. When National Assistance was introduced in 1948, it was intended as a safety net, and supposed to cover people who were not otherwise protected by the social security scheme. There were important exclusions, however; the benefits were not available to people who were working, or for people who could work but were not available for work. Over the years, the principles have changed, and more people are excluded. Unemployed people who are not available for work have never been covered, and there are other long-standing exclusions (such as people involved in trades disputes). Claimants under 18 are limited (though they can claim in certain special circumstances, including physical disability, lone parenthood and being at risk from their parents). School leavers are held to be dependent on their parents for a period after they have left school. Asylum seekers, who are now subject to special rules for income maintenance, are treated separately from the rest of the benefit system.

**Table 8.1: Recipients of the basic means-tested benefits (National Assistance, Supplementary Benefit, Income Support, Jobseekers Allowance and Pension Credit) (UK, 000s)[1]**

| | 1951 | 1961 | 1971 | 1981 | 1991 | 2001 | 2010 |
|---|---|---|---|---|---|---|---|
| Pensioners over 60 (Guarantee Credit post 2003) | 969 | 1,323 | 1,979 | 1,793 | 1,272 | 1,777 | 2,742 |
| Unemployed (on income-based JSA post 1996) | 66 | 142 | 407 | 1,384 | 1,335 | 690 | 1,116 |
| Sick/disabled | 219 | 280 | 321 | 213 | 375 | 1,017 | } 1,923 plus 199 ESA |
| Lone parents | 127 | 138 | 285 | 379 | 871 | 888 | |
| Others | 81 | 18 | 22 | 85 | 331 | 306 | |
| Total recipients | 1,462 | 1,902 | 3,014 | 3,873 | 4,487 | 4,678 | 5,980 |

---

[1] Main sources: Central Statistical Office, *Social Trends 1975*, table 5.24, for 1951-61; *Social Trends 1982*, table 5.6, for 1971; *Annual abstract of statistics 1986*, table 3.24, for 1981; and Department for Work and Pensions (2010) *Benefit expenditure tables*, table C1, for 1991-2010, (http://statistics.dwp.gov.uk/asd/asd4/alltables_budget2010.xls).

Although Table 8.1 shows movement in different directions, reflecting the fragmentation and complexity of the system, the general trend over the years has been for increasing numbers of people to depend on the basic means-tested benefits. The response of governments to the increasing numbers of claimants has been of two kinds. One has been to try to change other benefits to float people off the safety net. The fall in the number of pensioners claiming in the 1990s was because of improved insurance-based pensions.

The other response has been to reform the basic benefits, in an attempt to cope with growing numbers. A review in 1978, under the title *Social assistance*, tried to adapt Supplementary Benefit to its 'mass role'.[2] The review argued that it was simply not feasible to operate a mass scheme for millions of people and to pretend that it was possible to respond sensitively to everyone on an individualised basis. (That, ironically, is just what contemporary claims for 'personalisation' of the social security system claim can be done, despite millions more claimants, fewer offices and fewer staff.) *Social assistance* proposed major simplification of the Supplementary Benefit scheme, including fewer rates of benefit, simpler rules for assessment and the introduction of a short-term scheme; the creation of clearer rights to benefit; and reviewing the position of married women in the scheme. In the Social Security Act 1980, introduced by the Conservative government, the idea of a short-term scheme was dropped – it would create more bureaucracy, not less. The position of women remained unchanged until pressure from the European Community forced the government's hand. Before 1983, only the male of a couple could be the 'relevant person' in an 'assessment unit'; after 1983, females could also be relevant.

In the 'Fowler Reviews' of social security, which began in 1984,[3] the government introduced a number of further reforms – effectively an admission that the reform in 1980 had not worked. The reviews led to:

- renaming Supplementary Benefit Income Support;
- the introduction of premiums, payable to families, lone parents, pensioners and people with disabilities. Before 1988, the benefits distinguished between 'short-term' claimants (principally unemployed people) and long-term claimants. The main losers in the reforms were claimants under 25;
- the revision of housing assistance: extra money given to householders was removed, help with mortgage interest reduced and support was removed for water rates; and
- removal of the rights of most 16- to 18-year-olds to claim for themselves.

Four major changes have been introduced to Income Support since the 1988 reforms. One was the introduction of the Jobseeker's Allowance in 1996, which formally removed unemployed people from Income Support altogether, while allowing them an equivalent means-tested benefit. The second has been a change

---

2    Department of Health and Social Security (1978) *Social assistance*, London: DHSS.
3    Cmnd 9517-19 (1985) *Reform of social security*, vols 1, 2 and 3, London: HMSO.

in the structure of support for families. The premium for lone parents was abolished, initially planned by a Conservative government but implemented by Labour. It was followed in 2000 by a radical revision of the benefit scales affecting children, leading to a major increase in the level of income available to families. Labour argued that this revision led to a major reduction in child poverty. In 2004, the system for child support was changed so that allowances for children are now made through a combination of Child Benefit and Child Tax Credit, instead of Income Support. Third, pensioners have been taken into a new system, initially called the Minimum Income Guarantee and now incorporated in Pension Credit. Finally, in 2008 most people who would have received Income Support for sickness or disability were transferred to the new Employment and Support Allowance, while carers have been moved to a Carer's Allowance.

All of this means that Income Support is much less important formally than it used to be, and that is the way it looks in the official figures. The functions it used to perform are now shared with Jobseeker's Allowance, Pension Credit and ESA. At the same time, most of these new structures – the systems for unemployed people, pensioners and for people with long term illnesses – continue to reflect the structure and rules of the system of Income Support they were taken from. The common features of the benefits are the foundation for the combined calculation proposed for Universal Credit.[4]

---

## Box 8.1: The basic means-tested benefits, and how they work

A person's or household's resources are assessed in terms both of income and capital. Some income will be taken into account in full – possibly benefits (like National Insurance retirement pension), personal income (maintenance or occupational pensions) and some earnings (such as a retainer). Some income, such as earnings or money from boarders, will be disregarded only in part, up to a set limit. For example, a single person on Jobseeker's Allowance or Income Support can keep £5 of earnings before deductions are made. And some income will be disregarded completely, including some benefits (Attendance Allowance or Child Benefit) and income from capital. The rules relating to capital are different for different benefits: there is generally a lower limit of capital that is disregarded, there may be a deemed income above that level and there may be an upper limit, beyond which there is no entitlement to benefit.

Resources then have to be set against needs. There are four basic elements to the basic means-tested benefits.

1. *Personal allowances* These are supposed to cover all a claimant's normal needs – such as food, fuel and clothing – apart from housing costs. The rates in 1948 had a tenuous relationship to the minimum standards identified by

---

[4]   Cm 7957 (2010) *Universal Credit: Welfare that works*, London: DWP.

Rowntree, but repeated subsequent departures mean that the scale rates are not based on any calculation or measure of needs.

2. *Premiums*, or additional weekly payments for people in particular situations. The main form of extra weekly payment is made through the system of premiums, which increase the basic entitlement of a number of groups – particularly pensioners and people with disabilities. This goes some way towards recognising the extra weekly costs associated with disability, though the persistent exclusion of unemployed people and, after 1998, of lone parents, raises the suspicion that the distinction is really between 'deserving' and 'undeserving' poor.

3. *Housing costs* This mainly refers nowadays to mortgage relief for owner-occupiers; rent is dealt with separately through the Housing Benefit scheme, considered in the next chapter. The rules were developed as part of the Income Support scheme and have had to be duplicated for JSA and Employment and Support Allowance. Help with mortgages has been suspended for three months for first-time claimants, and nine months for most others. This implies that for most people who have been in work prior to claiming benefit, means-tested benefits are available only at a level that is far below basic liabilities. The introduction of a general cap on maximum benefit levels will also curtail the level of support available.

4. *Deductions* need to be distinguished from the calculation of the basic benefit. If someone's income goes up – for example, because they have been able to work for a brief period – their benefit goes down. This happens because they are only supposed to receive a fixed amount for the week, and if benefits are not reduced, they will receive too much. Deductions mean that people receive less in total than the basic rates. The idea of making deductions is problematic because of the general assumption that benefits are only just adequate to meet basic needs. If benefits are cut, they must then be less than is necessary.
Deductions are made:
   - where people are considered to be voluntarily unemployed, for example because they have refused appropriate work;
   - in the special case of strikers and others involved in an industrial dispute, who are not entitled to receive benefit even if they have no work and no income;
   - in order to cover certain debts, including fines, some essential goods like rent or fuel, and liability for child support; and
   - for the recovery of previous overpayments of benefit. If a claimant has been paid too much in a previous period, the benefit can be recovered – technically, only if the claimant had misrepresented or failed to disclose a material fact, but in practice clawing back is rather more widespread.

The government proposes to introduce additional sanctions, likely to include fixed-term suspensions for fraud and for failure to come to interviews.

## Means tests in principle

Means tests, and particularly the basic means-tested benefits considered in this chapter, are widely condemned in the literature.[5] Many of the arguments on each side are based in political ideology rather than practical experience. The first argument in favour of means tests is that they redistribute resources progressively; money is taken from richer people and given to poorer people. 'By definition', Whiteford writes, 'for a given expenditure level, a means-tested system will provide more generous benefits to the poor than universal or contributory benefits.'[6] The effectiveness of means tests in helping the poor varies considerably from country to country, because they are applied in different ways, in different contexts, from different starting positions,[7] but if you are attracted by the idea that the welfare state should be like Robin Hood, or by the idea 'from each according to his ability, to each according to his need', you should think about means testing. (The means-tested pension in Australia, for example, is redistributive, and not at all residual.[8]) Second, they concentrate resources on those who have least, so that the money is used most directly to alleviate poverty. By contrast with universal benefits like Child Benefit, means-tested benefits are far more effective in allocating resources to people in need; in Britain, non-means-tested benefits do much less work than means-tested benefits do to lift people above minimum income thresholds.[9]

The arguments against means tests equally begin with arguments about principles. The benefits are intrinsically residual, and all the criticisms made of residual welfare (considered in Chapter 3) are taken to apply to them. Means-tested benefits fail to reach the people they are intended to reach: there is a general problem of 'low take-up'. The problems include problems of ignorance about entitlements, complexity, stigma and intrusion into people's lives.[10]

---

[5] See, for example, A Deacon and J Bradshaw (1983) *Reserved for the poor*, Oxford: Blackwell; W van Oorschot (1995) *Realizing rights*, Aldershot: Avebury; D Piachaud (1997) 'The growth of means testing', in A Walker and C Walker (eds) *Britain divided*, London: Child Poverty Action Group; W van Oorschot (2002) 'Targeting welfare', in P Townsend and D Gordon (eds) *World poverty*, Bristol: The Policy Press.

[6] P Whiteford (1997) 'Targeting welfare: a comment', *The Economic Record*, vol 73, no 220, pp 45-50, p 45.

[7] D Sainsbury and A Morissens (2002) 'Poverty in Europe in the mid 1990s', *Journal of European Social Policy*, vol 12, no 4, pp 307-27.

[8] F Castles (1996) 'Needs-based strategies of social protection in Australia and New Zealand', in G Esping-Andersen (ed) *Welfare states in transition*, London: Sage Publications.

[9] K Nelson (2004) 'Mechanisms of poverty alleviation', *Journal of European Social Policy*, vol 14, no 4, pp 371-90.

[10] P Spicker (1986) 'The case for Supplementary Benefit', *Fiscal Studies*, vol 7 no 4, pp 28-44; Oorschot (1995) pp 33-4.

However, many of the criticisms made of means testing could be levelled at benefits that are not means tested.

There are good and bad reasons for the criticism of means testing. The bad reasons are first, an assumption that the way we respond to means tests is determined in some way by their history, rather than by current experience. Means testing was introduced during the period between the First and Second World Wars as a means of avoiding the stigma of the Poor Law, but its repressive administration soon earned it a similar reputation. If the responses to means tests depended on past experience, the problems should have started to die out after the Poor Law. That is not supported by the historical evidence: the problems have been consistent across many generations. There is no evidence that pensioners feel more stigmatised than others, and some studies in the 1970s suggested that if anything, pensioners were more likely to think of benefits as a right.[11] Another study from around the same time suggested that people of working age (25-60) were more likely to complain that they felt degraded or embarrassed.[12] This may be because this age group are expected to be independent and self-supporting.

A second bad argument is the assumption that means tests are somehow perceived differently from other benefits. This is a widespread view,[13] but I can see no evidence to support it. Claimants cannot tell the different types of benefit apart.[14] Pensioners tend to think that their pension is a right, whether or not it is means tested. Unemployed people tend to think of their benefit as a dole, and this was true even when it was insurance based.[15]

Third, means tests are taken to be conditional, and conditionality is strongly associated with measures that are moralistic, judgmental and punitive. However, the only elements in means testing that are intrinsically conditional relate to income and capital. Student grants, much missed, were means tested, but they were not moralistic or punitive; the scheme of Individual Learning Accounts now in operation in Scotland (unlike the failed scheme in England) works on a similar basis.[16] The other aspects of conditionality, like the insistence on family norms and sanctions against people who are not working, have certainly infected means-tested benefits, but they are not unique to those benefits. Sanctions

---

[11] E Briggs and S Rees (1980) *Supplementary Benefits and the consumer*, London: Bedford Square Press.

[12] J Ritchie and P Wilson (1979) *Social security claimants*, London: Office of Population Censuses and Surveys.

[13] Oorschot (1995).

[14] PSI (Policy Studies Institute) (1984) *The reform of Supplementary Benefit*, Working Papers, London: PSI; A Richardson and J Naidoo (1978) *The takeup of Supplementary Benefit: A report on a survey of claimants*, London: Department of Health and Social Security; Ritchie and Wilson (1979).

[15] Briggs and Rees (1980).

[16] ILA Scotland, (2010) What is ILA Scotland: Eligibility, www.ilascotland.org.uk/What+is+ILA+Scotland/Eligibility.htm

against voluntary unemployment have been part of the National Insurance system since 1911; the cohabitation rule applied to widows' benefits and One Parent Benefit, which was a supplement to the universal Child Benefit. The imposition of moral conditions affects every type of benefit, then, not just means-tested ones.

Those are just the bad arguments, but there are also good ones. There are other serious problems with means-tested benefits. The most obvious problem is that they are complex and difficult to administer. That much is also true of many other benefits – it is never straightforward to identify a person as 'unemployed' or 'disabled', and whatever the definitions there will be someone whose circumstances are not properly covered. But there are also special problems that are distinctively part of the process of means-testing, as opposed to any other test of need. The administrative complexities include:

- the problem of defining the threshold for entitlement – and the evident boundary problems that arise when someone just below the threshold is entitled and someone just above it is not;
- the changing and ephemeral nature of the condition that is being tested. Income changes constantly, particularly when people have no stable employment, and over any short period people are often not very sure what their income is.
- the treatment of saving – means tests are likely to penalise people for past savings;
- the aggregation and distribution of resources in the household. Some means tests assume that people in households share resources, which is not always true: some feminists have been critical of the effect on women in the household, who may have no independent resources.[17] Other means tests ignore the fact that people have shared expenses, which leads to inequities. The disparity in treatment between couples and an adult mother and daughter who live together is striking;
- the treatment of non-dependants in the household. Living with other people is typical of the lives of many people on low incomes: Millar and Gardiner suggest that it is a basic strategy for coping on a low income, and pooled resources of others who share the household (like adult children, lodgers, flatmates and friends) are essential for people on low wages to be able to manage.[18]

The second intrinsic problem with means tests is the problem of equity. How, for example, should capital be treated? If it is ignored, people with substantial resources will be treated in the same way as people who have none, which seems inconsistent with the purpose of means testing. Should

---

[17] For example, S Payne (1991) *Women, health and poverty*, London: Harvester Wheatsheaf.
[18] J Millar and K Gardiner (2004) 'Low pay, household resources and poverty', Social Policy Association Conference, University of Nottingham.

an inheritance be ignored? Does this apply to family heirlooms, like antique furniture? What about car ownership? Should someone who is buying a house be treated the same as someone who is renting? There have been times when people with substantial mortgages have been treated very favourably, despite considerable resources; arguably the pendulum has now swung in the opposite direction.

Third, means tests often fail to meet the aims for which they are introduced. The point of checking people's income, rather than conditions like unemployment or sickness, is to make sure that people with inadequate incomes are the ones who will receive help. Despite that objective, means-tested benefits often fail to provide an adequate income. There are many people on low incomes, and most benefits aimed at people on low incomes are mean-spirited. This reflects the practicalities, as well as cost: the more generous the benefits are, the higher the qualifying thresholds are set, and the more people who have to be dealt with. A similar criticism might be made of many other benefits. What makes it especially damaging for means testing is that financial need is precisely what means tests are supposed to be dealing with.

The general experience of means testing is that, whatever the theory, lots of things go wrong in practice. The benefits reviewed in this chapter are especially important. They are the basic method that is used to provide minimum income guarantees. They are also the basic method for getting resources to the people who are poorest and most in need. It follows that any fault in the design of the benefit is going to hit people particularly hard. Because means-tested benefits are complicated, they are often flawed. There is, then, a lot to criticise, and no-one who has been in contact with the system for any length of time will be unaware of at least some of the problems.

These are real and important problems, but none of them is quite enough to explain the special contempt in which means tests are held. If we look at who the poorest people in Britain are, and ask which benefits get most to them, the answer will almost certainly be the basic means-tested benefits – Income Support, income-related Jobseeker's Allowance, Employment and Support Allowance or the Guarantee Credit, which is the minimum income guarantee for pensioners. The most effective way we could help most poor people tomorrow would be to increase those benefits.

## Questions for discussion

Should policy makers be trying to avoid means tests?
What is the case for increasing the basic means-tested benefits?

# Chapter 9

# Means testing: income supplements

Some means-tested benefits are intended as supplements to income. They are available not just to people on very low incomes, but to many others. If benefits are given to people on low incomes, however, they must be taken away from people whose incomes go up, so the benefits are gradually withdrawn as income increases. This applies to Tax Credits, Housing Benefit and Council Tax Benefit. These benefits have many of the same problems as other means-tested benefits; beyond that, they tend to be particularly complex and inequitable. Nevertheless, Tax Credits have reached large numbers of people in the population despite the complexity and administrative problems.

Most of what is written about means testing has focused on the provision of a basic minimum. That is understandable, because of the especial importance of those benefits, but it is not the whole story. Some means-tested benefits are intended as supplements to income, and are available to people across a wide range of income. The main examples of this type of benefit are Housing Benefit and Tax Credits. If the Universal Credit planned by the current government[1] is ever implemented, it will work on the same principles.

- *Housing Benefit* This covers costs for rent. Over time, it has become one of the most important means-tested benefits. It goes both to Income Support claimants and to others on low incomes who might be in work. It is based on Rent Rebate, which was introduced in 1972, but the present system mainly dates from 1982. Unlike Income Support, it is not based on a simple income cut-off; the level of benefit depends on low income, the costs of rent and local rent levels, so that someone on a higher rent in one area may receive benefit on a higher income when another claimant in a different area receives less benefit on lower income.

- *Council Tax Benefit* Council Tax is a local property tax, used to pay for local authority services, and Council Tax Benefit reduces the amount that people have to pay. In most respects the rules are based on Housing Benefit. It is a very widely used benefit, going to over five and a half million recipients, but the transfer of responsibility and budgets to local authorities may mean that its role reduces in future.

---

[1]   Cm 7957 (2010) *Universal Credit: Welfare that works*, London: DWP.

- *Savings Credit* Savings Credit is an element of Pension Credit, but it deserves a special mention in this context. It is intended to allow pensioners with some limited savings or income, for example from an occupational pension, to gain some benefit from their savings. Pensioners who have a bit less than the level of the minimum income guarantee get to keep a proportion of their extra income; pensioners who have a bit more than the minimum income guarantee get a small extra amount in recognition of their extra savings, which is gradually withdrawn for higher incomes.
- *Child Tax Credit* This is a benefit for families with children, allowable across a wide range of income but which is reduced when the recipient moves into higher income brackets. More is paid for families with babies, and for children with disabilities. The benefit was called Children's Tax Credit between 1999 and 2003.
- *Working Tax Credit* has superseded Family Credit, Working Families Tax Credit and the Disabled Person's Tax Credit. It is administered in tandem with the Child Tax Credit, extending the coverage to people on low earnings without children as well as those with them. Claimants get a maximum benefit when their income is below a certain threshold, but the benefit gets reduced as income increases. Part of the calculation for families with children is based on an assessment of the costs of formal childcare – this is part of the WTC rather than the Child Tax Credit.

These benefits suffer from most of the problems of means testing – complexity, problems with take-up and the difficulty of responding to changes in circumstances – but they have two more. One is the problem of working out whether or not people are entitled. The process of reducing benefits is generally done as a percentage of extra income, referred to as a 'taper'. In principle there can be several tapers at different levels of income, in the same way as there can be different rates of taxation, but currently there tends to be one taper for each of the main benefits. However, the starting point is not the same for everyone. Entitlement to Housing Benefit depends on rent; entitlement to Tax Credits depends on family circumstances. Because people's entitlement gradually reduces from an individual starting point, it can be very difficult to work out just where the point is that someone ceases to be entitled, and if people are confused about whether or not they are entitled, or whether it is worth bothering, they may not claim at all. The same confusion is likely to blight the proposal for Universal Credit.

The other problem is the 'poverty trap', also known as the marginal deduction rate.[2] For each extra pound that a person earns, a claimant might lose some part of the extra income to tax (20%), some to the National Insurance contribution (11%) and some to the withdrawal of Child Tax Credit (39%, but it will go up to 41% in 2011–12). This makes up to 70p in the pound. Then there may be the withdrawal of Housing Benefit (65p) and Council Tax Benefit (20p). Those

---

2   Cm 7913 (2010) *21st century welfare,*, London: Department for Work and Pensions, p 11.

are calculated only after the other benefits have been taken into account, and that stops the poverty trap going above 100%. The calculation is complicated because the benefits cut in and out at different points, but it may help to focus just on Housing Benefit and Council Tax Benefit: for every £10 gained in other income, £8.50 is deducted. The interaction means that a person claiming benefits while working stands to gain very little through an increase in earnings. Getting out of poverty, Piachaud writes, is like getting out of a well – if you can't jump up far enough you simply slide back to the bottom again.[3]

In practice, because many people do not receive these benefits, they do not experience the poverty trap. People cannot lose benefits they do not receive in the first place. Limited numbers of people are on low incomes; half the households on low income are now in owner-occupation, which means they are not entitled to Housing Benefit; and take-up of all these benefits is moderate. According to the Treasury, only 70,000 families actually face marginal deduction rates of over 90p in each pound, and no-one is actually worse off (which they might have been in 1998). However, 2.57 million households have marginal rates through taxation and withdrawn benefits of over 60%.[4] These figures are calculated on the basis of actual experience, rather than what might happen theoretically; if more people claimed the benefits they were entitled to, the figures would be worse.

## Housing Benefit and Council Tax Benefit

### Housing Benefit

Beveridge failed to consider the problem of housing costs, and his benefits were not adequate to deal with them. From 1948 until 1982, housing costs were included as part of the basic benefit. People renting from a landlord would receive their rent in full; people who were buying a house received the interest on their mortgage payments. People on Supplementary Benefit received a minimum level of income inclusive of rent, rates or mortgage interest. A large number of claimants – including, at its peak, nearly 400,000 pensioners – had to claim Supplementary Benefit solely to make up the difference between their benefit and their housing costs. Until 1982, rent and rates were given as a part of Supplementary Benefit. People who were not on Supplementary Benefit received a different kind of help, that was not seen solely as a form of income maintenance.[5]

---

[3]   D Piachaud (1973) 'Taxation and poverty', in W Robson and B Crick (eds) *Taxation policy*, Harmondsworth: Penguin.

[4]   HM Treasury (2009) *Securing the recovery*, Cm 7747 (www.official-documents.gov.uk/ document/cm77/7747/7747.pdf), p 81.

[5]   See P Malpass (1984) 'Housing benefits in perspective', in C Jones and J Stevenson, *The yearbook of social policy in Britain 1983*, London: Routledge and Kegan Paul

Housing Benefit developed as part of an attempt to change the basis of housing subsidies.[6] Before 1972, council housing depended mainly on a 'general subsidy'; rents were deliberately kept low. The Conservative government of the day wanted to transfer subsidies from housing to individual families. They introduced a Housing Finance Act that trebled council rents, but that meant that most tenants could not afford them. This made it necessary to introduce benefits so that they could pay the increased rent – a Rent Rebate, in the form of a reduction of rent. Private rents were also increased by the Act, which started to ease controls, and Rent Allowances for private tenants were introduced in the following year. Rate rebates, which the Labour government had introduced in 1967 as an option for local authorities, became compulsory. The Thatcher government removed subsidies to council housing almost completely and the importance of Housing Benefit has grown. Most tenants of social housing now receive it.

Rent Rebate was based on one of the most complex calculations ever seen in UK social administration. When it was introduced, it was based on a 'needs allowance'. The needs allowance was easier to understand if one appreciated two essential principles: it had nothing to do with needs, and it was not an allowance. It was, rather, a nominal figure used for calculations. At the needs allowance, one received a proportion of rent or rates, and the benefit was gradually increased or reduced if income was above or below the allowance. (If some local authorities still prefer to refer to 'needs allowances', more than 20 years after the term was removed,[7] it may be that they feel that the term that replaced it, 'applicable amount', is even less comprehensible.)

When Rent Rebate and Rent Allowance were introduced in 1972, people with incomes equal to the needs allowance got 60% of rent and rates. The tapers were 17% for rent and 6% for rates for people above the needs allowance, and 25% for rent, 8% for rates for those below it. This led to a ludicrously complicated system, with predictable problems. The benefit added substantially to the poverty trap; there was considerable confusion because someone might be better off on Supplementary Benefit than Rent and Rate Rebate, and it took a difficult calculation to work it out; and perhaps most important, people could not work out for themselves if they were likely to be entitled at all – the 'needs allowance' gave no clear guide.

There were numerous calls to simplify the benefit, for example from the Supplementary Benefits Commission. The 'simplification' took place in 1982-83, starting with council rents and including private tenants in the second wave.

---

[6]   P Malpass (1990) *Reshaping housing policy*, London: Routledge.

[7]   For example, B C Gedling (www.gedling.gov.uk/index/fin-home/fin-benefits.htm), North Dorset District Council (www.north-dorset.gov.uk/index/living/benefits/ housing_benefit/how_housing_benefit_is_calculated.htm), or Sunderland BC (www. sunderland.gov.uk/index.aspx?articleid=2722), all consulted on 26 March 2010.

The job of dealing with housing costs was transferred from Supplementary Benefit to local authorities, bringing it together with Rent Allowance and Rent Rebate; that was why the scheme was described as 'unified', though it did not bring in every type of benefit for housing (mortgage payments continued on Supplementary Benefit). Claimants on Supplementary Benefit were to receive all their rent and rates. For other claimants, adjustments were to be made to the speed at which benefits were withdrawn. Unified Housing Benefit, however, proved to be unworkable. It is tempting to blame that on the complexity of the benefit, but that was not the main problem: local authorities were unable to cope with the administrative load. They had no staff and resources to deal with the problem, and at first no idea of the amount of work that was being dumped on them. They were rapidly overwhelmed, and there were massive delays in the payment of benefit. The government's response was to do nothing very much, blaming the local authorities rather than the policy. They decided the scheme was costing too much, and changed the rates for people above the needs allowance to reduce the benefit they were entitled to. They also introduced the principle that people should pay some contribution towards their rates regardless (a principle that has been carried forward into Council Tax Benefit).

## Box 9.1: How Housing Benefit works

Housing Benefit covers the costs from rent, at least in principle; it used to be related to the rent a person actually paid. It also used to include rates (the property tax used before the introduction of the Council Tax), but Council Tax is now treated by a separate benefit, Council Tax Benefit, which works by similar rules. Payments for social care or supported accommodation are not included — they are supposed to be separate from the rent.

The first step in calculation is to work out what the allowable rent is. Tenants in social housing have their annual rent divided by 52 to give a weekly allowance; many councils and housing associations give tenants some rent-free weeks, so the effect of this calculation is to produce a figure that is a little below the weekly rent. Housing Benefit for private tenants is now based on a local housing allowance — a notional figure, representing the amount that rent ought to be, instead of what it is. From 2008-11, it was based on median rental values; after 2011, it is limited by the 30th percentile, limiting support for tenants to the lower end of rental values in an area. The allowance varies according to family size and the number of bedrooms in a house. Younger single people are limited to the equivalent rent for a single room (an option which is rarely available in social housing). People sharing properties have benefits based on a nominal proportion plus £15. The situation is complicated by tenants before 2008, who are dealt with under different rules, and some tenants from before 1996, who are under different rules again.

The next step is to calculate income. Some income is disregarded (people in work consequently get more benefit than people not in work); there may be deductions for people living in the household, who are assumed to make a contribution. The benefit is calculated on the difference between income and the applicable amount. For every extra pound of income above the applicable amount, 65p is withdrawn from the payment towards rent, until the benefit is exhausted.

Housing Benefit for a local authority tenant is paid as a rebate, deducted from the rent. As the role of local authorities has diminished, this is becoming more uncommon. In most other cases, including housing association tenancies, it is paid to the tenant; direct payment to a landlord is possible, but unusual.

Housing Benefit has stumbled on, through a series of incremental reforms and adjustments. At first, the government planned to simplify the process of withdrawing benefit, but that was modified after protests that it would leave people worse off, and most subsequent changes in HB were marginal – additional rules, supplements and alterations to the tapers. In 1988, after the Fowler Reviews, an 'applicable amount', roughly equivalent to Income Support levels, was introduced in place of the needs allowance, so that all the tapers would work in one direction – a gradual reduction of entitlement as income increases. Other reforms relate to the assessment of rent. The rent allowable under the scheme has always been difficult to calculate – the obvious figure (what gets paid each week or each month) is rarely the same as the rent that is allowed for, because the costs are set against deductions, allowable costs, rent-free weeks and so forth. The rules introduced after the system of community care replaced most forms of specialised support previously treated as part of housing provision. The most important recent changes to HB, based on 'local housing allowances', have reduced the relationship of the benefit to rent further. When it was introduced, the local housing allowance was deliberately simple – a set figure, and for a time at least, if the actual rent was less, people could keep the difference. That provision expired in 2010, and the 2010 Budget introduced plans both to lower the allowance and to cap it.[8] The government also proposes to cap the sum of all benefits at a weekly maximum, equivalent to the median wage; that level of income cannot be reached from most other benefit rates, and it follows that the cap will mainly affect entitlements to housing..

There are many problems with the system of Housing Benefit, but at least four have been part of the scheme since its inception (and seem likely to be carried forward into the proposed design of Universal Credit). The most obvious problem is that potential claimants cannot tell at the outset whether they might be entitled or what they might be entitled to. The second problem is the taper. Housing Benefit and Council Tax Benefit are the principal elements in the poverty trap. The 'applicable amount' is based on income after tax, so the actual effect of withdrawing HB and CTB, when combined with tax and National Insurance, is to add just over 51% to the poverty trap. The third problem is equity. The needs of

---

[8]   HM Treasury (2010) *Budget 2010*, HC 61, London: The Stationery Office, p 33.

owner-occupiers are dealt with by different criteria from tenants, either through Income Support or through private insurance; the distributive results make little or no sense. Fourth, there is the dizzying complexity of the benefit, compounded by rules about rents, non-dependants and some bizarre transitional provision – it is still possible now for some cases to be assessed under the pre-1996 rules. The design of the benefit seems unsustainable. The main surprise is that, despite its defects, it has lasted so long.

The reason why Housing Benefit has survived is partly what political scientists call 'path dependency': once something like this has started it can be difficult to stop. Tenants have taken on leases, landlords have made investments and social landlords have taken out loans for development, all on the basis that HB will pay the rents. Dismantling an entire system, however badly designed it may be, and putting a completely new system in place, can be more trouble than it is worth to policy makers. Another reason for the retention of HB is that its aims stretch beyond the field of social security. The benefit is not just about supporting the incomes of people with limited resources; it is also intended to affect people's consumption of housing. In relation to the public sector, the intention was to change the pattern of subsidy from the general provision of housing to the specific circumstances of individuals. This has had a large effect, but there have been administrative problems for people with particularly complex needs, requiring extensive support. Housing Benefit has not really been geared to these circumstances, and the system of 'community care', where services are purchased by local authority social services departments, has usually been seen as more appropriate. There are recurring difficulties at the margins, and people who need lesser degrees of support have been the subject of various alternative funding arrangements. In relation to the private sector, Housing Benefit was seen as a way of bolstering the flagging private rented sector, which has been in decline since the rise of owner-occupation in the 1920s took away the most lucrative and secure part of the market. HB has a substantial effect on the rents that landlords are able to charge: landlords claim they want 'market rents', but a market depends on demand, not just supply, and while it is cheaper to buy than to rent there is little economic demand for renting. Without the benefit system, there would only be a very limited market for renting. This generates the suspicion that the rising costs of HB, and the levels of housing cost that are charged, are being fuelled by the benefit itself.[9]

Although Housing Benefit is about housing as well as income, the design of the benefit seems to be getting further and further away from its role in the housing market. It tends to be understood like other benefits, as a general supplement to the income of people on low incomes. Viewed in this light, its effects are not particularly coherent. The way HB works means that a person on a medium

---

[9]   See M Evans (1996) *Housing Benefit problems and dilemmas*, London: Suntory-Toyota Centre for Economics and Related Disciplines.

income with a higher rent can get more in benefit than someone on a low income with a lower rent. Social protection has effectively been suspended for many owner–occupiers, who are expected to take out private insurance to cover their liabilities instead. Whether it is viewed, then, as a housing subsidy, a form of social protection or a benefit for people on low incomes, Housing Benefit leaves something to be desired.

## Council Tax Benefit

Council Tax Benefit goes to large numbers of people, because unlike Housing Benefit it is not confined to people who are renting. The most unusual feature of the benefit is that a person on high income may be able to claim a rebate for a second adult on low income who is living with them but who is not liable for Council Tax – effectively, a subsidy to people who take in lodgers.

There is less to say about Council Tax Benefit than Housing Benefit; it mainly works by the same rules, but it covers smaller amounts of money. People need CTB because they cannot pay the Council Tax without it. Council Tax is higher than rates used to be, mainly because central governments in the 1980s cut the amount of funding made available to local authorities from general taxation. Single adults get a rebate of 25% in their council tax, and some types of accommodation (like student residences) are exempt, but in general terms most households have to pay the tax. The main effect of treating the calculation like Housing Benefit is that it is complex, it is difficult for people to work out what entitlement should be and many people do not actually receive it. Council Tax Benefit reaches 87% of eligible households where someone is receiving Income Support, and only 52% of other households.[10] This could mean that people who are hardy enough to claim IS are hardy enough to get their other entitlements, but more plausibly it seems to show that the way to get past the barriers of Council Tax Benefit is to be in contact with the social security system. In principle, delivering the rebate could probably be done much more simply by giving people in defined categories, such as pensioners or people on other benefits, lump sum rebates for six-monthly periods.

In the 2010 Spending Review, the government announced a general cut in CTB. More significantly, they proposed to make that work in practice by 'localising' the budget, leaving councils the choice as to how the system would be delivered. This seems to imply that CTB is going to be different type of benefit, operating like local authority education benefits on a discretionary basis.

---

[10] T Clark, C Giles and J Hall (1999) *Does Council Tax Benefit work?*, London: Institute for Fiscal Studies.

## Tax Credits

Tax Credits, Brewer suggests:

> illustrate the government's frustration with both the income tax and the benefits system as ways of targeting financial support: the income tax system does not allow sufficiently accurate targeting, and traditional means-tested benefits are seen as unacceptably complicated and stigmatising, and inappropriate for a programme that covers the vast majority of families with children.[11]

Income-tested benefits for people in work have been available since 1971. Family Income Supplement was introduced in 1971 to help families on low wages. Its design was simpler than some of its successors: it was reduced by 50p for every pound earned, but it was only adjusted every six months, which meant that incomes did not fluctuate too rapidly.[12] FIS was replaced by Family Credit after the Fowler Reviews, and that remained the position until the Labour government came into power with a commitment to relieve child poverty. That government introduced a minimum wage, but they set it at a low level, which would not be enough in combination with Child Benefit to guarantee an adequate income for families. So they opted, instead, for another set of complex means-tested benefits, based on the American Earned Income Tax Credit.[13]

There are two main benefits: the Child Tax Credit and the Working Tax Credit. The *Child Tax Credit* is a payment for people on low incomes who have responsibility for children, whether or not they are earning. The *Working Tax Credit* is a further supplement to low wages for people who either have a child or who have some kind of disability. It is calculated by taking a notional maximum, which can take account of parental responsibility, disability, an age allowance (marked for abolition in 2012-13) and the costs of formal childcare. The total entitlement for Tax Credits is tapered, like Housing Benefit. As income increases, they are reduced by 39%, soon to be 41%, of the difference between the minimum income and a person's actual income.

Operating this system as two separate benefits is an interesting approach. At a time when several portmanteau benefits have been created with lots of elements, and there is pressure to unify different systems, the government clearly

---

[11] M Brewer (2006) 'Tax credits: fixed or beyond repair?', in Institute for Fiscal Studies, *The IFS Green Budget 2006*, London: Institute for Fiscal Studies (www.ifs.org.uk/budgets/gb2006/gb2006.pdf).

[12] J C Brown (1984) *Family Income Support pt 1: Family Income Supplement*, London: Policy Studies Institute.

[13] R Walker and M Wiseman (1997) 'The possibility of a British Earned Income Tax Credit', *Fiscal Studies*, vol 18, no 4, pp 401-25.

felt that it made more sense in these case to have two distinct, overlapping benefits that work in combination to help families with children. The idea that Working Tax Credit is not really a social security benefit[14] was formed because it was initially thought of as a tax measure: initially, the intention was pay it through the pay packet. In practice, the benefits are calculated and paid in tandem, and it is difficult for claimants to distinguish them, especially as WTC is also paid to cover childcare expenses.

The Tax Credits have two key features distinguishing them from other benefits. First, they are administered by the tax authority, Her Majesty's Revenue and Customs. Reputedly the decision to base them in HMRC rather than the Department for Work and Pensions was based in the belief in the Treasury that keeping the benefits 'in house' would make them easier to control and keep track of. The side-effect of this has been a fundamental change in the nature of HMRC. Before the introduction of the Tax Credits, the main work of the former Inland Revenue was dealing with people who were returning tax forms – a small minority of taxpayers, usually self-employed or better off, because most workers had tax deducted by employers through the Pay As You Earn system. Tax Credits put HMRC in direct contact with millions of people, many needing urgent attention. There were problems with computers, with overload and with the management of claims.[15] HMRC has had to adapt rapidly.

Second, although Tax Credits are generally paid monthly, they are calculated on the basis of annual income, rather than weekly or monthly income. Where people's incomes fluctuate, there is a reason to alter the level of benefit in payment – and people's incomes fluctuate rather a lot. John Hills' work for HMRC suggested that the incomes of about a third of the households studied, mainly selected from the lower parts of the earnings distribution, were 'erratic' or 'very erratic'.[16] This has led to a situation where Tax Credits are not just paid unpredictably and irregularly, but where people can be asked for massive repayments, sometimes totalling thousands of pounds. The Ombudsman has commented:

> There are many for whom the experience has been, and indeed remains, highly distressing. Whilst they may be only a relatively small proportion of the overall numbers claiming tax credits, they are a significant number, and the impact on the customers

---

[14] N Wikeley, D Williams, I Hooker (2009) *Social security legislation 2009/10, volume IV: Tax Credits and HMRC-administered social security benefits*, London: Sweet and Maxwell, pp 110–11.

[15] Brewer (2006), pp 137–8.

[16] J Hills, R Smithies and A McKnight (2006) *Tracking income*, London: LSE Centre for the Analysis of Social Exclusion.

concerned, typically those on the very lowest incomes who are amongst the most vulnerable in society, is huge.[17]

Changes made in the rules to increase responsiveness have limited the size of some overpayments, but only at the cost of making income even less predictable. The Ombudsman questions 'whether a financial support system which included a degree of inbuilt financial insecurity could properly meet the needs of very low income families and earners'.[18] One option might be to recalculate benefits monthly, but a better way would be to restore the principle of assessing benefit for six-month periods, without seeking repayments when circumstances change. The government is apparently convinced that new computer systems will enable it, by 2014, to respond to changes in circumstances in 'real time'[19] on the basis that the technology that allows faster payments between banks can be extended to benefit assessments. This looks like wishful thinking. A computer system can only go as fast as the information that goes into it, and the complexity and confusion inherent in people's circumstances must lead to uncertainty, instability and delay.

## Timeline: support for people on lower income

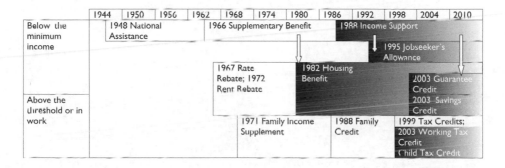

Despite the reservations, official statistics seem to suggest that Tax Credits have had a remarkable success. Child Tax Credits are apparently received by 5.8 million families in the UK, including 4.2 million families in work, out of the 7.8 million that receive Child Benefit.[20] The Tax Credits may be means-tested, but they are not very selective – the emphasis does not fall on excluding people are not

---

17  Parliamentary and Health Service Ombudsman (2007) *Tax credits – Getting it wrong?*, HC 1010, London: The Stationery Office, p 43.

18  Parliamentary and Health Service Ombudsman (2007), p 5.

19  Cm 7942 (2010) *Spending Review 2010*, London: HM Treasury; Cm 7957 (2010).

20  HM Revenue & Customs, (2010) *Child and Working Tax Credit statistics: Geographical analyses April 2010*, London: National Statistics, table 2 (www.hmrc.gov.uk/stats/ personal-tax-credits/cwtc-geog-apr2010.pdf).

entitled. The take-up of CTC is estimated at 79-84%[21] – which would mean that, even if take-up is at higher end of the range, well over a million more families are entitled. The figures are very different from the experience of other means-tested benefits. They seem to say both that relatively few families are not entitled to CTC and that the benefit has experienced few of the problems associated with the coverage of means-tested in-work benefits in the past.

## QUESTIONS FOR DISCUSSION

What are the alternatives to giving means-tested benefits to families on low incomes? How can the poverty trap be avoided?

---

[21]  HM Revenue & Customs (2010) Child Benefit, *Child Tax Credit and Working Tax Credit take-up rates* (www.hmrc.gov.uk/stats/personal-tax-credits/cwtc-take-up2007-08.pdf).

# Chapter 10

# Non-contributory benefits

Non-contributory benefits are provided without either a requirement to make a contribution or a means test. The main examples are benefits for people with disabilities, such as Disability Living Allowance and Attendance Allowance. Although these benefits were supposed to avoid some of the problems associated with means testing, they have problems of their own, and many of the problems attributed to selective benefits – cost, stigma, low take-up and inequities – apply to these benefits too.

The term 'non-contributory benefits' is ambiguous. Taken literally, it could refer to any benefit that is not based on insurance. The Department for Work and Pensions generally uses it to refer to benefits that are not based on insurance or on means testing. This leaves two different kinds of benefit. Some non-contributory benefits are based on a test of some sort, usually a test of need. The most important benefits of this kind are benefits for people with disabilities. *Attendance Allowance* is the main benefit for disabled people over retirement age – and most disabled people are over retirement age. Despite the name, Attendance Allowance is not actually given for 'attendance'; it is given for people who need care, which is defined by the disability rather than by the care. *Disability Living Allowance* is a more complex benefit for disabled people under 65. It has elements both to cover people's mobility needs and to cover 'care', though that really means severe disability – there does not have to be someone who delivers the care. The mobility component is for people who are unable to walk, though the interpretation is broad: the allowance is available to people with learning disabilities with behavioural problems. Like Attendance Allowance, the care component is for people who need attention or care, not necessarily those who actually receive it. (DLA is discussed in more detail in Chapter 16)

The second main class of non-contributory benefits are benefits aimed at everyone: examples are Child Benefit and the non-contributory pension for people over 80, also referred to as Category D Retirement Pensions. These are very different from the first class of non-contributory benefits, because they do not rely on a test of need. I have dealt with them under a different category, that of 'universal' benefits, in Chapter 12.

## The provision of non-contributory benefits

The defining characteristic of non-contributory benefits is that they reach people who are not reached by insurance-based benefits. One of the central arguments for doing this is the extension of solidarity, or 'social inclusion'. The first use of the term 'exclusion' was in France, where it was used to apply to people who were not covered by the completion of the coverage of the insurance system.[1] People who are not protected otherwise will be left out, or excluded. Non-contributory benefits can be seen as an extension of the principle of mutual responsibility represented by insurance to people who have not been able to make contributions.

The main example of this kind of extension in Britain is the development of benefits for disabled people. If the issue was only about social inclusion, it could be argued that means tests would provide a safety net. There are other reasons for introducing non-means-tested benefits instead. Some are negative — a desire to avoid the problems associated with means testing. Some are pragmatic, because there are identifiable groups of people (like people with a learning disability in long-stay institutions) who did not seem to be provided for in other ways. Arguably recognition of the personal needs of people with disabilities is another kind of reason again: some benefits are justified in terms of compensation for the extra costs that disabled people have to bear when others do not.[2] And there seem to be circumstances where government might have wanted to recognise an obligation, such as the introduction of Vaccine Damage payments in place of compensation in the courts. If governments wish to recognise a moral obligation to people, insurance — which requires beneficiaries to have made a contribution — may not be enough.

One of the best examples of this kind of moral obligation are benefits related to military service — recognition of the 'military covenant'. There are non-contributory allowances attached to the award of the Victoria Cross and the George Cross, the military and civilian medals for valour. War Disablement Pensions (popularly known as War Pensions) are non-contributory. There is a range of additional allowances given for war pensioners in different circumstances:

- allowance for a lowered standard of occupation
- age allowance (for older war pensioners)
- clothing allowance
- comforts allowance (an addition for more severely disabled pensioners)
- constant attendance allowance

---

[1]   R Lenoir (1974) *Les exclus*, Paris: Editions de Seuil.
[2]   T Burchardt (1999) *The evolution of disability benefits in the UK: Reweighting the basket*, London: London School of Economics Centre for Analysis of Social Exclusion.

---

- exceptionally severe disablement allowance (not the same as Severe Disablement Allowance)
- funeral expenses
- invalidity allowance
- mobility supplement
- severe disablement occupational allowance
- unemployability supplement.

Although the core of the benefit relates to the status of ex-servicemen and women, these allowances recognise a range of different principles: need, financial disadvantage and compensation. The issues are returned to in Chapter 16, on disability.

The reasons for providing non-contributory benefits, then, go well beyond the initial arguments discussed at the beginning of this book. Contributory benefits are used to provide finance for social protection; means-tested benefits are associated with financial need, the relief of poverty and income maintenance. Non-contributory benefits can be applied flexibly to a range of other issues, including desert, compensation and needs that go beyond financial needs. In principle, they could be extended to meet other purposes, including actions to influence behaviour or to promote different kinds of economic activity. We tend not to think of them in this light, because when governments do provide grants and subsidies to different groups – start-up grants for small businesses, support for farmers or grants for cultural work – we do not necessarily class them as forms of social security. The same arguments and administrative issues apply in those cases, however, as they do to social security benefits.

## Box 10.1: Attendance Allowance

Attendance Allowance is a benefit for people over the age of 65 with relatively severe disabilities. Despite the name, it is not really about 'attendance': it goes to disabled people, not to their carers, and people get it because their disability is serious enough to need attendance, not because anyone is actually providing it. However, people who are receiving full-time care in care homes cease to be entitled. The disability, and the attention that people consequently need, has to be related to bodily functions. People get it if they are terminally ill, or receiving kidney dialysis. The tests for whether or not people can receive Attendance Allowance are, then, tests of need, not of income.

There are two rates of payment, depending on the severity of the disability. The tests are tighter than for Disability Living Allowance, which offers support for a lower rate of disability when Attendance Allowance does not. So, for example, in one leading case a woman whose daughter was having to sit in with her, helping with shopping and housework and offering support and stimulation for several hours a day, was not eligible for Attendance Allowance. If DLA had been available, she would have been eligible for that.[3]

Claimants are asked what their illness is, but they are also asked to respond to questions like 'Do you have difficulty or do you need help with washing, bathing, showering or looking after your appearance?' and 'Do you stumble because of your illnesses or disabilities?' Help the Aged comments that Attendance Allowance recipients 'value the benefit, but found claiming it to be a tiring, repetitive and confusing process'.[4] Another study of Attendance Allowance complains that claimants lost money because of problems with the process, and some died before the benefit came through.[5]

## Needs testing

Most non-contributory benefits are supposed to offer recipients benefits on the basis of need. Notionally, at least, the benefits avoid the problems of means testing. In practice, however, needs-based benefits exhibit many of the same problems as means-tested benefits. The benefits are complex, and they add to the complexity of the benefits systems overall. They are often difficult to understand, and claimants cannot easily tell whether they are likely to be entitled.[6] A study of Disability Living Allowance records that

> many applicants were unsure of, or misunderstood, the level of severity of care and mobility needs that would be required for a claim to be allowed. As one sciatica sufferer put it: 'I didn't think I was that bad because there are a lot of people that are very bad, but then again I don't know how serious is bad, you see what I mean?'[7]

The process of claiming is often burdensome and stressful. It may be stigmatising. These problems are, of course, the problems of selectivity – the problems of any system designed as much to keep people out as to bring them in. The fact that they occur in the context of needs testing emphasises the importance of not treating selectivity as only being about income. In Chapter 2 I listed five main

---

[3]  D Bonner, I Hooke, R Poynter, N Wikely, P Wood (2009) *Social security legislation 2009/10, volume I: Non means tested benefits and Employment and Support Allowance*, London: Sweet and Maxwell, p 123.

[4]  Help the Aged (2006) *Benefits and takeup: Help the Aged policy statement*, London: Help the Aged.

[5]  G Nososkwa (2004) 'A delay they can ill afford', *Health and Social Care in the Community*, vol 12, no 4, pp 283-7.

[6]  R Sainsbury, M Hirst and D Lawton (1995) *Evaluation of Disability Living Allowance and Attendance Allowance*, London: Department of Social Security.

[7]  A Thomas (2008) *Disability Living Allowance: Disallowed claims*, London: Department for Work and Pensions, p 20.

disadvantages of selectivity. Because many people will have read those as being the disadvantages of means testing, it is worth restating them here to show how they apply to non-contributory benefits that test people's physical needs.

- *Boundary problems* Selective benefits depend on making a distinction between the people who qualify and the people who do not. Inevitably, tests of need rest on judgements about people's relative position. It is almost impossible to distinguish between people's conditions fairly and consistently: judgements are often finely balanced, and people's personal needs change frequently (people can do on some days what they cannot do on others). Even if it were possible to judge this accurately and consistently in every case, however, lines would have to be drawn somewhere: some people will qualify, and others will not, even though there is very little to distinguish between their circumstances. Disability Living Allowance depends on information about capacities, like a person's ability to walk. An evaluation of DLA found that even though the criteria were clearly defined, there was no obvious distinction between the circumstances of people identified as having disabilities at the lower rate from those on middle or higher rates, while the distinction between unsuccessful applicants and those on the lower rate was 'blurred'.[8] The coalition government has announced the intention to call for medical assessment of all claims.[9]

- *Incentives* It may seem strange to talk about 'incentives' in relation to personal needs like disability, but the issue discussed under this heading before was not simply about whether people respond to financial reward; the term is also used to stand for circumstances where people can be rewarded or penalised for different kinds of situation. A considerable majority of people of working age who suffer from a disability later cease to be disabled.[10] Needs testing has sometimes led to people seeing themselves as unable to work, and withdrawing into early retirement.[11] It can seem perverse, too, that a person who learns to walk with the aid of an artificial limb should lose benefit. It seems unlikely that anyone would be persuaded by the lure of Disability Living Allowance to give up trying to walk, but there is something not quite right about the idea that people like stroke victims who push themselves through fear, pain and embarrassment to regain relatively limited movement should be disadvantaged financially as a result.

---

8   Sainsbury, Hirst and Lawton (1995).
9   HM Treasury (2010) *Budget 2010*, HC61, London: The Stationery Office, p 33.
10  T Burchardt (2000) *The dynamics of being disabled*, London: London School of Economics Centre for the Analysis of Social Exclusion.
11  S Yeandle and R Macmillan (2003) 'The role of health in labour market detachment', in P Alcock, C Beatty, S Fothergill, R Macmillan and S Yeandle (eds) *Work to welfare*, Cambridge: Cambridge University Press.

- *The administrative cost* Tests of needs are expensive to administer. The assessment of benefits for people with disabilities is complex, and adjudication may involve expert medical examination. More appeals take place in the benefits system on the assessment of disability than on any other subject.
- *Stigma* Benefits based on need can also be stigmatising. For example, some people do not want to classify themselves as 'disabled':

> Somebody had mentioned DLA a long time ago when my eyes were really bad, and it was something that I'd always said, no I'm not going to do it because if I do, that's writing myself off.[12]

If it is in any way better to admit that you cannot use the toilet unaided than to state you are on a low income, it is far from being self-evident. This illuminating discussion of whether or not a claimant needs help to use a commode comes from the *Disability rights handbook*:

> It is important to explain why you need particular types of attention or supervision. There may be simpler, more practical ways of meeting your needs. ... A typical simpler method is the use of a commode or portable urinal. If you could use one without help, it is often said you don't reasonably require help with trips to the toilet. Doctors often write that you can use a commode without thinking about all the practical issues involved (eg privacy, handwashing etc) and without thinking about the effect on your morale or general health.[13]

In other words, the test doesn't stop at having to say whether or not you can use the toilet, or with the type of toilet you have to use; you may have to argue about it.

- *Take-up* Take-up is uncertain. Despite initial confidence that non-means-tested benefits would not have the same problem, many people fail to claim these benefits, and take-up campaigns among people with disabilities have had an important effect. On the basis of the prevalence of disability in surveys, estimates of take-up for Attendance Allowance are roughly between 40% and 60% of eligible claimants; the care component of DLA has a take-up of 30-50%, and the mobility component has a take-up of 50-70%.[14] The

---

[12] Thomas (2008) p 62.

[13] I Greaves (2009) *Disability rights handbook* (34th edn), 2009-April 2010, London: Disability Alliance, p 23.

[14] P Craig and M Greenslade, cited in D Kasparova, A Marsh and D Wilkinson (2007) *The takeup rate of Disability Living Allowance and Attendance Allowance: Feasibility study*, London: Department for Work and Pensions

take-up appears to be higher than that among people registered blind,[15] but the fact of registration in itself probably indicates that this group were better linked than others to services; and the study which found this also found that a fifth of the recipients had at first been refused, and had had to appeal.

This all indicates that the problems which people assume are characteristic of means-tested benefits are not unique.

None of this is generally considered an obstacle to the extension of benefits on the basis of a test of need. Some governments like to respond to needs by restructuring existing benefits, in the greatest reform since Beveridge — we have had two or three of those. Others like to make incremental adjustments, and new benefits spring up as they pass. When 'new' needs — that is, specific unmet needs — are discovered by politicians or the press, non-contributory benefits offer a route to provide specific, conditional, limited benefits. Examples have included, among others, Mobility Allowance, Severe Disablement Allowance, Invalid Care Allowance and Vaccine Damage Payments. (Only one of these, the last, still has the same name and form it started with.) Governments seem to like the way that non-contributory benefits combine apparent generosity with a limited commitment in practice. We can probably expect, then, to see more benefits along these lines.

## QUESTIONS FOR DISCUSSION

Can we provide for disability without having a test of need?
Can this be done without stigma?

---

[15]  G. Douglas (2008) *Network 1000 DLA takeup study*, London: RNIB (www.rnib.org.uk/aboutus/Research/statistics/prevalence/Documents/2008_2_Network_1000_DLA.doc).

# Chapter 11

# Discretionary benefits

Discretion is used to fill in gaps in the system, covering circumstances that are difficult to predict or generalise about. The most important benefit of this type currently is the Social Fund, which offers a range of grants and loans, including help in emergencies and help for people with problems of budgeting. Every social security system needs some element of discretion. The Social Fund, however, is being used not just for unpredictable or special needs, but to make up for the inadequacy of other benefits.

Discretionary benefits are benefits given not as of right but at the discretion of officials or professionals. The most important discretionary benefits in Britain are provided by the Social Fund, which is a cash-limited fund administered by the Department for Work and Pensions. Another has been the Independent Living Fund, a 'non-departmental body' – effectively a government-sponsored charity - which gave awards to severely disabled people, but its abolition was announced late in 2010. Social services and social work departments also have residual powers to make cash grants in certain cases – principally for child care or community care – though this is not widely done. In the 1970s, local authorities were responsible for rather more discretionary benefits, particularly in relation to education; recent steps to return certain benefits to local authority control, including Council Tax Benefit and Education Maintenance Allowance, seem to be a prelude to the extension of the role of discretion.

There is a tendency to think of discretionary benefits simply as a sub-category of means-tested benefits. There are, however, various forms of discretionary provision, and some distinct principles apply. Some benefits are discretionary because they are highly personalised; some are discretionary because they depend on resources and political decisions; some, like business start-up grants, have been available to encourage individuals, rather than being provided as of right. The most important, however, are discretionary because they are designed to plug holes in coverage. Because some needs are unpredictable, many social assistance schemes have some kind of discretionary element to deal with urgent or exceptional needs. Where social assistance is tied to social work, discretionary payments may also be used as a means of encouraging and directing appropriate patterns of behaviour. The criticisms that are made of the Social Fund, which is discussed in more detail later in this chapter, often muddle three issues: the meanness of the Fund itself, the problems of relying on discretion and the fact that people have to rely on the Fund because their basic benefits are not high enough. What is happening is that where other benefits are inadequate to meet basic needs, discretionary benefits are liable to be called on more frequently than is appropriate administratively, and frequent use makes the process of claiming an act of personal supplication. But there is still a case for having some kind of flexible system to deal with emergencies, special cases and circumstances that the rules fail to take account of. Even if benefits were much higher, some provision for discretionary benefits would still be necessary.

## The nature of discretion

The idea of 'discretion' refers to choices and decisions that are remitted to the people who administer the service. Discretionary systems are systems that rely on administrators to make decisions, rather than setting rules. Social work with families, for example, largely rests on the discretion of the social worker; the delivery of medicine depends largely on the discretion (or 'clinical judgement') of the doctor. Social security in Britain typically depends on rules, rather than discretion. This was done deliberately in the period after the Poor Law. The Poor Law had relied largely on the discretion of its administrators, and this was associated with the humiliating and degrading practices of the system. Avoiding discretion was seen as a way of reducing the scope of degrading treatment.

It is difficult to avoid the situation where officers make judgements about claimants. Nearly every administrative action, no matter what it is, requires officers to make some kind of judgement. If the rules say, for example, that benefits will be paid when someone is out of work and actively seeking work, someone has to take a statement to establish that the criteria are met. The need for officers to exercise judgement is unavoidable. This is not quite, however, what we mean by 'discretion'. Discretion usually comes into play whenever there are gaps and uncertainties in the rules.[1] In the case of 'actively seeking work', people are expected to take steps to find employment, but it is difficult to predict every contingency which might constitute a 'step' (and sometimes difficult to know what 'employment' is). People's lives are complicated, and whatever the arrangements are formally, there will be someone, somewhere, for whom the application of the rules is not clear.

The post-war system of social security was intended to reduce the scope for discretion, and this led to some extraordinarily elaborate rules. These rules were referred to, paradoxically, as the exercise of 'discretion',[2] but the discretion was exercised by the centralised administration – for a long time, the Supplementary Benefits Commission – not by individual local officers. Whenever someone

---

[1]  K C Davis (1966) *Discretionary justice*, Baton Rouge, LA: Louisiana State University.

[2]  See M Hill (1969) 'The exercise of discretion in the NAB', *Public Administration*, vol 47, no 1, pp 75-90; J Bradshaw (1981) 'From discretion to rules', in M Adler and S Asquith, *Discretion and welfare*, London: Heinemann.

came in with a case that did not fit the rules, new rules had to be made. Over time, the rules for the operation of the basic means-tested benefit — known at first as the 'A Code', then later incorporated into the 'S Manual' — grew more and more detailed. The extensive set of rules did not mean that no discretion was possible. It did mean that the scope of discretion was strictly confined, in an attempt to offer consistent decisions without making claimants subject to the personal preferences of the officer they were dealing with.

Within this complex system, there were several remaining areas which were still not covered by explicit rules. Some benefits have to be available on a discretionary basis, either because the decision to pay them rests on complex circumstances that are difficult to codify, or because there needs to be some provision to respond flexibly. Examples of the first case have typically included benefits based on medical assessment, or some judgements about disability — the discretionary element may be removed to doctors, but that does not mean that it is not discretionary. Where there is a demand for flexibility, it generally requires local officers to be given the authority to make decisions. In Guernsey, where I was a consultant on policy, they used to have a system of 'Procureurs of the Poor', who handed out cash directly (and personally) to applicants. On the face of the matter, this is disturbing: the arrangements are potentially degrading, there are extensive-opportunities for abuse and the personal contact risks having seriously deterrent effects. The case for the practice was made to me by a probation officer, who argued that in the absence of rules governing the position of people being discharged from prison, a flexible system had to be better than having no provision at all. It was possible to abolish the system only when alternative provision was made to bring the people who were left out into mainstream income support. The general rule in such cases is not to do things that will leave poor people worse off.

## The operation of discretionary benefits

No matter how extensive the rules are, there will be some circumstances that fall outside them. There are over twelve million pensioners, two to three million poor children and over six million people with disabilities. In a system that deals with millions of people in constantly changing circumstances, some people, somewhere, will find themselves in a situation where they fail to fit the pre-defined categories. If systems do not make allowance for the unpredictable, they are unable to do anything when the situations arise.

In principle, it is possible to make rules for nearly every circumstance. There is much to be said for doing so. Even if the book of rules becomes extraordinarily complex, it is easier and more comprehensible both for administrators and for claimants if they are able to look up the answer that applies to them. Despite that intention, there will always be circumstances that go beyond the specification that has been made in the rules.

The problem with this sort of rule is that it becomes, in itself, potentially intrusive. Richard Titmuss expressed concern about the rules he had encountered in New York, where people were entitled to an inventory of items, including, for example, a toothbrush.[3] The problem with systems of this kind is not that they are rule-based, and not that they are discretionary; it is that they have been applied to the normal needs of people who are too poor to afford basic items. The benefits are not adequate, and if people cannot afford to replace essential items, then a minimal system is liable to be forced to consider what the need is. The problem with both kinds of system, discretionary and rule-based, is that they have been forced to deal with huge administrative and personal problems generated by the simple fact that people do not have enough money to live on.

This argument reflects part of the experience of the British system. In the period before 1980, there was provision in the system for three main kinds of discretionary payments. The first were Urgent Needs Payments, made (as the name suggests) to cover circumstances that were exceptional and urgent – for example, to protect someone whose house had burned down. Second, there were Exceptional Circumstances Additions, weekly payments made because the person had special needs. Third, there were Exceptional Needs Payments, which were meant to cover the kinds of need that were not allowed for in the weekly benefit rates. The weekly benefit rates allowed (supposedly) for such expenses as the normal replacement of clothing through wear and tear; they did not allow for the replacement of clothing damaged through accidents. The advice of the Chief Supplementary Benefit Officer was that clothes worn out through normal wear and tear, like shoes that were worn out from playing football, were not to be considered as the basis for an ENP, but clothes damaged during accidents could be claimed for. So, it would not be possible to claim if trousers were torn climbing trees, but it would be possible to claim if a child fell out of a tree and damaged their trousers.[4]

Although the benefits were supposed to be for 'exceptional' cases, in practice about half of all appeals were made for clothing, and more and more money was being spent on such payments towards the end of the 1970s. The review of Supplementary Benefit, *Social assistance*, argued for the creation of a system of regular lump sum payments, the confinement of other payments to exceptional circumstances and the replacement of administrative discretion by defined rights.[5] The kind of extra payment that was available included, for example, an extra 30p for each bath needed for medical reasons, above the normal one per week nominally allowed for in the basic scale rates. The shift away from exceptional

---

[3]  R M Titmuss (1987) 'Welfare rights, law and discretion', in R Titmuss, *The philosophy of welfare*, London: Allen & Unwin.

[4]  D Carson (1981) 'Recent legislation', *Journal of Social Welfare and Family Law*, vol 3, no 1, pp 101-20.

[5]  Department of Health and Social Security (1978) *Social assistance,* London: DHSS.

additions was part of the adaptation of the benefit to its 'mass role'; it is not really possible to run a system with seven million dependants and test for each one how many baths it is appropriate for them to have. However, the idea of regular lump sum payments was rejected. In place of Exceptional Circumstances Allowances, there were to be 'additional requirements' paid as of right. Exceptional Needs Payments were replaced by the single payments scheme, which replaced the previous system of discretionary payments by defined rules (and stopped most payments for clothing). A right of appeal to Social Security commissioners (snappily renamed in 2008 as the Administrative Appeals Chamber of the Upper Tribunal) was established. Urgent Needs Payments remained in place as the only discretionary provision for special cases.

The 1980 Social Security Act was intended to save money. The effect was the reverse; the establishment of rights meant that people were able to prove their case much more easily.[6] The number of claims fell from 1,130,000 in 1980 to 830,000 in 1981 – then climbed steadily to 4,730,000 in 1986. The government at first attempted to restrict the range of payments that could be made – most important, gradually removing the rights of most claimants to receive payments for furniture. The 1988 reforms removed the rights to single payments introduced in 1980 and replaced them with the Social Fund, marking a return to discretion. The Social Fund is limited in the funds available and the grounds on which it can offer help.

## The Social Fund

The Social Fund gives grants to people in certain cases, mainly funeral expenses, cold weather payments (an important concession introduced after the initial legislation) and 'community care', a term which in this context covers not only older people, people with disabilities and other recipients of social care, but also 'families under stress'. For others, there are only loans, given either as 'crisis' loans (a provision which replaced Urgent Needs Payments) or 'budgeting' loans, for people who are short of funds.

### Box 11.1: The discretionary Social Fund

The Social Fund has three main elements: grants, budget loans and crisis loans. Applications are considered in batches, but the decision on any application should not take more than 28 days. An officer has to consider:

- the nature of the applicant's need
- the resources the applicant has
- the possibility that someone else might meet the need

[6] R Cohen and M Tarpey (1988) *Single payments: The disappearing safety net*, London: Child Poverty Action Group.

- whether and when the loan will be repaid
- the budget, and
- official guidance.

*Crisis loans* are mainly for emergencies and disasters, although they may also cover loss of money, the time up to the first payment of benefit, money to get lodgings, people stranded away from home and people barred from benefit because of capital they cannot realise.

*Budgeting loans* are for people on low income who have been on the basic means-tested benefits for at least six months. They are not available for most fuel costs. High priority is given for items important for health or safety, essential furniture or household equipment, bedding, removal costs or fuel connection charges. Other furniture, clothing and redecoration are medium priority. In practice, budgeting loans have to be repaid at higher weekly rates than either crisis loans, or deductions made for debt like arrears; the rationale for this is not very clear.[7]

When the Social Fund was based in local offices, there was a strict local budget, and once that was exhausted no more loans could be made. The Fund now operates regionally and this is much less likely to be an issue.

The system of loans is the most controversial part of the Social Fund. The requirement for claimants to repay means that people with very low incomes have to sacrifice future income. Loans are interest free, but they have to be repaid within a reasonable time – 15% of benefit may be deducted for up to 18 months – and claimants have to be judged to be capable of paying before the loan is made. There are strong arguments for loans. One is that loans give the flexibility for people to respond to fluctuating circumstances. They also give flexibility to the agencies: it clearly makes sense for a benefits office that has not been able to work out benefits for someone in urgent need to be able to loan them the money and to set it against benefits when they come into payment. Another important argument is that claimants are likely in other circumstances to obtain credit at high interest – in some cases from loan sharks, but more typically from shops that have been eager to offer credit to all comers.

One of the worst features of the Social Fund no longer really applies, however. When it was introduced, there was a cash limit for local offices. Whether people could get payments mainly depended not on their needs, or on national priorities, on whether the local office judged their case to have priority, or even on the views of the officers running the system, but on competition from other people locally. This comment is from a Social Fund inspector:

---

[7]  S Collard (2003) 'Making it better?', in T Buck and R Smith (eds) *Poor relief or poor deal?*, Aldershot: Ashgate.

> The system isn't fair because different parts of the country have more or less demands on their budget. It may well be that people in North Worcestershire can have anything they ask for at the moment, providing they can afford to repay the money and their debt isn't over £1,000. Whereas, parts of Scotland, you can barely get a cooker.[8]

The variation was exacerbated because loans are treated as expenditure: offices are not able to set the money repaid against the cost to the Fund of making the loan. The poorer the area, the greater the pressure. The situation was challenged in the High Court, which ruled that budgetary considerations are secondary to need and relative priority.[9] Subsequently the move to telephone claims rather than claims in local offices has meant that local limits no longer apply, and a centre that is dealing with a million claimants should not have either the variation in practice or the unmanageable pressure on resources that smaller localities experience.

The Social Fund has been roundly condemned in the literature. Roger Smith, for example, questions whether 'the Social Fund has made any real contribution to alleviating poverty at all'.[10] That view is reinforced by Legge and her colleagues, who express concern about the difficulty of getting help for some claimant groups, including pensioners and those in minority ethnic groups, and the impact of having to repay loans.[11] Buck and Smith identify four persistent problems with the discretionary Social Fund. Running costs are high; there is no consistency in decision making; the scheme is unresponsive to needs; and despite the claim that the Fund offers flexible discretion, it has been hemmed in by rules.[12]

The main problem with the Social Fund is not that it is discretionary. Whatever the system, and no matter how good it is, there has to be some provision for special needs. Nor is it necessarily a problem that it is partly based on loans, in a world where poor people are routinely exploited by loan sharks charging penal rates of interest for modest short-term loans, the existence of a secure, interest-free loan system could be valuable. The basic problem is that the Social Fund

[8]  M Rowe (2003) 'Decision making processes', in T Buck and R Smith (eds) *Poor relief or poor deal?*, Aldershot: Ashgate, p 133.

[9]  Cited in Child Poverty Action Group (2010) *Welfare benefits and tax credits handbook 2010/2011*, London: CPAG, p 503.

[10]  R Smith (2003) 'Claimants, applicants, customers or supplicants?: the social fund, safety nets and social security', in T Buck and R Smith (eds) *Poor relief or poor deal?*, Aldershot: Ashgate, p 101.

[11]  K Legge, Y Hartfree, B Stafford, M Magadi, J Beckhelling, L Predelli and S Middleton (2006) *The Social Fund: Current role and future direction*, York: Joseph Rowntree Foundation.

[12]  T Buck and R Smith (2004) *A critical literature review of the Social Fund*, London: National Audit Office.

is being used to bolster a system of benefits that is not adequate to meet basic needs. Half of all Social Fund claimants never have money left over from their benefit, and a third of Social Fund claimants run out of money every week.[13] If benefits were delivered at an adequate level, many of the problems attributed to the existence of the Social Fund would disappear.

## QUESTIONS FOR DISCUSSION

Should the Social Fund be abolished?
Should other benefits have a discretionary element?

---

[13] N Finch and P Kemp (2004) 'The use of the Social Fund by families with children', Paper presented to the Social Policy Association Conference, University of Nottingham.

# Chapter 12

# Universal benefits

Universal benefits go to broad categories of people, without specific tests of means or needs. The most important is Child Benefit. There have been many proposals for extending the principle further, such as proposals for Negative Income Tax or Citizen's Income, but none of the general systems proposed is able to deal with the diversity and complexity of circumstances that social security has to respond to. The main scope for universal benefits is to provide, like Child Benefit, an element of income that is stable, secure and predictable.

Universal benefits are benefits given to whole categories of a population, like children or old people, without other tests. The best known example is Child Benefit, which is available to everyone caring for a dependent child, but there are others, such as the free TV licence for the over 75s, free prescriptions for children and pensioners, and Winter Fuel Payments, which effectively go to every pensioner.

The general arguments for universality were considered in Chapter 2. They include basic rights, simplicity and effectiveness. The central criticism of universal benefits is that they spread resources too widely: if benefits are going to everyone, then either they will be very costly, or they will have to be set at very low levels. This dilemma can be avoided. One option is that universal benefits can be reclaimed through the tax system – a process referred to as 'clawback'. This has an effect similar to means testing, with two important differences: first, that everyone receives the benefit, and second, that the examination of means is also done for everyone. Another option is that even if the entitlement is universal, the benefit is not actually paid to everyone. The non-contributory pension for people over 80 is universal, but it is also residual    it goes to every person over 80 who does not otherwise have an entitlement to the National Insurance pension.

## Child Benefit

Child Benefit is a universal benefit, paid to parents for each child living with them. Currently it is paid at a slightly higher rate for the first child.

The idea of family allowances developed in the UK during the First World War, when they were paid to help servicemen's families. A committee formed in 1917 was to become the Family Endowment Society, which argued for allowances. The National Union of Societies for Equal Citizenship, under Eleanor

Rathbone, argued for a flat-rate family allowance. The influence of Keynes led to acceptance of the principle in 1941 – before the Beveridge report. Family Allowance was introduced in 1945, ahead of the 'welfare state'. It was not made available for the first child.

Tax allowances for children were first introduced in 1909. Titmuss, in 1955, made the important argument that tax allowances and benefits were really two aspects of the same thing,[1] a principle which has gradually gained acceptance since then. The Child Poverty Action Group, founded in 1965, has been the main advocate of Child Benefit. They argued to extend family allowances for the first child, and to unify tax allowances and benefits. In 1975, the Labour government passed an Act introducing Child Benefit, which was not at first implemented. Copies of cabinet minutes were leaked to Frank Field, at that time the director of CPAG, showing that the cabinet had decided they could not bring in the benefit.[2] In most cases, Family Allowance was paid to the mother and the tax allowance to the father. The cabinet thought that men would see Child Benefit paid to the mother as a cut in their pay packet and press for higher wages, when the government was trying to run an incomes policy. When this argument became public, the unions denied it, and the reform went ahead.

Child Benefit is not age-related. Older children are more expensive than younger children, and there is a good case to say that teenagers, who are still growing, are more expensive than adults, so this needs some explanation. The case against age relation is partly that it is simpler not to relate the benefit to age, but more importantly it is true that poorer families tend to be those with younger children. That mainly happens because while the child is young, the woman in the family is unable to work. The argument for paying more for the first child, which is a relatively recent measure, is more complex. This runs counter to the early practice of Family Allowance, which was not available for the first child at all; it also runs against a common perception that larger families present a greater financial challenge. Families with one child tend, on the whole, to be on lower incomes. Such families are younger on average (as people get older, they may have more children) and younger adults tend to have lower incomes than older adults. This could also be an argument for having higher benefits for young children: in France, there is an additional benefit for children up to the age of three. This would run counter, however, to perceptions about the increasing cost of children.

---

[1] R M Titmuss (1955) 'The social division of welfare', in R M Titmuss, *Essays on the welfare state* (2nd edn 1963), London: George Allen & Unwin.
[2] F Field (1976) 'Killing a commitment', *New Society*, 17 June.

The basic arguments for Child Benefit are:

- it is normally paid to the mother, who may have no other income
- it is not means tested and take-up is very high (it is estimated at 96-98%)[3]
- it is simple to administer
- it avoids problems like the poverty trap and stigma, and
- it helps to protect the position of the working poor.

The arguments against are:

- it is inefficient: like any universal benefit, some of it goes to people on higher incomes; and
- the redistribution is horizontal – from people without children to people with children – rather than vertical, from rich to poor. Child Benefit may redistribute from a poor single person to a better-off family.

For much of its history, there was another argument against Child Benefit. Poor people on Income Support did not get any net income from it, because it was deducted directly from the IS payment. This position changed in April 2004, and people on the basic means-tested benefits and Jobseeker's Allowance now get Child Benefit and Child Tax Credit in place of the previous dependants' allowances.

The literature emphasises the apparent simplicity and high take-up associated with Child Benefit.[4] This needs to be treated with some caution, because it cannot necessarily be generalised to other universal benefits. First, the take-up of Child Benefit is not as straightforward as it at first appears. Many parents do not receive the benefit in the first few months of their first child's life because it takes time to realise that they are entitled, and that they have to claim. Once they have claimed the benefit carries on – that, rather than the universal acceptance, is why take-up is so high. Second, Child Benefit works, not just because the benefit is universal, but because so few conditions are attached. Some other non-contributory benefits are simple for the same reason, like payments to people holding the Victoria Cross. Passported benefits (where entitlement depends on receiving another benefit) are simple, too. Benefits become complicated when they impose conditions, and they become particularly complicated when those conditions are liable to change. (For example, One Parent Benefit, an addition to Child Benefit which was abolished in 1997, had a cohabitation rule. That

---

[3]  HMRC (HM Revenue & Customs) (2010) *Child Benefit, Child Tax Credit and Working Tax Credit take-up rates* (www.hmrc.gov.uk/stats/personal-tax-credits/cwtc-take-up2007-08.pdf).

[4]  For example, A Walsh and R Lister (1985) *Mother's life line*, London: Child Poverty Action Group; J Brown (1988) *Child Benefit: Investing in the future*, London: Child Poverty Action Group.

is unavoidable, because the absence of the second parent is what a 'one parent benefit' is about.)

Child Benefit is simple because, in most cases, it needs relatively few rules. The basic qualification for the benefit is relatively simple – to have a child under the age of 16. But people's lives are complicated, and Child Benefit also becomes complicated when the rules have to take that complexity into account. Many families undergo separation or divorce. Nominally, the rules say that Child Benefit is payable only to the person who has the child in care. Initially, this was calculated on a daily basis, so that if parents shared child care, Child Benefit could be split between them. The position was difficult to assess, and complicated by the definition of a day as running from midnight to midnight, because that meant that a child who went to different parents on alternate evenings would not attract benefit. The rule was reformed, then, to say that parents would receive Child Benefit if they were responsible for a child during the week in question. This is a much better approach, but it does leave open the possibility that more than one person could be entitled during a week for the same child. To avoid that situation, the benefit rules stipulate an order of priority between competing claims – first the person the child is actually living with, then the parent, the mother, a partner where there is a written agreement, and so forth, with at the end the opportunity for adjudication in the event of a dispute. Although this is explicit and manageable, HM Revenue & Customs (which administers Child Benefit) does make rather a meal of it, and tends to delay the process of applications whenever there is the possibility of disputes. This also implies that the government's step to curb entitlement for higher earners will complicate the system, as people with changing incomes, changing households or those who lose employment, move between states where they may be entitled at some times and not others.

## Other demogrants

The basic principle behind Child Benefit is sometimes called a 'demogrant' – the term has been credited to James Tobin, a Nobel-Prize winning economist. Awarding universal benefits on the basis of a broad category, like childhood, has some notable advantages over other benefit systems. The first is that it is relatively simple to administer – it is much easier to establish whether someone is under 16 than, for example, whether they are a tenant on a low income. The second is that it is long term – once a determination is made, it stays made unless there is some reason for radical revision. The third is that it seems to be economically fairly neutral – if there are any negative implications for economic behaviour or outcomes, they have been difficult to detect.

At the same time, the use of demogrants has been very limited. There have been calls for a universal state pension, of the sort given in New Zealand;[5] the coalition government is actively considering the idea. The National Insurance pension and Pension Credit would be replaced by a simple flat-rate, universal pension. The same principle has been supported by the World Bank and applied in some developing countries, because it offers a simple, practical way of distributing money to a poor population. (Even this is not without its problems; in countries where many people have no formal address, benefits can be difficult to track.)

Some countries have been represented as extending the same kind of idea to disabled people, but these benefits are not really universal; there is usually a test of need or of a person's capacity for work. In principle, it would be possible for some narrowly defined benefits for disabled people to work like a demogrant. A Blind Person's Allowance, for example, could be introduced for people with specified levels of sight loss. Although there could be problems in defining the boundaries, it would have some of the features of a demogrant – in particular, relatively straightforward qualification rules and long-term payment. However, many cases of disability can be difficult to identify or based in fluctuating circumstances, and it would be difficult to make this the basis for a more general universal distribution.

## Basic Income and Negative Income Tax

Although there are not many examples of universal benefits in practice, they have often been prominent in debates about benefits. This because, beyond what a benefit like Child Benefit can actually achieve, it gives us a glimpse of a different kind of social security system. The principle behind universal benefits was first put by Tom Paine[6] as a model for ensuring that everyone – man, woman and child – could have a basic income, as of right. This model used to be called a 'social dividend', and it has also been called a 'state bonus', but it is now usually referred to in the contemporary literature as 'Basic Income' or 'Citizen's Income'.[7] A Citizen's Income would be tax-financed and unconditional.

Imagine, for the sake of argument, that every man and every woman in the UK received £80 per week and every child received £40. Most other basic benefits, like Income Support, Retirement Pension, Pension Credit, Jobseeker's Allowance, Child Benefit and Tax Credit, would be abolished. There would be no cohabitation rule, no separate means test and no conditions about work. All income would then be taxed, without any tax reliefs. A system like this would be simple, easy to administer and should achieve complete coverage and take-up.

---

5 A O'Connell (2004) *Citizen's pension: Lessons from New Zealand*, London: Pensions Policy Institute.

6 T Paine (1791) *The rights of man*, part 2, ch 5.

7 P van Parijs (ed) (1992) *Arguing for basic income*, London and New York: Verso.

There are three main problems. The first is cost. A scheme like this would not be absurdly expensive, because the figures would be largely offset by very large savings in benefits, tax allowances and tax reliefs, but it would cost more than the current system, and that would imply a higher tax rate. The second problem is equity. Some people would be better off under such a system, while others would be worse off. The people with most to lose are often those with greatest needs: on the figures I have suggested, many of the losers would be people who are currently on benefits. The third problem is the difficulty of predicting effects on behaviour. There are fears that some people would stop working if they had the option of benefits without the conditions imposed at present. An experiment with a guaranteed income in the United States was profoundly inconclusive on this point[8] – which does not mean that there is no evidence, but rather that there is some evidence to suggest it would not make much difference.

In the early 1970s, the Conservative government of the time proposed a smaller-scale version, called the Tax Credit scheme.[9] It is not very much like the Tax Credits introduced by the Labour government in the late 1990s, which are means-tested benefits. Rather, it was a scheme to integrate the concept of basic income with the tax system. Instead of actually giving people money, tax would be calculated as if they had been given the money; at the end, some people would receive the money and others would pay it. This has the same effect as a Citizen's Income, with the advantage of keeping the money off the accounts of public spending. At the time the scheme was proposed, it was so limited that no one felt it could do any good, and it won no support.

The main alternative to Basic Income schemes are schemes for negative taxation. They generally involve the unification of the social security and tax system into one income maintenance system, and strip away the existing structure of benefits. People who are poorer have money directed toward them; people who are richer have money taken away. The *Reverse Income Tax*, proposed by the Institute of Economic Affairs in 1970, is one of the simplest schemes. They proposed abolition of all existing benefits, a guaranteed minimum income for all and taxation for all above the minimum income.[10] The problem with this is that all people below the minimum will have any income up to that level taken away.

An earlier scheme, *Negative Income Tax*, avoids this problem. Milton Friedman's scheme for NIT worked up to a set level by giving people half the amount between their income and a set level. (This principle was used in 1971 for Family Income Supplement.) Above that level, people would be taxed.[11] The Institute for Fiscal Studies once proposed a similar system, arguing that all benefits can be administered through the tax system, and that benefits can be increased

---

[8]   C Green (1967) *Negative taxes and the poverty problem*, New York: Brookings.
[9]   Cmnd 5116 (1972) *Proposals for a tax credit system*, London: HMSO.
[10]  IEA (Institute of Economic Affairs) (1970) *Policy for poverty*, London: IEA.
[11]  M Friedman (1962) *Capitalism and freedom*, Chicago, IL: University of Chicago Press.

and taxation cut by concentrating resources on those who are poorest.[12] The coalition government's proposals for a Universal Credit scheme come from the same stable. [13]

The core problems with NIT are the problems of means testing. It is all very well to say that there will be a smoothly administered system, but a scheme of this sort requires constant adjustment to people's continually changing circumstances. The government apparently believes that can largely be achieved through a new computer system. There are grounds for scepticism: what seems to be called for is not just error-free and instantaneous information processing, which no other computer project has achieved, but a fundamental restructuring of the character of the labour market.

The main differences between Negative Income Tax and Basic Income are differences of method rather than principle. It is possible to devise negative income tax, basic income or tax credits in such a way that people would end up with exactly the same amount of money at the end of the day as they would with any of the others.[14] The issue is how the money is paid.

Although these schemes are interesting as a thought experiment, I am not convinced they can be used as widely or exhaustively as their proponents hope. The simplified schemes tend to assume that social security is about redistribution and the relief of poverty. Social security is not just about giving money to poor people; it does lots of other things, including for example compensation for disability, encouraging or discouraging different patterns of behaviour, or helping to maintain the economy.

Even if the principles could be agreed, though, there are many issues of practical operation. Will there be a different scheme for people who receive money and people who pay money in? Who will claim in the family? Will benefits be delivered automatically, in the same way that tax is deducted, or will people have to claim? What happens to special cases? Most of the schemes for radical simplification founder because they attempt to impose an artificial rationality on a complex environment. Social security covers many contingencies. There are special rules for all sorts of situations – for local councillors, people with contagious diseases, prisoners on remand, people undergoing gender reassignment, people who have worked in more than one country, and so on. The system is complicated because people's lives are complicated. That means, inevitably, that benefits have to be adapted to meet the circumstances. The apparent simplicity of these schemes is often superficial. As Jonathan Bradshaw argued during a debate on the issue in the 1980s, many rules have been introduced

---

[12] A Dilnot, J Kay and C Morris (1984) *The reform of social security*, Oxford: Clarendon Press/Institute for Fiscal Studies.

[13] Cm 7913 (2010) *21st century welfare*,, London: DWP.

[14] See A Atkinson (1983) *The economics of inequality*, Oxford: Oxford University Press.

to deal with people's real problems, and if the benefit system has grown unruly, it is not necessarily a bad thing.[15]

The general case against integrated universal systems does not undermine the argument for a more extensive use of universal benefits. The main arguments raised against broadly universalist schemes are concerned with practicality, equity and flexibility; the arguments about cost and incentives are more contentious. But few of these very general arguments seem to have much to do with Child Benefit in practice. What Child Benefit offers is a modest but secure element of a family's general income, something that is fairly predictable and secure. It is the only element of income that seems to continue to function reliably in situations where people are moving in and out of work or where their income is unstable and unpredictable. That seems to me something which is valuable and important, and the principle could be more generally extended.

**QUESTIONS FOR DISCUSSION**

Should there be more universal benefits?
Should we introduce a Basic Income?

---

[15] J Bradshaw (1985) 'A defence of social security', in P Bean, J Ferris and D Whynes (eds) *In defence of welfare*, London: Tavistock, pp 227-55.

# Chapter 13

# Claiming benefits

The process of claiming has been transformed, following the movement away from local administration and paper-based assessments to computerised calculations managed by call centres. There is still a general assumption that the onus of claiming falls on the claimant, and this chapter tries to give some idea of what someone needs to do to receive a benefit. The system is complex, and many people do not claim the benefits they are entitled to. Welfare rights and advice have developed to help guide people through the difficulties.

For several years, the Department for Work and Pensions has been referring to claimants as 'customers'. This is apparently intended to represent a change in the relationship between the agency and the service user, though if so, it is not clear what the change consists of. People who claim benefits are not like the 'customers' of a commercial enterprise.[1] Customers, in a commercial setting, have a contingent contractual relationship. It is contingent because either party can withdraw. Being contractual implies that there is a voluntary agreement. Neither of those is really true of the benefits system. People claim benefits because that is how they have to proceed; because they have legal entitlements, the agencies administering benefits cannot withdraw.

As a general proposition, people who receive social security benefits are expected to claim them. It is the responsibility of the person who is entitled to demand the benefit; it is not the responsibility of the service to provide it. (Late claims lose money, especially for people with disabilities. This is a minor point in the discussion of social security policy; it looms much larger in welfare rights work.) In technical terms, social security is a 'subjective right', which depends on the actions of the claimant, rather than an objective one, imposing a duty on other people. Claimants have to take the initiative. The main consequence is that many people do not receive the benefits they are entitled to, of which more shortly, but it also means that where people ask for the wrong benefit, they lose out. This is from a recent report from Citizens' Advice Scotland about Employment and Support Allowance:

> Unless the applicant explicitly states that they wish to be considered
> both for income-based and contributions-based benefits – and many

---

[1]  N Flynn (2002) *Public sector management*, London: Pearson, ch 9.

clients are unaware of this requirement – their assessment is made on a contributions-based component only. This situation has left clients financially distressed as they have had to wait till the process is restarted before receiving any payments.[2]

The idea that the process has to depend on people making a claim is far from obvious. We do not give people the choice about paying tax; parents have a legal obligation to register the birth of their children; people do not necessarily have to apply to receive other basic services, like having their rubbish collected. In the unusual case of the Child Trust Fund, families on low incomes did not have to claim the supplementary contribution from HM Revenue & Customs – HMRC were required to identify the families and deliver the benefit.[3] There are some benefits that we could not deliver automatically, because they are subject to conditions that require detailed examination of personal circumstances, but there are certainly benefits that could be delivered without a claim. Child Benefit, old age pension or benefits for funerals could be delivered on the basis of other information, without special claim forms. (One possible explanation for the slowness of many people to claim Child Benefit in the first few months after the birth of their first child may well be that they are simply expecting the benefit to arrive, and do not realise that they have to claim.)

The arguments for requiring claims are hazy. Part of the argument is a legacy of the Poor Law, when claiming was something that needed actively to be discouraged. Part is a belief that true rights are those that people can decide whether they want to exercise – though, as this does not seem to apply to education or health care for children, it is not at all clear why it should apply to benefits for children. Part of the reason is a feeling that money which people do not actively claim is more likely to be wasted. For example, people with severe learning disabilities were able to claim non-contributory benefits after 1975, but the take-up was not always good, and even when people did claim, there was sometimes a problem of funds slowly building under the tutelage of health and social care authorities because the recipients were not able to spend the money. This did not, in principle, stop those authorities spending the money on their clients' behalf – but that requires thought, care and administrative effort. It was not until the community care reforms of the 1990s that the issues really started to be dealt with.

Claiming is probably necessary for circumstances where the provision of benefit depends on the definition of need – for example, unemployment, sickness, disability

---

2   Citizens' Advice Scotland (2009) *Employment and Support Allowance*, Briefing paper 44, Edinburgh: CAS

3   N Wikeley, D Williams, I Hooker (2009) *Social security legislation 2009/10, volume IV: Tax credits and HMRC-administered social security benefits*, London: Sweet and Maxwell, p 266

and low income. This is because it would not be possible to deliver benefits automatically without retaining a great deal of information about the eligible individual. However, the Department for Work and Pensions has been exploring the idea of making claims more automatic despite those limitations. Kotecha et al identify a spectrum of approaches that might be used to make processes more automatic:

- sending people an estimate of their entitlement if they claim;
- sending them a 'pre-populated' form, filled in with data already held;
- paying people for a short trial period;
- fully automatic payments, where recipients do not have to claim at all.[4]

In an interesting experiment, a pilot scheme in 2010 is delivering Pension Credit – a complex, means-tested benefit – to people who have not claimed. Two thousand recipients are being given the benefit for 13 weeks and invited to follow this up with a claim.[5]

## The process of claiming

Claiming makes considerable demands of claimants and staff alike. The image that sometimes emerges from the popular press is one of gullible, smiling benefit officers showering claimants with money like confetti as they walk into the office. The reality is very different. Claiming is a complex, time-consuming and often puzzling process.

The first problem is making contact at all. The transfer of responsibility from local offices means that most claims are processed over the telephone, though Jobseeker's Allowance can now be claimed online and an online application is being piloted for the State Pension. Once the call is made, the details asked for are extensive. When the forms were on paper, an unemployed person, coming to Jobcentre Plus, received a 'Jobseeker's Allowance Claim Pack', containing a pack of leaflets and forms. In the pack there were forms which included 14 pages about a claimant's availability for work, eight pages as a record of efforts to look for work, four pages of an outline Jobseeker's Agreement, a 37-page claim form for Jobseeker's Allowance and claim forms for Housing Benefit and Council Tax Benefit. Now that the forms are usually held on a computer screen, it is more difficult to give a sense of just what is involved. The target

---

4   M Kotecha, M Callnan, S Arthur and C Creegan (2009) *Older people's attitudes to automatic awards of Pension Credit*, DWP Research Report 579, London: Department for Work and Pensions (http://research.dwp.gov.uk/asd/asd5/rports2009-2010/rrep579. pdf).

5   Pensions Client Directorate (2010) *Pension Credit payment pilot*, London: Department for Work and Pensions (www.dwp.gov.uk/docs/pension-credit-payment-pilot-response. pdf).

for the telephone interview in the call centres is an average of 22 minutes for an interview. Claimants have to answer a long series of questions – perhaps a hundred or more – which are recorded as the telephone interview progresses; applicants online are recommended to allow for 30-60 minutes. Subsequently the forms will be returned to the claimants for signature and verification (as they are in the Pensions Service) or subject to meetings for assessment (the procedure for Jobcentre Plus). The script that operators follow, or 'mandatory text', is complex, convoluted and inflexible; there are long passages where they have to run through legalities, and lists of benefits and circumstances which have to be reeled off. I am personally sceptical that people can answer many of the questions they are asked accurately in the course of a single phone call (like their partner's National Insurance number or the type of Tax Credits they get), but the front-line officers I have spoken to in the contact centre assure me that the scripts do not pose problems – on the contrary, they have been surprised at how few claimants now have to be referred on to the Jobcentres for the alternative interview procedure. This perception is not universally shared by claimants, who complain that it is difficult to get the right forms, that the forms repeatedly ask for the same information, that the questions are not clear and that they take far too long to fill in.[6]

The factors that contribute to the complexity of claiming for people without work are:

- the *work test*;
- the *means tests*, which demand as many questions again. The idea that means tests are solely, or even primarily, responsible for the problems is illusory. They certainly contribute to the difficulty of claiming, but any benefit based on unemployment would need to ask the other questions about work, education and employment history;
- the *rules relating to families*, which lead to questions about partners, children and co-residents. Joint claims, where both husband and wife are unemployed, are more complicated still;
- the *existence of multiple benefits*. The distinction between income-related Jobseeker's Allowance, Housing Benefit and Council Tax benefit did not exist 25 years ago; an unemployed claimant in the 1970s would have claimed one benefit, Supplementary Benefit, to cover all three circumstances. Although it would be possible in principle to reduce some of the duplicated information – names, addresses, declarations and the like are required because the forms will be distributed to different offices – most of the information requested is additional material applying to the conditions for which the benefit is provided.

---

[6]  D Finn, D Mason, N Rahim and J Casebourne (2008) *Delivering benefits, tax credits and employment services*, York: Joseph Rowntree Foundation, pp 37-8.

The central administration of the Department for Work and Pensions is apparently convinced that errors are often a result of mistakes by the computer operators: 'Error occurs when our people, for whatever reason, fail to follow agreed business processes ....'[7] It has consequently tried to limit the scope for wrong entries by blocking officials who have not recorded answers appropriately. The problem with this is that the people the officials are dealing with are in diverse, often unpredictable, circumstances, and it can be hard to fit them in the boxes. Officers in First Contact centers have to start filling the forms again if the unfortunate claimant remembers a detail too late. The Benefit Delivery Centres and the Pensions, Disability and Carers Service have officers whose role is to identify, report and warn other centres of faults. In some cases, the officers have to enter different information that at least won't crash the system; in others, they may have to pull the file off the computer to work it by hand. An example I was told about in 2007 was for people with same-sex partners, which the computer insisted was an error. Another example, from 2009, was that the computers could not cope with medical evidence relating to Employment and Support Allowance covering a different period from the period of unemployment. A senior DWP officer — who described the ESA procedures as 'an absolute horror story' — told me that her unit had taken deliberately to entering different dates, to avoid creating unnecessary problems for claimants. I think we too often underestimate the professionalism, commitment and competence of benefits staff.

## Claiming and take-up

The problems of low take-up have been a recurring theme in the literature on benefits. The history of the Poor Law meant that, at the time of the foundation of the welfare state, administrators and politicians were very familiar with the barriers to claiming and the reluctance of people to claim. This was referred to in general terms as the problem of 'stigma'. The idea of stigma was used generally to refer to a bundle of negative attitudes. The Poor Law had used a combination of deterrence, humiliation and a distinction between 'deserving' and 'undeserving' claimants. When it became clear in the 1960s that many pensioners were still reluctant to claim, it was assumed that this was a survival of attitudes left over from the Poor Law.[8] But there were doubts about the concept. Research on school meals seemed to show that negative attitudes had no effect on take-up at all.[9] Klein, for example, suggested that stigma was only an excuse for an

---

[7]  Department for Work and Pensions (2007) *Getting welfare right*, London: DWP, para 1.12

[8]  Ministry of Pensions and National Insurance (1965) *Financial and other circumstances of retirement pensioners*, London: HMSO.

[9]  B Davies, with M Reddin (1978) *University, selectivity, and effectiveness in social policy*, London: Heinemann Educational Books.

explanation. It was, he suggested, 'the phlogiston of social theory'. (Phlogiston was the imaginary substance which scientists thought, before the discovery of oxygen, might account for things burning).[10]

Subsequent research tried to break down the different factors explaining people's behaviour. There were two main competing models. The first model was one proposed by Scott Kerr, a psychologist.[11] Kerr suggested that people had to go through several steps before claiming, and each one had to be passed before they would go on to the next. The steps were:

- *perceived need:* people had to feel there was a need;
- they had to have enough *basic knowledge* to know where to go;
- *perceived eligibility:* they had to think they might be eligible;
- *perceived utility:* they had to think it worthwhile. The value of Housing Benefit or the Guarantee Credit may be marginal, and there is very little advantage for some people in claiming both Child Tax Credit and Housing Benefit simultaneously. The amount of money might not be worth claiming for the effort involved;
- *beliefs and feelings:* claiming had to be acceptable, despite stigma or personal beliefs;
- *perceived stability or circumstances:* they had to think their condition would last long enough to make it worthwhile; and
- *claiming:* they had to go through the process of applying.

Kerr's model was highly influential, and it dominated the model of research done in the Department of Health and Social Security.[12] It was useful, because it led to research which looked at a series of influences, but the framework depended on a questionable assumption: the steps it outlines are not distinct. What people know about benefits is not distinct from what they think about them; some people suppose that benefits are not for people like them, and some do not want to know.[13]

The other model was proposed by Weisbrod.[14] Weisbrod suggested that the demand for services should be seen in terms of an assessment of the costs and benefits of receiving payments. The costs included the costs of information, the time and trouble of claiming and the cost of shame and humiliation. The benefits of claiming had to be judged against the level of payment – many pensioners who did not claim Supplementary Benefit were failing to claim for relatively small

[10] R Klein (ed) (1975) *Social policy and public expenditure*, Bath: Centre for Studies in Social Policy, p 5.

[11] S Kerr (1983) *Making ends meet*, London: Bedford Square Press.

[12] See P Craig (1991) 'Costs and benefits', *Journal of Social Policy*, vol 20, no 4, pp 537-66.

[13] P Spicker (1984) *Stigma and social welfare*, Beckenham: Croom Helm, ch 2.

[14] B A Weisbrod (1970) *On the stigma effect and the demand for welfare programmes*, Madison, WI: Institute for Research on Poverty, University of Wisconsin.

amounts of money – but more importantly (because claimants are often very unclear about how much money they might gain) against the needs they hope to meet. This approach is less clear-cut than Kerr's, but it is a better description of the process people go through. The approach prompts a focus on removing barriers to claiming – the reduction of costs, for example, by simplifying applications or passporting benefits. Equally, it may be possible to weight the positive benefits, for example through advice agencies. Ritchie argues that for people to claim, it is important to tilt the scales in favour of claiming.[15]

The figures on take-up are generally confined to means-tested benefits: the official estimates are shown in Table 13.1. Take-up by expenditure consistently seems to be higher than take-up as a proportion of people who are entitled; the implication is that the amounts of money that are not being claimed tend to be relatively small. The Child Tax Credit figures are surprising. HMRC acknowledges problems of confusion, complexity and some alienation of former claimants who have been forced to pay large sums of benefits paid through miscalculation, and consequently have refused to claim again.[16] If take-up is affected by ignorance, complexity, stigma or barriers to access, the take-up of CTC might reasonably have been expected to be markedly lower.

## Table 13.1: Estimates of take-up[17]

| Benefit | Proportion of people entitled | Proportion of total expenditure claimed |
|---|---|---|
| Pension Credit | 61-70% | 70-78% |
| Income Support | 78-88% | 85-93% |
| Housing Benefit | 80-87% | 85-91% |
| Income-based Jobseeker's Allowance | 52-60% | 54-65% |
| Child Tax Credit | 79-84% | 86-92% |
| Working Tax Credit | 55-59% | 72-01% |

[15] For example, C Davies and J Ritchie (1988) *Tipping the balance: A study of non-takeup of benefits in an inner city area*, London: HMSO.

[16] Department for Work and Pensions (2009) *Income-related benefits: Estimates of takeup in 2007-08* (http://research.dwp.gov.uk/asd/income_analysis/jun_2009/0708_Publication.pdf); HM Revenue & Customs (2010) Child Benefit, *Child Tax Credit and Working Tax Credit take-up rates* (www.hmrc.gov.uk/stats/personal-tax-credits/cwtc-take-up2007-08.pdf).

[17] P Gerrard (HMRC Transformation Programme Director) (2008) 'Tax credits and Child Benefit', DWP Annual Forum, Glasgow, 20 November; see also Parliamentary and Health Service Ombudsman (2007) *Tax credits – Getting it wrong?*, HC 1010, London: The Stationery Office, pp 3-4.

There has not been much independent research on take-up for many years, because it is expensive and difficult to do, but local surveys in the past tended to cast doubt on the official estimates.[18] It cannot be said with confidence that the independent researchers were right and the government was wrong. The figures are puzzling, however. Why, one has to ask, should take-up by unemployed couples with children (74-88%) be so much lower than take-up by lone parents on Income Support (93-97%)?[19] Both groups face deterrents, and uncertainties about their position. Is it plausible that nearly all the expenditure entitlement of Income Support for people of working age is claimed – implying that people of working age who fail to claim IS are not claiming for small amounts, but that pensioners are not claiming for large amounts? Most pensioners have another source of income (the State Pension), while other IS claimants do not. And why are figures only published on income-tested benefits, when the problems of ignorance, confusion about eligibility, complexity and stigma apply so much more widely? The figures produced by government have shown the same patterns over a long time. That may show that the findings are robust, but they may also reflect a lack of adequate examination of the problem.

## The rights of claimants

Legal rights are rules that can be enforced by the person who holds them. Under the Poor Law, claimants were treated as 'paupers', and often they were denied legal rights on that basis. The modern social security system has an extended system for the redress of grievances. Claimants can ask for a revision of a decision; where circumstances change, they can ask for 'supersession' of the decision, or they can appeal formally. Complaints are dealt with through internal review, appeals to 'first tier' tribunals, and appeals which go at first to the Upper Tribunal and after that to the higher courts. The nature of the legal system, however, is that the higher courts are concerned with supervision, rather than review of cases and evidence; they are generally concerned with errors of law, not with whether they agree or disagree with the decision taken.[20]

---

[18] For example, D Page and B Weinberger (1975) *The take-up of rent rebates and allowances in Birmingham*, Birmingham: Centre for Urban and Regional Studies; M Noble, G Smith and T Munby (1992) *The takeup of Family Credit*, Oxford: Oxford University Press.

[19] DWP (2009) pp 102 and 18.

[20] P Craig (2008) *Administrative law*, London: Sweet & Maxwell, chs 14-5.

The system of tribunals was initially intended to offer an alternative to formal legal processes, which tend to be slow, expensive and inaccessible.[21] The stress on informality did not always work well: in the days when tribunals were largely conducted by lay people, they were often judgmental and heavily biased against claimants. (One tribunal chairman I used to appear before always gave a little speech: 'we have to be fair to you, but we have to be fair to the taxpayer as well ....') In the 1980s, tribunals were given much more independence, the chairs had to have some legal competence and lay members were trained. The system was restructured in 2008, bringing together appeals on a range of benefits, including local authority benefits and tax credits; the first tier tribunal is now headed by a judge, legally qualified, who may draw on advice from a doctor and in some cases a 'person with experience of disability'. Rowland and White question whether the new arrangements, in which tribunal decisions can be overruled by the Secretary of State, give the tribunals sufficient independence, and they think the reform may be open to legal challenge.[22]

The process of appeals still plays a major part in advice work in social security, even if the scope of the appeals system has reduced. Hartley Dean has argued that the character of the appeals process has also changed because they deal with different kinds of circumstances than they used to. Three benefits – Disability Living Allowance, Incapacity Benefit and Industrial Injuries Benefits – have accounted for about two thirds of all social security appeals.[23] These appeals tend to be about matters of fact rather than law, and in areas where the facts are subject to dispute, like the extent of a person's disability, a good half of all appeals are successful. That means, Dean suggests, that the process has become much less like a court, and much more like the complaints procedures of consumer-based organisations.[24] If that analysis is right, the creation of the new service is unlikely to make the appeals process as formal as the constitution of the tribunal suggests.

The process of appealing can slow down the smooth processing of individual claims, but the process is important and valuable. From the point of view of the claimant, it means that decisions can be challenged, and corrected where appropriate. From the point of view of the administration, the testing of rights provides a constant check on the actions of the agencies. Over time, it has produced an extensive system of general rules and principles that administrators

[21] K Bell (1969) *Tribunals in the social services*, London: Routledge and Kegan Paul.
[22] M Rowland and R White (2009) *Social security legislation 2009/10, volume III: Administration, adjudication and the European dimension*, London: Sweet and Maxwell, p 1214.
[23] H Dean (2004) 'Losing appeal?', *Benefits*, vol 12, no 1, p 5.
[24] H Dean (1996) 'Who's complaining? Redress and social policy', in M May, E Brunsdon and G Craig (eds) *Social Policy Review 8*, London: Social Policy Association.

have to apply. The process has certainly made the system more complicated, but it has made it more consistent, and more defensible, over time.

Reports on decisions from the Upper Tribunal and the courts on tribunal cases give a valuable insight into practical problems, and the decisions serve to establish important rules. At the same time, there are important limits to the role of the law. The process of appealing is relatively slow and cumbersome; it relates to people with limited resources, often in conditions of urgent need. When cases are decided, they are more likely to be used to affect future practice than to rectify past mistakes. The Child Poverty Action Group's Citizens' Rights Office has followed a 'test case strategy' for over forty years, seeking to select cases that will establish legal rights for claimants.[25] One of the most perplexing rules in the system, however, is the 'anti-test case' rule, a statutory rule by which the government refuses to apply principles retrospectively where it is found they have made an error of law.[26] This places administrative convenience above the issue of fairness, reasonableness or proper conduct. It is palpably unjust.

## Welfare rights and advice

The complexity of the benefits system has led, over time, to an increasing emphasis on the importance of people to advise and help claimants over the obstacle course. This falls under the broad heading of 'welfare rights', though the field of welfare rights covers a range of other related activity. There are four main kinds of welfare rights work:

- *Advice and support* for individuals who are claiming. 'Advice' consists of information about benefits. 'Support' goes beyond this by helping a person with a claim – helping the person to fill in forms, writing letters on someone's behalf or going to a benefits office with the person.
- *Advocacy and specialised advice* Second tier agencies can take referrals from other groups, though some deal directly with the public. If advice and support is sometimes referred to as 'first tier' advice work, this is 'second tier' work. Advocacy at tribunals and in appeals processes serves two functions: it offers a degree of specialist support, but it also serves to test the system, helping to establish rules and precedents in difficult circumstances.
- *Publicity* Welfare rights agencies try to promote knowledge about benefits and entitlements, and try to persuade people to claim. Many agencies see this as central to their work.[27]

---

[25] A Prosser (1983) *Test cases for the poor*, London: Child Poverty Action Group.
[26] Child Poverty Action Group (2010) *Welfare benefits and Tax Credits handbook 2010/2011*, London: CPAG, pp 1124-5.
[27] R Berthoud, S Benson and S Williams (1986) *Standing up for claimants*, London: Policy Studies Institute.

- *Campaigning* Welfare rights work is often linked to political argument and policy work — for example, in the work of CPAG.

The agencies that are engaged in welfare rights work are very varied. They include voluntary and community agencies, which usually work at first tier level, and generalist advice agencies, like the Citizens' Advice Bureaux. There are charitable and public groups, including law centres, specialist groups dealing with disability or particular types of circumstance (the Royal British Legion, for instance, generally offers help relating to War Pensions). There are local authority agencies, which may have broad remits concerned with publicity and income generation as well as specific roles in advice. There are also increasing numbers of solicitors and private financial advisers who can offer some support with benefit issues on a commercial basis. In England and Wales, many advice services have been brought under the umbrella of the Community Legal Services Partnerships, which are an attempt to ensure that there is systematic coverage of people's needs for advice in an area.

From the perspective of claimants, the role of the welfare rights adviser is partly to provide information about services, but it is also to provide support and help with claims. Advisers can act as representatives, putting the best case for the claimant; beyond that, they also effectively act as witnesses, helping to provide evidence about a person's circumstances. In legal cases, people need representation, not necessarily because they need an expert in law, but because they need someone who is emotionally detached from the situation, and because representatives can say things that participants in a legal action can't do effectively. ('My client is a fine upstanding citizen' carries much more conviction than the claim that 'I am a fine upstanding citizen'.) This is why lawyers don't defend themselves in criminal cases. The same principles apply to advice and assistance with benefits.

## QUESTIONS FOR DISCUSSION

How could the barriers to claiming be reduced?
Should there be a right to advice?

# Chapter 14

# Understanding complexity

The benefits system has grown progressively more complex. Some of that complexity is intrinsic: the design of benefits can be complex in its conception, its operation and its structure. Some of it comes from the interaction of different benefits, the complexity of the rules that are applied, and the practical difficulties of managing a system for millions of people. Part, however, reflects the complexity of people's circumstances and needs. Despite periodic attempts to simplify the system, it is difficult to do this in a way that will not imply considerable problems for benefits and for the people who receive them. Some of the complexity is avoidable, but much is not.

Why is the benefits system so complicated? Part of the answer is historical: the benefits system has simply grown this way. Part is practical. The problem with trying to change it is that, without a great deal more money, changes can only be made by taking money from some people and giving it to others. That would mean that some very poor people are made worse off. The idea of simplifying benefits returns periodically to the policy agenda. It was on the agenda in the 1970s, with the Conservative Tax Credit scheme[1] and the reform of 'social assistance',[2] and in the 1980s with the Fowler Reviews,[3] and it has been central to the proposals for Universal Credit.[4] But an understanding of complexity is essential before we can work out where some simplification might be possible.

## Five types of complexity

In a report published in 2005, the National Audit Office identified five types of complexity: problems of changing design, patchwork changes, horizontal links between benefits, vertical interfaces (between higher and lower levels of the administration) and 'delivery interactions', between the service and the user.[5] They published their report eighteen months after I had sent them a paper called

[1]  Cmnd 5116 (1972) *Proposals for a tax credit system*, London: HMSO.
[2]  Department of Health and Social Security (1978) *Social assistance*, London: DHSS.
[3]  Cmnd 9517-19 (1985) *Reform of social security*, vols 1, 2 and 3, London: HMSO.
[4]  Cm 7957 (2010) *Universal credit: Welfare that works*, London: DWP.
[5]  National Audit Office (2005) *Dealing with the complexity of the benefits system*, HC 592 2005-06, London: The Stationery Office

'Five types of complexity',[6] but they did not use my classification, and I am not going to follow theirs.

## 1. Complexity by design

Some benefits are intrinsically complex. They can be complex in their conception, structure and operation. These elements cannot really be separated in practice, but it is possible to give examples of each. Complexity in *conception* arises because the benefits are supposed to deal with complex circumstances or problems. Jobseeker's Allowance deals with complex circumstances: it requires consideration of employment status, contribution entitlement and financial status. The Savings Credit deals with a complex problem: people on means-tested benefits are liable to lose the value of occupational pensions or independent income. The complex design of Pension Credit stems from the difficulty of dealing with this problem adequately. And claimants for Disability Living Allowance are clearly baffled as to its purpose, criteria and rules.[7]

Complexity in conception overlaps with complexity in *structure*. Some structures are complicated simply because the design of the benefits is complicated, such as Housing Benefit or Pension Credit. But the problems are greatly exacerbated when benefits are intended to take multiple issues into account: the more elements that have to be considered to establish entitlement, the more complex a benefit becomes. Housing Benefit, regardless of the details of benefit calculations, depends on consideration of personal circumstances, financial circumstances and housing circumstances; the same will be true of Universal Credit. Until recently, Child Support required calculation on the basis of circumstances, finance and liabilities of two families – six elements in total. The White Paper on Child Support notes that over 100 pieces of information were required to make an assessment.[8] The attempted simplification of those rules has been somewhat spoiled by the development of rules governing departures from the formula, which has added another component element.

Complexity in *operation* is intrinsic when benefits try to do too much. The transfer of claimants from Incapacity Benefit to Employment and Support Allowance requires the assessment or re-assessment of 1.5 million claimants; the coalition government has undertaken to follow this up with as many Disability Living Allowance claimants, 'to ensure payments are only made for as long as a claimant needs them'.[9] One of the core problems is trying to keep up when

---

[6] Published as P Spicker (2005) 'Five types of complexity', *Benefits*, February.

[7] A Thomas (2008) *Disability Living Allowance: Disallowed claims*, London: Department for Work and Pensions.

[8] Department of Social Security (1999) *A new contract for welfare: Children's rights and parents' responsibilities*, Cm 4349, London: The Stationery Office.

[9] HM Treasury (2010) *Budget 2010*, HC 61, London: The Stationery Office, p 33.

the circumstances that the benefit addresses fluctuate. This is the fundamental problem with means testing: income can change from day to day or week to week. Unemployment and employment status change with great rapidity, especially in the current labour market. Increasingly the same is true of child care, which is often shared between different adults.

Complexity that is intrinsic to the design of benefits can only be modified to a limited extent. Complexity in conception and structure cannot be responded to without changing benefits fundamentally. Complexity in operation can be reduced by reducing the number of times an operation has to be performed. That was the argument for the 26-week period of Family Credit and Working Families Tax Credit. Changes in circumstances for Working Tax Credit have to be reported within three months, and others do not, making it rather more complex in operation than its predecessors.

## 2. Extrinsic complexity

The second form of complexity is external to specific benefits: it depends on how benefits relate to others. Some complex benefits (such as Jobseeker's Allowance or Income Support) could as easily have been designed as three or four benefits with common rules; and State Pensions really consist of several benefits bundled up together. There are, however, further problems that arise because there are multiple overlapping benefits – for example, the relationship of Tax Credits to the rest of the benefits system.

The central problem concerns the *interaction of benefits*. Some benefits are taken into account when calculating others. The level of the basic means-tested benefits depends on a calculation of income from other benefits. Housing Benefit and Tax Credits interact (which is one of the principal sources of the poverty trap). The Social Fund has to be used for urgent payments when other benefits fail to deliver in time. There is considerable scope for rationalisation here. The treatment of child support has been an important model of how it can be done: taking Child Benefit and child maintenance out of the calculations for the basic means-tested benefits has had a huge effect on both the stability of people's income and the effectiveness of those provisions.

There is also a growing problem of *interaction between agencies*. A welfare rights officer described a case where grandparents had responsibility for child care, and the Pensions Service and HMRC could not resolve who was responsible for payment: 'One department was passing the buck to the other.' The new divisions of labour in relation to benefits for children should avoid some of the most common confusions, but there are continuing issues to be resolved in the relationship between Tax Credits and other income-tested benefits. It is difficult to see how complexity can be reduced here, short of a structural redesign. The balance between agencies has to be thought through; that requires more guidelines, not fewer.

## 3. Complex rules

The third form of complexity concerns the rules developed for benefits. Some rules are intrinsic: the points scheme for Employment and Support Allowance is (supposedly) a way of establishing who meets the criteria and who does not. Many rules are not intrinsic, but are imposed for a variety of other reasons. There are two main classes of imposed additional rules. One concerns *conditionality*. Some benefits are rationed. The use of age limits for disability benefits or the rules relating to residence extend beyond the definition of the circumstances the benefits are supposed to meet. Some benefits are conditioned morally: rules about voluntary employment and availability for work are illustrative. And there are rules covering deliberate exceptions, such as either rules governing deductions for overpayment or departures in the Child Support rules.

The other basis of complexity in rules is *administrative*. These are concerned with administrative operations and delivery of benefits. National Insurance entitlements are based on records for the calendar year preceding the financial year: any number of more comprehensible alternatives are available. The periods over which benefits are paid – typically weekly or fortnightly, with some daily benefits – are wholly arbitrary.

There is one other relatively minor but perplexing source of complexity, which relates to the issues I referred to at the start of this chapter – history, and the fear of making people worse off. Several benefits have rules inherited from previous regimes. Transitional arrangements, legacy benefits and earned entitlements claims mean that some people are still receiving Graduated Retirement Benefit (related to contributions before 1975), Severe Disablement Allowance (which was closed to new business in 2001), Income Support for incapacity (otherwise ended in 2008) or the Reduced Earnings Allowance for industrial injuries (for accidents before 1990), while Housing Benefit recipients claiming before 1996 still have rent treated under the old rules. The House of Commons Select Committee on Work and Pensions has suggested that these residual entitlements should be bought out.[10] The DWP replied that this would be 'very expensive'[11] – which is questionable, because the value of compensation for entitlements bought out will usually be slightly less than their future cost. If they mean only that they have not budgeted for buy-outs when they calculate the cost of a reform, the answer is simple – they should.

---

[10] House of Commons Work and Pensions Committee (2007a) *Benefits simplification*, HC 461 (www.publications.parliament.uk/pa/cm/cmworpen.htm).

[11] House of Commons Work and Pensions Committee (2007b) *Third special report* (www. publications.parliament.uk/pa/cm200607/cmselect/cmworpen/1054/105404.htm).

## 4. Management issues

Some of the complexities of the benefit system are created not by benefits, but by the management procedures that have been developed to deliver them. The landscape of the benefits system changes with startling frequency. Local offices have undergone several forms of radical restructuring, including the shift to Jobcentre Plus, and the establishment of the Pensions, Disability and Carers Service. This is far from being the only major change in recent years: the last twenty years have included agencification, computerisation, the new public sector management and radical changes in the division of labour between different agencies, including call centres. Both internally within the offices and externally in welfare rights, there is some alarm at the way in which changes have deracinated staff, leading to a loss of expertise in the delivery of specific benefits.

Three changes in administrative procedure have added massively to the complexity of benefits administration. The first is computerisation, which took the best part of fifteen years to deliver a system that could be said to be effective. There is much less down time since the system transferred to the internet, but the basic programmes still cannot cope with the complexity of the operations required. At irregular intervals, cases have to be pulled off the computer and worked by hand.

The second is information management. The computers cannot store paper copy, which means that, at least until the scanning pioneered in the PDCS is generalised, there have to be two files. However, files have to be put into store after a month, even if they are still live. The system of storage has been 'contracted out', or privatised, and all files are 'migrating' to central storage. Offices have then to pay to retrieve the paper copy subsequently, which means in practice that they cannot reasonably get hold of them. If this is done properly, there will be three files for a live case – the computer file, the archived file and the recent paper file in the office. If, on the other hand, a file is being put together in bits, successive items of correspondence are not necessarily going to be reunited with the main file. The old system, despite popular preconceptions, did not often lose material from files, but because a file could legitimately be in several places, it was not designed to find them when requests were made. This system makes the files inaccessible to everyone.

Third, there is the growing division of labour between the offices. This leads to confusion about who is responsible for which parts of processing a case. One welfare rights officer described the administration of overpayments, which locally depends on a division of labour between a local office, a regional office and the national agency at Salford, as the 'Bermuda Triangle' of benefits.

## 5. The claimant experience

This category is the largest omission from the National Audit Office's report on complexity. There is an aspect of complexity which, though it can be described in terms of benefits, is not attributable to the benefits system at all. Janet Allbeson, from One Parent Families, commented to the Work and Pensions Committee: 'The models do not take on board how swiftly people's circumstances change, particularly those of working age. Tax credits made that mistake, Child Support has made that mistake. The systems just cannot cope with it.'[12] Even if the DWP and HMRC do get in place the new, integrated, instantaneous information systems that Universal Credit is supposed to rely on, the same problems will dog the new system.

The administration of claims tends to rest on the assumption that people know what their situation is, and relies on them to report it. Life is not like that. People in a casualised labour market do not always know if they are employed or not. With the growth of marginal employment, such as short-term contracts, casual and intermittent patterns of work, this uncertainty has increased. People do not know whether they are disabled: disabled people often have fluctuating physical capacities, combined with a variable appreciation of their own potential or limitations. (This makes survey estimates of the extent of disability notoriously unreliable.) Because child care is so often shared, people are not sure when they are responsible. Because of the problem of determining when relationships begin and end, it is difficult to know whether a person is a lone parent.

Income fluctuates; the benefits offices have to recalculate and attribute it to different time periods. From the perspective of the claimant, it is not surprising that sometimes they get it wrong. The focus groups of claimants that I have talked to – small groups that may not, of course, be representative – express feelings of puzzlement, indignation at the imputation of dishonesty and some resentment. Overpayments are actively pursued – in the case of Tax Credits, without regard to claimants' ability to pay. The Ombudsman comments:

> I continue to receive a significant number of complaints where the overpayment complained about has arisen solely as a result of the annualised system operating as intended. Despite HMRC's efforts so far, it is clear that many people simply do not understand that it is possible for them to have provided all the correct information, and for their award to have been properly assessed on that basis, but that because of changes in their circumstances towards the end of the tax year, they could find themselves with a significant debt to repay when their award for the previous year is finalised.[13]

---

[12] House of Commons Work and Pensions Committee (2007a), para 292.

[13] Parliamentary and Health Service Ombudsman (2007) *Tax credits – Getting it wrong?*, HC 1010, London: The Stationery Office, p 10.

---

The benefits that work best are those that are paid long term, to people in stable circumstances: examples are State Pension and Child Benefit. This is not just about means testing. There is a risk of error in any benefit where circumstances change – even in Child Benefit, where errors occur because children leave school, move between separated parents, spend time with grandparents or leave residential childcare. However, because Child Benefit mainly deals with people in situations that tend not to change much over time, the problems welfare rights officers have told me about – long delays in payment, disputes about priority for claims, and HMRC's excessive caution about the possibility of duplicate claims – are not repeated once the benefit comes into payment.

## Coping with complexity

Complexity is difficult to manage, but it may be possible to work around some of the problems. Whatever else happens, part of people's income needs to be stable – unaffected by temporary changes in circumstances or fluctuations in income. That is one of the main advantages of Child Benefit, which continues through most changes in income or employment status. There is no reason in principle why this should not be extended to other benefits like Housing Benefit or Tax Credits, where previous rules were based on calculations for six-monthly periods.

Second, there needs to be a different approach to changes in circumstances, going rather beyond recent measures to make sure that people do not have to report changes of circumstances several times. Even Child Benefit does not continue through all changes in circumstances – it is most typically affected by partnering or re-partnering when both partners have children. HMRC have recently reviewed their procedures so that the benefit is no longer automatically suspended in such cases. That is a precedent that could usefully be extended to other benefits: if continuity of income is crucial, the practice of suspending benefits during recalculations needs to stop.

Third, where benefits are supposed to reflect changes in circumstances, it is important to slow down the rate at which changes in circumstances are reflected in benefits. There have been significant changes in relation to means-tested pensions, with some changes not being reflected for up to five years. This is not practical for most working-age benefits, but it does seem clear that longer time periods and less sensitivity to fluctuations are important for stability. Currently, changes in income are reflected almost immediately in most working-age benefits. In France, the benefit rules make rather more allowance for changing and unpredictable circumstances. Benefits are calculated and paid monthly, which means that fluctuations and changes in circumstances in the course of a month are cumulated and resolved retrospectively. This avoids many of the problems associated with lack of 'synchronicity', or common time frames. The use of standard pay days also means that income flow is predictable, that it tends to fall in line with payments when people move into or out of work, and utility companies and public sector agencies have been able to bring billing into line.

This kind of change is a long way from fundamental reform, and I know that some readers will be disappointed that I have not been more enthusiastic about some of the radical reforms, like single working-age benefit, Universal Credit or Citizen's Income, which critics have advocated. This is not just because I am suspicious about the effect that simple rules have on complex lives, but it also reflects a view about what social security ought to do – that it is about many things, not just one or two core principles. Social security needs to respond to a wide range of circumstances, and unless there is a radical change in the way that people live, the main effect of imposing basic, common rules will be to help some at the expense of creating hardship for others.

## Does complexity matter?

The social security system is an intricate, unwieldy, often incomprehensible structure. But the main issue is not whether the system can be understood as a whole: it is whether it makes sense to claimants. Take a single example, which is the National Insurance State Pension. It is a complex benefit, with four main elements: a basic benefit, depending on contributions through a person's working life; the graduated pension, based on the value of earnings-related contributions made between 1961 and 1977; the State Second Pension, based on later earnings-related contributions; and various additions, including age-related and dependants' additions. Pensioners may, of course, have other sources of income, including occupational pensions, private income or means-tested benefits (principally now the Pension Credit). Very few pensioners have much idea how their benefit has been calculated, or if it has been calculated correctly. As far as I can tell, not many people clearly understand the difference between insurance-based benefits and means-tested benefits anyway. But it is not obvious that any of this makes much difference. Pensions are calculated rapidly, the calculations do not seem to detract from the operation of the benefit, and despite a series of reforms that at times seem designed to dismantle any procedure that actually works, they are still delivered with considerable efficiency.

The comparative literature on social security policy is no longer very interested in the detailed rules and regulations affecting benefits. It has become increasingly common to look not at specific benefits like 'retirement pensions' or 'industrial injuries benefits', but rather at the 'income package' as a whole. People are likely to draw a series of benefits drawn from different sources. What matters to people is not so much whether their benefit is insurance based or means tested – in practice, they are likely to be both – but how much they get, and what they have to go through to get it.

There is an argument, then, to say that complexity is not important in itself. Complexity becomes important when it interferes with the objectives of the social security system – preventing the effective delivery of benefits. There are some genuine problems here. They are most evident in the way the benefit system responds, or fails to respond, to the changing conditions of people in complex circumstances – situations that lead to confusion, administrative error and accusations of fraud.

Some aspects of complexity are defensible. Some do not make much sense, but they are there anyway, like the weather and the tides, and there is not much hope of changing them. We cannot ask claimants to live simpler, more orderly lives. Dealing with intrinsic complexity requires a root-and-branch reform of benefits. Dealing with extrinsic complexity is attractive, but only part of the issues can be easily resolved, for example through common claim processes and passporting (that is, using entitlement to one benefit to allow automatic claims to others). The problems of relationships between agencies may have been predictable and avoidable, but that is the way the world now is, and the issues are not going to be settled in the near future.

There is much more scope for addressing the other issues – conditionality, administrative rules and administrative procedures. If we seriously hope to reduce complexity and increase the effectiveness of the benefits system, that is where we need to concentrate.

## QUESTIONS FOR DISCUSSION

How can benefits be adapted to the reality of people's lives?
How else can the system be simplified?

# Part IV
## The principal contingencies

The idea of 'social protection' was introduced in Chapter 1. The form it generally takes is provision for particular circumstances or contingencies. There are certain circumstances that social security commonly provides for – typically old age, unemployment and disability. Richard Titmuss called them 'states of dependency'.[1] They are not equivalent to low income, but people in these circumstances are likely to have low income, and social protection implies the creation of an institutional framework to support people in these circumstances.

This part of the book is concerned with groups in need, but it does not look at every group or category of people affected by the benefits system. Many texts on social security look at the effects that social security has on people in different groups, such as minority ethnic groups or women. This part has a different purpose. There are no benefits specifically for women or minority ethnic groups, but there are benefits for pensioners, people with disabilities and so forth. The aim of this book is to understand the benefits system, and provision for a range of categories is part of that system. The groups being considered here are those for whom the benefits system makes distinct provision.

This way of understanding the benefits system has become increasingly important. In the period since the mid-1990s, the benefits system has been slowly reconstructed around the principal states of dependency. Provision for elderly people has been substantially located in one agency. Benefits for children have become increasingly centred on the tax authorities. Provision for unemployed people is now centred in the Jobseeker's Allowance, and although the key agency, Jobcentre Plus, is being decentralised and some of its functions are being privatised, the system for unemployed people is becoming more distinctive. The reform of incapacity benefits in 2008 has begun the process of creating a similarly unified structure for people of working age who have disabilities and long-term illnesses.

This part discusses the situation of people in a wide range of situations:

- pensioners
- people with disabilities
- people who are unable to work through sickness
- children
- lone parents

---

[1] R M Titmuss (1955) 'The social division of welfare', in R M Titmuss, *Essays on the welfare state* (2nd edn 1963), London: George Allen & Unwin.

- unemployed people and
- perhaps most controversially, benefits for 'the poor' – controversially because the terminology is potentially stigmatising, and much of the point of the post-war welfare state was to move us away from this kind of focus.

The devil is in the detail. Social security benefits have been developed to provide for people in a wide range of circumstances, with very different needs. In each of these categories, there is still a range of benefits, delivered on different assumptions, through different structures. It is not possible yet to make sense of the system by focusing solely on these groups, but equally it is not possible to understand the system without them. This part looks at the states of dependency that are recognised by the benefits system, the range of benefits available for them and the issues that arise.

The chapters in Part IV are not wholly self-contained. Because I have already dealt with the structure and organisation of benefits, these chapters are more concerned with identifying the issues, and arguments about the structure and pattern of benefits are taken as read.

# Chapter 15

# Pensioners

The main benefits for retired people are the State Pension, the Pension Credit and a complex system of private and occupational pensions. The State Pension has important deficiencies, but increasing numbers of pensioners are coming to have more adequate earnings-related pensions through the private sector. The state system is partial in its coverage, unstable and difficult to understand. Occupational pensions have become increasingly individualised and commercially oriented, but they may not be sustainable.

More than 12 million people in Britain receive some form of state pension on account of their age (there are rather more old people than there are pensioners, but many of them live with someone else who actually receives the pension). The vast majority of pensioners in Britain have National Insurance pensions, but in some cases the National Insurance is not enough to provide a basic minimum income. Those who do receive National Insurance tend to be often just above the basic minimum benefit, but many have incomes below the threshold: more than 2.7 million people receive Pension Credit. If it is right that the take-up of Pension Credit is 61%-70%, there could be another 1½ million people who are eligible but not claiming.

Pensions in the UK have gained a reputation for being too little to live on. This is less true than it once was, but it reflects a long history when many pensioners were seriously deprived. In the 1970s, most of the people on the lowest incomes were elderly people;[1] in the years since then, other groups have become relatively poorer, and this has become much less likely to be true. There are important generational differences between people in Britain currently aged 65 and those aged 85. Those who are now 85 were born in the 1920s, and they were in their teens at the time of the Second World War. Large numbers of them were deprived in childhood, and their early adulthood would have been lived in times of relative austerity, but there was a marked improvement in living standards in the later part of their working life. People who are 65, by contrast, were part of the post-war generation. On the whole, they were better housed, better fed and altogether more likely to be prosperous. The position of older people, and so of pensioners, has been steadily improving throughout the last thirty years.

---

[1] R Layard, D Piachaud and M Stewart (1978) *The causes of poverty*, Royal Commission on the Distribution of Income and Wealth Background Paper No 5, London: HMSO.

Many pensioners — a minority, but still many — have limited resources. They tend to live in older housing; savings have been eroded by the inflation of the 1970s and 1980s; and they are less likely than others to possess certain items, such as washing machines and cars, that have become part of the modern household. At the same time, pensioners nowadays are probably not as badly off as unemployed people. The support offered to pensioners from the Pension Credit makes their benefits substantially higher than those of unemployed people, both in the level of the minimum guarantee and in allowances for savings. Pensioners tend to have accumulated resources, like carpets, furniture and clothing, that younger people may not have. And unemployed people are more likely to have dependent children, for whom benefit rates have been particularly inadequate.

The pensioners who are best provided for are those with an occupational pension. Although the amounts paid by private pensions are often quite marginal, they play a crucial part in lifting people above a minimum income. By the same token, other benefits besides the state pension or Pension Credit can be an important part of the package of income that pensioners have, and a quarter of the cost of state benefits for pensioners is accounted for by benefits such as Housing Benefit, Council Tax Benefit or benefits for disability.

## Retirement

Most pensioners have something very basic in common: that they have a pension, which generally they draw not just on the basis of old age, but because they have retired from their previous employment. Financial dependency is the result of withdrawal from the labour market. In the 1960s, it was still common for people to delay their retirement; about a quarter of all men kept on working after the age of 65. By the 1990s, fewer than one in 12 did. There has been a tendency to delay retirement longer since the late 1990s, but most workers withdraw from the labour market in their mid-sixties.[2] For many, early retirement has become much more common: men over 60 who are unemployed are no longer required to be available for work. There is nothing about old age that means people are unable to work, but we have instituted a system that means that it is expected that they should not, and withdrawal from the labour market is not just legitimate, but almost required. The average pensioner is now likely to spend about a third of his or her adult life in retirement — over 20 years for

---

[2]  R Wild (n.d.) 'Estimating the average age of the withdrawal from the labour force' (www.statistics.gov.uk/downloads/theme_compendia/pensiontrends/ EstAveAgeWithdrawalLabForce.pdf).

men, and over 25 for women.[3] The position of old people has been described, by Alan Walker, as 'structural dependency'.[4]

When Old Age Pensions were first introduced, at the beginning of the 20th century, they were for people over 70. The current age of retirement is 65 for a man, 60 for a woman. The pension age is set to go up, and the difference between men and woman is in the process of being removed, after a long debate about equalising the age of retirement for men and women. Women's pension age was increasing gradually from 2010, but from 2016 it will increase rapidly, and by 2020 women will retire at 66, the same age as men. The Barber judgment in the European Court of Justice, which identified pensions as a form of pay, has required governments to remove sexual discrimination. Bringing the age of retirement of men down to 60 would have had the apparent advantage of releasing about two million jobs in short order, but it would be more expensive than benefits paid for unemployment, and permanent. Standardisation at 63 would have had little or no cost; increasing the retirement age of women will save money. However, if the Pensions Commission is right, this situation will not last; as the number of pensioners increases, and the value of the pension improves, the pension age will have to increase.[5] The age at which state benefits will be paid may be set to rise above 65, but this is not necessarily reflected in other systems. Retirement, Arkani and Gough suggest, is often a transitional process; people gradually withdraw from the labour market. People with occupational pensions generally find this easier than others.[6]

The immediate implication of retirement is that retired people need to have a substitute income. Pensions have been represented in many ways: as a form of saving, as a form of solidarity between generations, as 'income smoothing' by redistribution across age groups,[7] and as a form of redistribution. Each of these views are true of some arrangements, but not of others. Some pensions have nothing saved; some put everything in a fund, and pay benefits from the accumulated capital; and there are increasing numbers of private pensions where the fund is closed to new custom, denying the opportunity to future generations to buy in. 'Income smoothing' is based on an individualistic model, where benefits are geared to the contributions that each person has made. Redistribution, by contrast, depends on the idea that workers pay for pensioners, as they pay for

---

[3]  Pensions Commission (2005) *A new pension settlement for the 21st century*, London: The Stationery Office, p 97.

[4]  A Walker (1980) 'The social creation of poverty and dependency in old age', *Journal of Social Policy*, vol 9, no 1, pp 42-75.

[5]  Pensions Commission (2005), ch 5.

[6]  S Arkani and O Gough (2007) 'The impact of occupational pensions on retirement age', *Journal of Social Policy*, vol 36, no 2, pp 297-318.

[7]  N Barr (1991) 'The objectives of old age pensions', in T Wilson and D Wilson (eds) *The state and social welfare*, London: Longman.

other people who are financially dependent, because these kinds of payments are essential for people to live.

## Pensions

When people retire, their pension can be determined by a range of criteria. The most common are financial need, minimum income, work relation and income replacement.

- *Financial need*  Pensions based on financial need are generally means tested (because that is how financial need can be established), and consequently liable to exclude people on higher incomes. This is the basis of the system in Australia;[8] in Britain the Pension Credit is the principal means-tested benefit for older people.
- *Minimum income*  Minimum incomes can be related to need, but they do not need to be. They can be higher, because governments want to make sure that people have enough to live in reasonable comfort, or lower, because governments want pensioners to make up their income from different sources. (National Insurance in Britain was, for many years, below the minimum income offered by Supplementary Benefit and Income Support, largely because it excluded housing costs.)
- *Work record*  Many schemes, both occupational and state-funded, base pension entitlements on the work record of the retired person. Contributory schemes often have a notional relationship between the financial value of contributions and entitlement, but more typically they will be based on qualifying periods when payments have been made.
- *Income replacement*  Many schemes aim to replace a proportion of the retired person's former income, based either on final salary or proportionately to their income, as measured by previous contributions.

Different types of payment are related in principle to different types of benefit. Work-related and income replacement schemes are generally contributory. Schemes based on financial need are typically means tested. Minimum income provision can be based on either, and (although it is unusual) it could be universal, like the non-contributory pension in Britain for people over 80.

The most common distinction between forms of pension lies between funded and solidaristic schemes. Funded schemes built up reserves: contributions are used to save or invest for the future and pay benefits from the fund. This is particularly true of occupational and commercial pension schemes, but it is rare in government schemes. The Beveridge scheme was supposed to be funded, maturing over 20 years. The arguments for having a national funded

---

[8]  F G Castles (1996) 'Needs-based strategies of social protection in Australia and New Zealand', in G Esping-Andersen (ed) *Welfare states in transition*, London: Sage Publications.

scheme are not very strong, which is why it never happened. A funded scheme would be a visible proof of contributions, and it has been supposed (without much evidence to support the view) that governments would find it difficult to keep out of a funded scheme, or to abolish the entitlements. But it would also find it difficult to keep pace with rising incomes, to cope with changes in monetary values, or in changing circumstances like longer life expectancy. (These are all problems that funded schemes have at present.)

Solidaristic systems are rather more common. Solidarity is based on pooled risks and resources. In a 'pay as you go' scheme, current contributions are used to pay for current benefits. This relies on trust for the future: people pay benefits now in the expectation that future generations will pay for them. It is generally true that as economies have grown over the years, pensions paid in this way have been able to improve, and pay as you go has the advantage that there is no problem in taking account of inflation. Its main weakness is political: it depends on the willingness of current politicians to accept the costs.

The other crucial distinction lies between public and independent provision. Until very recently, the British system has been dominated by state provision, leading to a striking uniformity in the pattern of provision, at least for older retired people. 'Independent' provision does not have to mean 'commercial' or 'private'; many pension schemes in Europe are based in mutualist, non-profit-making insurance.

## Box 15.1: State Pensions

There are four main elements to the State Pension:
1. The basic Retirement Pension, which is based on National Insurance contributions paid during a person's working life. Entitlement depends on contributions, either from employment or self-employment. From 2010, pensions will be based on contributions for a working life of 30 years, but there are credits given for periods of 'home responsibility' (caring for children or people with disabilities), and voluntary contributions can also be purchased to fill some gaps.
2. The State Second Pension, the earnings-related element based largely on contributions for SERPS (State Earnings-Related Pension Scheme) since 1977.
3. Graduated Pension, based on contributions made between 1961 and 1977.
4. Miscellaneous additions, including additions for dependants and special allowances for those over 80.

There are also means-tested benefits, of which the most important in this context are the two types of Pension Credit – the Guarantee Credit and the Savings Credit. The Guarantee Credit is the element of Pension Credit which brings people up to a minimum income. The Savings Credit is a complex additional benefit. It cuts in when pensioners have extra income that is not enough to bring them above the minimum guarantee, and is gradually phased out for people above the minimum level. What makes the calculation complicated is that the Savings Credit does not pay anything to people on relatively high or low incomes: it only pays people in a band in the middle. Because Pension Credit comes in two parts, however, the combined effect of the two elements is to give people more benefit when their income is below the minimum, and to reduce it gradually over a range of income. It does, however, mean that:

- the amounts people receive will be difficult to work out;
- people will have very little idea whether they are entitled, or if the benefit has been correctly calculated; and
- people with more money will sometimes get more benefit than people with less.

## Pensions in Britain

Pensions could be different. Britain has opted for generally available insurance pensions at a low level. Several countries in continental Europe developed mutual insurance for pensioners offering income replacement. The average pensioner in France is, unbelievably from the perspective of people in Britain, better off than the average worker.[9] This happens because the level of earnings-related pensions are related to a person's best earning years.

In Britain, by contrast, the system of state pensions was never intended to replace people's earnings in old age. Beveridge wanted pensions to be 'adequate', but there were elements in his scheme which meant that they would not really be adequate. Flat-rate benefits meant that the benefits were set at a low, general level. Flat-rate contributions meant that the contributions had to be notional, because many people could not afford to pay enough contributions to give adequate benefits. Beveridge tried to get around this with the proposal for a very large contribution from the Exchequer, but this never happened.[10] The low commitment meant that benefits were kept low and contributions high.

In the 1950s, the Labour Party set out a plan, *National superannuation*, for a different system.[11] This proposed earnings-related contributions, and a flat-rate benefit with earnings-related supplement. The argument for earnings relation was that it was proving, elsewhere in Europe, to offer better pensions; it did so at the cost of perpetuating the inequalities of the workplace into old age. The Labour scheme was designed to be a progressive form of redistribution. There would be a 25% Exchequer contribution, and funding over 20 years, with inflation proofing to protect the fund's value.

The Conservatives introduced a modest reform of pensions in 1959, under the title of the 'graduated pension'. Most people currently retiring in Britain have

---

[9]  O Guillemin and V Roux (2002) 'Le niveau de vie des ménages de 1970 à 1999', Données Sociales, November (www.insee.fr/fr/ffc/docs_ffc/DS065fr.pdf).

[10] J Veit Wilson (1992) 'Muddle or mendacity? The Beveridge Committee and the poverty line', *Journal of Social Policy*, vol 21, no 3, pp 269-302.

[11] Labour Party (1958) *National superannuation*, London: Labour Party.

contributed under this scheme, which operated from 1961 to 1977; that will continue to be true until at least 2026, which is when people aged 16 in 1977 can expect to retire, and unless the entitlement is abolished some pensioners will continue to receive payments for 30 years or so after that. The Act created a pay as you go scheme with flat-rate contributions and benefits, but with earnings-related supplements. It also introduced 'contracting out' of the earnings-related supplement, in favour of occupational pensions. These provisions were the small beginnings of occupational pensions in Britain. In many cases the entitlements they gave were very limited: pensioners retiring with an occupational pension in the 1970s typically had only a few pounds, enough to lift them above the level of Supplementary Benefit but not to replace the State Pension as the main source of their income.

Major reforms of the pension system began in the late 1960s, with Labour's 1969 White Paper, *National superannuation and social insurance*.[12] This proposed earnings-related contributions and benefits. The scheme would be solidaristic, but it would be backed up by two reserve funds, intended to give the scheme greater financial security. It was intended to mature over 20 years. In other words, pensions would still be paid for out of current contributions, but the pension would not go up until most current pensioners were dead. The journal *New Society* commented, in an editorial, that the effect of phasing in a pay as you go scheme over 20 years is that we were promising ourselves better pensions, paid for by our children, but were not prepared to pay for our parents now.[13] That comment is worth bearing in mind, because the principle behind it has been consistently breached in pension reform ever since.

Labour lost the 1970 election, and the 1969 scheme was never brought into force. The same fate befell the Conservative's replacement scheme, *Strategy for pensions*,[14] which was passed in Parliament in 1973. This proposed earnings-related contribution with flat-rate benefit — breaking the link between contributions and benefits, and taking more from the better-off — pretty much the principle that Labour had proposed in the 1950s. The scheme was to be PAYG with a funded reserve scheme, and there would be contracting-out for occupational pensions.

Labour came back into power in 1974. The Social Security Pensions Act 1975 abolished the Conservative Act of 1973. It introduced earnings-related contributions, and a flat-rate benefit with earnings-related supplement (SERPS, the State Earnings Related Pension Scheme). There was only an 18% Exchequer contribution. There would be inflation proofing before retirement, pay as you go with 20 years maturity (which was open to the same objection as the 1969 scheme). The most progressive feature was the protection for women, who were offered a shorter qualifying period for pension (the best 20 years), and protection

---

[12]  Cmnd 3883 (1969) *National superannuation and social insurance*, London: HMSO.
[13]  *New Society* (1969) 'Pensions progress', 30 January.
[14]  Cmnd 4755 (1971) *Strategy for pensions*, London: HMSO.

for time spent at home with responsibility for dependants. Very oddly, the scheme offered complete protection for occupational pensions, which would be guaranteed inflation proof at the expense of the state. The Conservative opposition welcomed the scheme; it went further in promoting and protecting the private sector than they had previously proposed.

This bipartisan agreement lasted until the mid-1980s. The effect of increasing pensions seemed to the Conservatives to represent an impossibly onerous financial commitment. They estimated that by 2035 there would be only three workers for every two pensioners. 'It would be an abdication of responsibility to hand down obligations to our children which we believe they cannot fulfil.'[15] The Social Security Act 1986 withdrew the pledge to support private schemes, and greatly reduced the proposed commitment to the state earnings–related pension. Initially, the Conservative government proposed to abolish SERPS. After opposition, they arranged to cut the level of pensions that SERPS will provide in the long term – but not immediately – and based SERPS on 40 years' earnings instead of the best 20, which undermined the rights of women.

The intervening years saw increasing reliance on private and occupational pensions, and correspondingly less emphasis on the role of the state pension. SERPS matured fully in 1998-99, but its abolition followed shortly after. From April 2002 SERPS was replaced by the State Second Pension (sometimes referred to as S2P, more jargon run riot), which makes more generous provision for people on lower incomes and those whose contributions were less complete. Following the recommendations of the Pensions Commission,[16] the scope of the State Second Pension has been scaled down and the general movement has been towards the obligatory addition of a private pension supplementing the pensions provided by the state.

It is still difficult to tell what the full impact of these changes will be, largely because the private and occupational pensions that have been such a large part of retirement planning are in a state of flux. Nearly all of these schemes in Britain are funded, at least in part – the same is not necessarily true in other countries – and the value of funds depends largely on investment. Many people were mis–sold personal pensions and have found themselves worse off as a result. The fall in stock market values in the late 1990s left many schemes with important deficits. Private schemes were forced either to reduce their commitments, or to close final salary schemes to newcomers. Public sector schemes, which are protected to some degree by their solidaristic elements, have been better able to shore up commitments. The importance of the State Second Pension largely rests on the circumstances of those people who do not have adequate incomes from other sources; at the time of writing, it is not fully clear how people will be affected, or how many will be. Glennerster suggests that the combination of unstable private

---

[15] Cmnd 9517 (1985) *Reform of social security*, vol 1, London: HMSO, p 18.
[16] Pensions Commission (2005).

pensions with means-tested minimum guarantees is unsustainable – 'a recipe for eventual collapse'.[17]

## Pensions now

The State Pension is only part of the picture. The idea that the state pension is crucial reflects British experience; it is not necessarily true of other countries. When people look up the rates of basic pensions in different countries, they are not comparing like with like. Much more important than any comparison of formal arrangements is an understanding of the income package – the amount of money that people end up with when they have received everything from different places.[18] There is no basic 'pension' in France in the way we have them in Britain. The pension system there is a patchwork quilt; it depends on sticking together income from a range of different sources. The system integrates elements of state benefits with independent, work-based provision. The problem with this approach is that it is very, very complicated. The agencies begin calculations two and a half years before retirement. Sometimes they might have worked out the details before the person retires, and sometimes they might not. The Pension Commission's claim that 'the UK has the most complex pension system in the world'[19] is puzzling; it may be difficult for policy makers to understand, but it is far from being the most complex from the point of view either of pensioners or of administrators.

Falkingham and Johnson point to five main criticisms of state pensions in Britain. The first is inadequacy – state pensions are limited, and they have become less important than other sources of income in retirement. Second, there is eligibility. The reliance on an unbroken contribution record means that women are far less likely to be entitled to a full pension: they refer to projections suggesting that although women who retire are expected to have their own pension by 2011, women's entitlement will be 83% of the full rate.[20] Third, there is a gender bias (though the difference in pension ages is now being removed). Fourth, there is the problem of instability: constant changes in the rules mean that people cannot predict future payments with any certainty. Fifth, the system is opaque – people cannot tell what is likely to happen or why. This affects the way people respond to savings, contributions and proposed changes. The good news is that, since this critique was written, considerable progress has been made both with the

---

[17] H Glennerster (2009) *Understanding the finance of welfare*, Bristol: The Policy Press, p 151.

[18] L Rainwater, M Rein and J Schwartz (1986) *Income packaging in the welfare state*, Oxford: Oxford University Press.

[19] Pensions Commission (2005), p 66.

[20] J Falkingham and P Johnson (1993) *A unified funded pension scheme for Britain*, London: Suntory-Toyota International Centre for Economics and Related Disciplines.

inadequacy of benefits and the differences in entitlement. The bad news is that the system is still partial in its coverage, unstable and incomprehensible. To those problems, however, must now be added the complexities associated with private pensions – the insecure financial base, the inadequate protection of schemes, the record of abuses in the private sector and the loss of political support.

Recently, there have been proposals for a universal old-age pension, like the 'Citizen's Pension' in New Zealand.[21] A Citizen's Pension would not replace every benefit for old people – they would still need to claim benefits like Attendance Allowance, Housing Benefit or the element of the Pension Credit for people with severe disabilities – but it could in principle replace the basic State Pension, the Pension Credit and the Savings Credit. The main advantages of the scheme would be the relative administrative simplicity of the scheme, the avoidance of problems for people who have only a partial work record, especially women, and the removal of the 'disincentive to save' that people think is implicit in means-tested pension provision like the Pension Credit. The main disadvantage is an issue in equity: extending a universal pension to people who do not currently qualify for the Guarantee Credit (that is, the minimum income guarantee) would work to the advantage of better-off pensioners who have opted not to contribute.

In the latest plans for a Citizen's Pension in Britain, the government is suggesting that the new pension will not affect the position of existing pensioners; it will only apply to new claimants, a process which will take many years to mature. This poses a dilemma. On one hand, the arrangement the government is proposing implies that universal pensions will be available for the current generation of workers, at their children's expense, but that they are not ready to protect the position of current pensioners. At the same time, if the government were simply to abolish existing earned entitlements, that would invite a storm of protest. A practical alternative would be to introduce the scheme, not for younger pensioners, but for older ones. If the scheme were to open with a universal pension for everyone over 90, and gradually extend the coverage downwards, most of the problems of the transition would be overcome.

## Timeline: pensions

| | 1944 | 1950 | 1956 | 1962 | 1968 | 1974 | 1980 | 1986 | 1992 | 1998 | 2004 | 2010 |
|---|---|---|---|---|---|---|---|---|---|---|---|---|
| Means testing | | 1948 National Assistance | | | 1966 Supplementary Benefit | | | 1988 Income Support | | | 2003 Pension Credit | |
| National Insurance | 1948 Retirement Pension | | | 1959 Graduated Pension | | | 1975/78 State Earnings Related Pension Scheme (SERPS) | | | 2002 State Second Pension | |
| Non contributory | | | | | | | | 1975 Non-contributory Retirement Pension (Category D) | | | | |

[21] A O'Connell (2004) *Citizen's pension: Lessons from New Zealand*, London: Pensions Policy Institute.

## Key issues in pension provision

The key issues that have dominated pension provision in the past have been the questions of whether pensions should be earnings related, whether they should be funded or solidaristic, and the extent to which they should be delivered by the private sector. For better or worse, each of those issues seems to be settled. Pensions have become substantially work related, and earnings related, in practice. They are based in a mixed economy, in which private and independent provision have a substantial role. Schemes in the independent sector are usually funded; solidaristic pensions are largely provided by the state. This is not the only way that things could be, and in other countries they are done differently – for example, in other countries there are independent and occupational pensions which are provided solidaristically. However, it seems unlikely that these basic policies will alter in the UK in the foreseeable future.

The key issues for the future are likely to be different. The central problem in pensions provision is sustainability. The changing population base, which was raised as a concern in the Conservative reviews of the 1980s, implies a growing number of pensioners. Pensioners are living longer, their pensions are generally improving and the numbers of workers supporting them are falling. None of this is crucial: the ability of the economy to support dependent people depends on the amount that is produced, not on the number of people who are doing it. But that does not mean that the growing dependency ratio is not problematic. In broad terms, the effect of greater longevity and the increasing level of pensions means that the average cost of each pensioner has increased greatly; the costs of pensions are an important political issue in their own right. Viewed more narrowly, the established entitlements of beneficiaries have posed problems for specific benefit schemes, which is why some schemes in Britain have had to close to new business; they cannot afford to take on further liabilities. In France, there have been particular problems with the pension schemes for railway workers and miners, where contributions have been limited because of the decline of those industries. The main policy has been to get round this by redistribution between schemes, referred to as a form of 'solidarity'.

A second key issue is responsiveness to changes in circumstances. Many pension entitlements are built over a long time: people work for 40 years or so and are dependent for 25 years after that. Undertakings that are given to people when they start to contribute are liable to evaporate: either they are relatively meaningless, like the graduated pension, or they are written on water, like the rights given to women in 1975. Increasing longevity, higher benefits, earlier retirement and the availability of alternatives to the state pension have all served to excuse a weakening public commitment to pensions. But there are also real problems: the interruption of many people's working lives by mass unemployment has broken the chain of contribution for many, and the extended dependency of old people on inadequate incomes has exacerbated their need. Pensions used to be given to support a family, rather than just an individual. The Beveridge scheme was conceived at a time when families were relatively stable. Now divorce is more frequent, and pension rights are often the most important capital asset after the house that people have to divide up. It takes a long time for changes in the labour market to be reflected in changes in the distribution of pensions, but many women have worked, and have some pension entitlement; in due course, most women will have occupational pensions in their own right.

The reliance on the private sector, savings, personal investment and stakeholder pensions seems increasingly fragile in the current economic climate: the crisis of underfunding in many occupational and private schemes preceded the 2008 crash in the values of stocks and shares. Growing numbers of old people have long-term dependency, which in Britain brings them into the realm of means-tested social care; several countries, in a move pioneered by Germany,[22] have modified their social insurance systems to cover issues of long-term care. It seems likely that only solidaristic schemes – that is, schemes paid for by current taxpayers or contributors, bolstered by a broad cross-pooling of risk – can cope with the erratic and unpredictable changes experienced in recent times.

A third issue has been individualisation. Pensions in the private sector have become individual commodities, attached to a single person, and the trend has been reflected in the way that national insurance pensions operate – more than a million pensions are in payment to older Britons who live abroad. There have been arguments for extending the principle of individualised, transferable pensions throughout the state sector, crediting people with 'notional defined contributions', which is done in Sweden and Italy.[23]

The movement towards treating pensions as the property of the individual was presented as a 'new insurance contract', offering a greater degree of security.[24] The emphasis has increasingly fallen on individual responsibility through personal or 'stakeholder' pensions. There are pressures to allow people to realise or capitalise their pensions, allowing them to use funds and entitlements for a range of purposes. That degree of flexibility is unlikely to be extended to entitlements to state pensions, but state pensions are not necessarily the most important part of pensions overall. The report of the Pensions Commission takes individualisation of pensions very much for granted.[25] It should not have done. Individualisation has introduced a considerable degree of variability, and some unpredictability, into the system. It also carries the implication that while some people will have individual entitlements, others will not. The change in the character of pensions takes them

---

[22] U Götting, K Haug and K Hinricks (1994) 'The long road to long-term care insurance in Germany', *Journal of Public Policy*, vol 14, no 3, pp 285-309.

[23] Pensions Commission (2005), pp 104-5.

[24] P Ring (2002) 'The implications of the "new insurance contract" for UK pension provision', *Critical Social Policy*, vol 22, no 4, pp 551-71.

[25] Pensions Commission (2005).

far away from the idea of redistribution and solidarity. The establishment of a Citizen's Pension could do a great deal to redress the balance.

## QUESTIONS FOR DISCUSSION

Why are pensions so much more generous than other benefits?
Should pensions depend on a person's work record?

# Chapter 16

# Benefits for people with disabilities

Disability is a complex set of issues, and benefits are given on a wide range of principles, including, for example, need, compensation, rehabilitation, the needs of carers, and desert. The main benefits for people with disabilities are Income Support or Employment and Support Allowance, Disability Living Allowance, Attendance Allowance and the Working Tax Credit. The system has been complicated by attempts to offer distinct benefits while trying at the same time to save money, often by excluding large numbers of potential claimants.

## The nature of disability

'Disability' is a broad term, covering a complex set of issues. In its initial work on the classification of disabilities, the World Health Organisation distinguished impairment, disability and handicap. This classification has now been replaced by a different form of words: disabilities are classified as problems in bodily function or structure, problems relating to activities and problems related to social participation.[1]

Problems in bodily function and structure, or impairments, generally refer in the WHO's terms to 'anatomical, physiological or psychological abnormality or loss'. This approach to disability is used only in a limited context. An example from Britain is the system used for assessing compensation for industrial disablement. It includes, among many others, ratings like these:

| | |
|---|---|
| Very severe facial disfiguration | 100% |
| Absolute deafness | 100% |
| Amputation below shoulder | 80% |
| Loss of a hand | 60% |
| Loss of four fingers | 40% |
| Loss of all toes | 20% |
| Loss of part of big toe | 3% |

The 'percentages' in this scale represent judgements of value, rather than any precise statement of functional ability or capacity.

---

[1] World Health Organisation (2000) ICIDH-2, Geneva: WHO.

Problems in activities, or disability, refer to functional limitations in ordinary activity. The test is not the impairment, but how impairments or chronic physical conditions affect behaviour. The term '80% disabled', widely used in Europe, refers to a loss of 80% of physical or mental capacity, judged by medical examination; blind people are taken to be 100% disabled. (There is still some ambiguity as to how far the measure of disability can be taken on the basis of impairments, and how far it should consider functional capacity. British schemes mix both criteria. In France, the 80% test used to be based on the scales introduced in 1919, which were concerned principally with impairment; since 1993 they have been based on a test of functional limitations.[2])

The third element, problems in social participation, has replaced the related idea of 'handicap'. Handicap was intended by the WHO to refer to the social issues surrounding disability − the production of the social status of a 'disabled person'. The UN defines handicap as:

> the loss or limitation of opportunities to take part in the life of the community on an equal level with others. It describes the encounter between the person with a disability and the environment.[3]

The term 'handicap' is now considered unacceptable by many people in the disability movement, and the idea of a 'social model of disability' has been adopted in its place, but the condemnation of the WHO definition found in some texts[4] is misconceived: the term 'handicap' was clearly intended to refer to the same issues as the social model of disability. The primary emphasis in services based on this model has been 'normalisation'[5] (not in the sense of 'independence', but the promotion of autonomy and 'social role valorisation') and 'empowerment'.[6]

## Benefits for people with disabilities

Disability has not always been recognised as a grounds to receive benefit. The only main benefits available until the 1960s were the Industrial Injuries scheme (1896/1946), the contributory Sickness Benefit (1946), and War Pensions (1917).

---

2 A Deveau (1995) 'Un nouveau barème', *Informations Sociales*, vol 42, pp 40-6.
3 United Nations (1994) *The standard rules on the equalization of opportunities for persons with disabilities*, New York: UN, p 9.
4 For example, M Oliver (1996) Understanding disability, London: Macmillan; P Abberley (1998) 'The spectre at the feast', in T Shakespeare (ed) *The disability reader*, London: Cassell.
5 W Wolfensberger (1972) T*he principle of normalization in human services*, Toronto: National Institute of Mental Retardation.
6 P Ramcharan, G Roberts, G Grant and J Borland (eds) (1997) *Empowerment in everyday life*, London: Jessica Kingsley Publishers.

The main benefit received by people with disabilities was National Assistance, the basic means-tested benefit.

Pressure for improvement came from three sources. One was the Disablement Income Group, at first a one-woman pressure group: Megan du Boisson wheeled herself around Whitehall, persuading officials that they needed to establish that disability was an issue. Second was the Thalidomide case, which brought a group of people with severe disabilities powerfully to public attention. Third, research by the end of the 1960s pointed to the extent of disability, suggesting that there were millions of people affected (though the limited definitions used in that study held down the figure to about three million, with arthritis appearing as the main single factor). The Chronically Sick and Disabled Persons Act 1970 made certain aids available, including telephones, and prompted further research into the extent of disability. It was really from that point that awareness of disability developed in official services; the commitment of local authorities to an initial provision of services revealed a deep well of unmet need. Some providers feared it might be a bottomless pit.

The Attendance Allowance, one of the final pieces of legislation of the outgoing Labour government in 1970, was the first general allowance available to people on the grounds of severe disability. The name of the benefit caused (and continues to cause) some confusion: it was not for people who received attendance, and it was not given to carers; it was for people who needed attendance, whether or not they actually received it. It was given for people who need, by day, 'frequent or constant attention in connection with their bodily needs' or by night, 'prolonged or repeated attention'. These definitions were very broad ranging, and later legal decisions applied them to issues like blindness and problems with communication. At that stage, the extent of disability was still believed to be limited, and the terms of the benefit were much more generous than many benefits that followed subsequently. In 1971, the Conservative government introduced Invalidity Benefit, an insurance-based benefit for long-term sickness; in the absence of other supports for people with disabilities, it became an important element of support for disability as well. (The relationship with benefits for people who are sick and incapacitated will be considered further in Chapter 17.)

The Labour government, 1974-79, introduced several benefits for people with disabilities: they included the Mobility Allowance, for people who were unable to walk; Non-Contributory Invalidity Pension, for people who did not qualify for the National Insurance benefit; and Invalid Care Allowance, for people who were forced not to work to look after someone with a disability. By the mid-1970s, however, there was both a much greater awareness of the extent of disability, and an economic climate that led governments to be cautious. There are two fairly striking examples of this caution. The first was the Mobility Allowance, introduced in 1975. After campaigns by the Tricycle Action Group, the 1974 Sharp Report recommended the phasing out of invalid tricycles, which were unpopular and widely seen as dangerous. The government was not prepared to finance cars for disability, believing that the cars would likely benefit 'helpful' relatives rather than the disabled people themselves. Instead, they came up with Mobility Allowance, which was for people who were unable to walk. Mobility Allowance was not well received by pressure groups. Alf Morris, the minister for disabled people, said 'I don't know what they want.' This was an easy point to answer: they wanted cars. Motability, a government-sponsored 'charity', was set up for people to lease a car with their Mobility Allowance. The advantage of using a charity is that it does not have to explain its use of discretion in the way that a government agency does.

Mobility Allowance was subject to some extraordinary restrictions. First, it was limited to people who could not walk 'with or without the aid of a prosthesis', or artificial limb. People who learned to walk with artificial legs were not entitled − a rule that has now been modified in later benefits. Second, it was limited to people who could not walk for an attributable organic reason. Most cases of learning disability have no attributable organic reason, so someone who had not learned to walk, or who had to be guided to walk in a particular direction, would not necessarily qualify. Third, Mobility Allowance was limited by age. At first it was confined to people under 55; it was later extended to those under 65. This is a simple restriction, but it had a massive effect. Since more than two thirds of all disabilities are experienced by people over 65,[7] this excluded the majority of people who cannot walk on the grounds of age alone.

The second example was the introduction of Non Contributory Invalidity Pension in 1975. This was available to people who did not qualify for Invalidity Benefit. It was only for people of working age − excluding, again, most people with disabilities − and it was not available to married women. (More than thirty years later, the discrimination seems unbelievable. Be reassured that it was scarcely more believable then.[8]) In 1977, HNCIP was introduced: the 'H' stands for housewives. There was a test of a woman's ability to perform normal household duties. A married woman could claim only if she was substantially impaired in her ability to do housework. However, too many women claimed and the rules were changed in 1978 to restrict claims further; from 1978, married women could claim only if they were unable to do housework 'to any substantial extent'. The change of wording meant that before, if a woman had been unable to do half the expected household duties, she would have qualified; after, she would still have been able to do half, so she would not qualify. (A similar trick has just been pulled with the rules for Employment and Support Allowance, which is considered in the next chapter.) Pressure from the European Community to remove sexual discrimination from benefits led to the replacement of NCIP in 1980 by Severe Disablement Allowance.

---

[7] J Martin et al (1988) *The prevalence of disability among adults in Britain*, London: HMSO.
[8] See Equal Opportunities Commission (1981) *Behind closed doors*, Manchester: EOC.

Severe Disablement Allowance was based in a different test: claimants needed to be '80% disabled', a test borrowed from European benefits. After 2001, new claims for SDA have been suspended and Incapacity Benefit was made available to people under 20 in its place. (At the time of writing, SDA is still in payment to about a quarter of a million people; it is scheduled to disappear only in 2014.) The main people to be excluded by this process will therefore be people who become disabled over the age of 20 but who do not have a record of contributions. The Department of Social Security justified this by saying that it would 'direct more help to those for whom it was intended'.[9] It may be possible to say who SDA helped, but it is very unclear who it was 'intended' for. Bonner et al argued that the structure of the benefit was self-contradictory:

> SDA is an earnings-replacement benefit. Therein lies a difficulty ... because a non-contributory benefit for people incapable of work is likely to be payable to a large number of people who would not have been working even if they had been able to do so.[10]

If it was intended to help people without a contribution record, Burchardt suggests, it did not reach them; and it was never explicitly directed at children.[11] Its role was limited, but it was to prove particularly important for people living in residential institutions and for some people with learning disabilities who would not receive other benefits. The first of these groups are also those who will be affected by the withdrawal, after 2012, of the mobility component of Disability Living Allowance for those living in residential care.

The third main introduction by the Labour government was the 1976 Invalid Care Allowance. This was for people of working age looking after someone who received Attendance Allowance. Once again, the rules were restrictive: claimants had to be out of employment (the benefit was intended for people who had given up their jobs for full-time care); the care had to be 'regular and substantial' (being with someone who might fall was not enough); they had to be looking after someone for at least 35 hours per week in the daytime; and it was not available to married women. That last point was successfully challenged in the European courts in 1985, and the benefit was extended to married women after that – the government's defence, that this was not a social security benefit under European rules, won little sympathy. The benefit was renamed Carer's

9   Department for Work and Pensions (1998) *A new contract for welfare: Support for disabled people*, Cm 4103, London: The Stationery Office, p 9.
10  D Bonner, I Hooker and R White (2003) *Social security legislation 2003: volume 1, Non means tested benefits,* London: Sweet and Maxwell, p 121.
11  T Burchardt (1999) *The evolution of disability benefits in the UK,* London: London School of Economics Centre for the Analysis of Social Exclusion.

Allowance in 2003, and the benefit has been extended to allow people over retirement age to claim.

For most of the 1970s and 1980s, Attendance Allowance was the main benefit for people with disabilities, because the restrictions on the other benefits made them very limited in their scope. From 1988, disabled people on Income Support received a premium equivalent to the premiums for pensioners aged 60-75. A severe disablement premium is given for people who receive Attendance Allowance, but who have no-one to look after them. However, there was an element of 'rough justice' in this – the position for many disabled people became worse than in the previous system, when additions were given for special needs. Premiums for carers were introduced in 1991. The Invalid Care Allowance was not worth anything to carers on IS because it was deducted from their benefits. The introduction of a special premium on IS offered a small supplementary amount.

There was a further substantial reform in 1992, with the introduction of Disability Living Allowance and Disability Working Allowance. This led to a split between benefits for younger and older disabled people: older people continued to receive Attendance Allowance, but younger people received DLA. The DLA has components for mobility and 'care', or attendance, and replaced the Mobility Allowance and Attendance Allowance for people under 65. The Disability Working Allowance was a means-tested benefit for disabled people who were working for a low wage. Very few people received the benefit – few were eligible, and only a fifth of those took it up – and it was regarded as a failure.[12] It has now been replaced by the Working Tax Credit (briefly named the Disabled Person's Tax Credit before it was combined with the main Tax Credit for low-income families).

The most recent change has been the introduction of the Employment and Support Allowance in 2008. Existing Income Support claimants are remaining on that benefit, but new claimants will not receive IS at all, and over time the distinction between IS and ESA will disappear. Existing Incapacity Benefit claimants are being retested, a process that is scheduled to take three years, and entitlement to benefit on the basis of contributions is being time-limited, so that for most claimants ESA will be a means-tested benefit. (In some of the published documents about incapacity, IS claimants with disability premiums are already counted together with Incapacity Benefit claimants, and some of the historical figures have been revised.) The main differences between ESA and Incapacity Benefit are the use of means-testing and the emphasis on establishing a person's capacity for work.

This is not a full account of all the possible benefits. There is a patchwork quilt of provision available to people in particular circumstances. They include Industrial Injuries Benefit, for people injured by industrial accidents, and some prescribed diseases; War Pensions, for people injured in military action; and

---

[12] N Cockett (2003) 'Disability Working Allowance', *Benefits*, vol 11, no 3, pp 175-9.

Vaccine Damage Payments, a half-hearted attempt in one very specific set of circumstances to replace the system of civil compensation overseen by the courts. There is also a wide range of discretionary benefits, because within the system of community care local authority social services or social work departments are able to provide assistance with home helps, holidays, telephones, aids and adaptations, recreational facilities, educational facilities and transport. The Family Fund, a central government fund administered by the Joseph Rowntree Foundation, helps families with severely disabled children on a charitable basis, and the Independent Living Fund did the same for disabled adults.

## Timeline: disability and incapacity

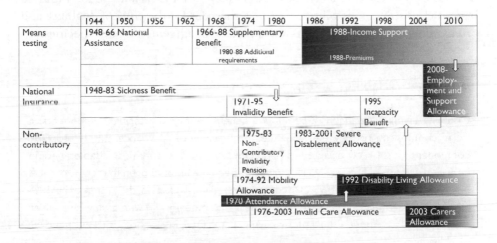

The Disability Alliance for many years argued for a national disability income – essentially, universal provision for all disabled people.[13] The advantages of such a scheme should be, in principle, that it would offer a basic minimum income to every disabled person, and that it should avoid invidious distinctions between people with similar disabilities. There are serious disadvantages, however. There are very large numbers of disabled people – one count puts the number at 8.6 million[14] – and because most of them are elderly, it is not certain that many, or even most, have consequent financial disadvantages that are attributable to their disability. A universal benefit could be very expensive and not very equitable. Another has been that the same distinctions between disabled people often reflect genuine concerns about fairness; the idea of 'compensation' is based on the principle that someone should be treated according to their individual circumstances. Many people with disabilities, like war pensioners, have privileges

---

[13]  C Barnes (1991) *Disabled people in Britain and discrimination*, London: Hurst, pp 219-21.
[14]  R Berthoud (1998) *Disability benefits*, York: Joseph Rowntree Foundation.

they would not want to see eroded by a different system. The other is that disability can be very difficult to define and identify. Some people are able to identify themselves, clearly and firmly, as 'disabled'; many cannot. Some conditions fluctuate, like mental illness; some are inconsistent and unpredictable, and they may leave people over some time confused about their status and possible future. This applies to some serious chronic illnesses like multiple sclerosis (where sufferers commonly have some period of temporary respite, and are uncertain about the likely rate of deterioration) and stroke (where people begin with incapacity but may hope to recover).

As so often happens in social security, idealised models are liable to founder on the rock of practical realities. In Ireland, there were proposals in the 1990s (from the 1996 *Commission on the Status of People with Disabilities*[15]) for a unified benefit consisting of disability pension, a payment for the costs of disability and carer's allowances. The idea sank through lack of agreement about specifics.

## Box 16.1: Disability Living Allowance

Disability Living Allowance is a compound benefit, with two principal components: a 'care' component, roughly equivalent to the Attendance Allowance, and a 'mobility' component. It is largely directed to people of working age, and most disabled people in Britain are too old to receive it. However, people who have been in receipt of DLA before reaching the age of 65 can continue to claim it afterwards, and that has the advantage of allowing claimants to receive help with mobility and with care with a lower level of disability. About a third of the payments for DLA in practice go to people over working age.[16]

The mobility component is available for people who are 'unable or virtually unable to walk'. It is paid at higher and lower rates, and the higher rate is available only for people who cannot walk for physical reasons. The lower rate is mainly for people who cannot walk out of doors. Walking with severe discomfort is supposed to be disregarded. People with severe mental impairment and behavioural problems, so that they need someone to intervene for them to get about, can also qualify.

The care component has three rates – low, middle and high. The rules, and the difficulties of qualifying for the benefit, are similar to Attendance Allowance. The low rate is for people who need care for a significant part of the day; the middle rate, for people who need frequent attention during the day, or care at night; and the highest rate, for people who need such care day and night. This causes considerable confusion, and

---

[15] Government of Ireland (1996) *Report of the Commission on the Status of People with Disabilities*, Dublin: Stationery Office.

[16] Department for Work and Pensions (2010) *Benefit expenditure tables* (http://statistics.dwp.gov.uk/asd/asd4/alltables_budget2010.xls), table 3.

evaluation suggests that in practice no clear distinction can be made between people on different rates.[17]

DLA is also very poorly understood by claimants. A revealing study of unsuccessful claimants showed that they did not understand what the benefit was for, what the criteria were or how the system worked. Applicants were expecting a benefit for being disabled or an out-of-work benefit, and thought the process of claiming was largely a matter of luck.[18] The researcher commented that often 'applications for DLA had been made as part of a speculative trawl across a number of possible sources of benefit without any attempt to understand the specifics of any one in particular'.[19] Beyond that, DLA also suffers from many of the problems of selectivity. A study focusing on the treatment of people claiming DLA with Chronic Fatigue Syndrome complains of arbitrariness, stereotypical judgements and stigma.[20]

Despite the restrictive conditions attached to Disability Living Allowance, the number of claims has been increasing, and a growing proportion of claimants have been receiving DLA in respect of mental health problems.[21] The same research suggests that DLA has been acting in practice as a top-up for Incapacity Benefit,[22] which is surprising, because the tests for DLA insist that a very substantial need for attention or restricted mobility is needed, and the tests for Incapacity Benefit do not. This trend has raised concerns as to whether the benefit is functioning as intended, and from 2013 on, the government intends to introduce medical assessment as part of the gateway for DLA.[23] The new assessment will introduce new criteria. However, the conditions that lead to people receiving DLA tend to be serious, chronic and long term, which makes it questionable whether review can possibly produce the drastic reduction in the numbers of claims the government is looking for. A more likely result is one that has been visible in the assessment for Employment and Support Allowance: 37% of claimants drop out of that process before they are assessed.[24] The Treasury has confirmed that they expect both the process and the savings on DLA to be similar to those for the ESA assessment.[25]

[17] R Sainsbury, M Hirst and D Lawton (1995) *Evaluation of Disability Living Allowance and Attendance Allowance*, London: Department of Social Security.

[18] A Thomas (2008) *Disability Living Allowance: Disallowed claims*, London: Department for Work and Pensions.

[19] Thomas (2008), p 19.

[20] C Hammond (2004) 'A poorly understood condition', *Social Policy and Administration*, vol 36, no 3, pp 254-74.

[21] C Beatty, S Fothergill and D Platts-Fowler (2009) *DLA claimants – A new assessment*, London: Department for Work and Pensions, pp 13-14.

[22] Beatty, Fothergill and Platts-Fowler (2009), pp 13-14.

[23] HM Treasury (2010) *Budget 2010*, HC 61, London: The Stationery Office, p 33.

[24] K Dryburgh (2010) *Unfit for purpose*, Edinburgh: Citizens' Advice Scotland.

[25] HM Treasury (2010) *Budget 2010 policy costings*, London: The Stationery Office, p 36.

## The principles of distribution

Benefits for disability are given on a number of principles.

- *Compensation for disability* Industrial disablement or action in the courts assumes that people should be paid if something unpleasant happens to them. This does not extend to those who simply become ill or to those born with disabilities. (Part of the rationale for compensation is preventative: penalising those who are responsible is assumed to encourage more responsible action. Prevention is not, however, a primary aim of benefits in themselves.)
- *Special needs* Allowances can be made, for example, for personal care, transport and medical goods.
- *Desert* In some cases compensation depends on a moral evaluation of the reason for disability. War Pensions are the main example.
- *The protection of carers* People caring for a disabled person may be limited in their capacity to seek work and to earn.
- *Rehabilitation* Benefits may be concerned to change the status of the disabled person – for example, through training or the provision of special equipment.
- *Promoting employment* Some benefits are geared specifically to the promotion of employment for disabled people, as a desirable end in itself. The Working Tax Credit does so by altering the calculation of costs and benefits made by disabled people or by employers.
- *Improving low income* Low income may reflect incapacity or disadvantage in the labour market. Many disabled people on low income rely on forms of social assistance benefits, intended for anyone who is poor. Support for disabled people on low earnings is another example. The disability element of Working Tax Credit takes into account the disadvantage that disabled people have in finding employment.
- *Equal opportunity* Rehabilitation and the promotion of employment can both be seen as means to further equality of opportunity for people with disabilities. This is an express objective of the UN World Programme of Action concerning Disabled Persons.[26]
- *Participation in society* This encompasses rehabilitation, employment and income support; it is also a justification for a range of benefits in kind intended to promote social inclusion for people with disabilities, including housing, transport, leisure, cultural and educational benefits.
- *Market-based and voluntary provision* State intervention that is based on support of the voluntary sector necessarily reflects to some degree the principles that inform voluntary action. The voluntary sector has a wide range of objectives, including humanitarian, religious, mutualist and commercial aims. In the special case where market-based criteria apply, the services

---

[26] United Nations (1994).

provided, like mobility aids, nursing care or help with domestic tasks, are dominated by services for elderly people. This is because commercial services develop according to economic demand rather than abstract principles.

## QUESTIONS FOR DISCUSSION

Why should the level of disability be directly related to financial support?
Should governments compensate people for disability?

# Chapter 17

# Incapacity

Incapacity is different from disability; it is principally concerned with people's relationship to the labour market. People who are unable to work for medical reasons are being gradually transferred from Incapacity Benefit or Income Support to Employment and Support Allowance. To qualify, people have to pass a 'Work Capability Assessment' to show they are unable to do any work. This is not consistent with the widespread use of the benefit as a route to early retirement through sickness.

## Incapacity and sickness

Incapacity arises because people are unable to work. Medical incapacity happens because of sickness or because of some impairment (an anatomical, physiological or psychological abnormality or loss) that prevents a person from working. This might mean either that someone is unable to undertake the employment which he or she would usually do, or that he or she is unable to do any work at the time. Incapacity can overlap with disability, but it is not necessarily the same thing. There are disabling conditions (like amputation or disfigurement) which do not necessarily impair the ability to work, and problems that incapacitate people – like frequent illness, backache and stress-related disorders – which are not usually described as disabilities. Although benefit regulations in Britain tend to refer to the broader definition of incapacity, in other places incapacity relates to functional ability in a specific context. In France, the test of incapacity is whether or not a person is able to earn two thirds of a previous wage.

There are different kinds of incapacity: the most basic distinction made falls between short term and long term. Short-term incapacity covers most episodes of interruption of work and earnings; there is a presumption that the person who is incapacitated in the short term will return to work subsequently, in an equivalent position. Short-term incapacity has to be understood in the context of the person's own occupation. Different standards apply to a surgeon, a bus driver and a clerical worker. Sicknesses such as influenza or backache do not usually imply an inability to do any sort of work; they offer a legitimate reason for temporary interruption of employment, which is not inconsistent with performing at full capacity overall. In the short term, people are encouraged to enter the 'sick role'. Parsons defines four principal features:

1. The sick person is discharged from ordinary social obligations. He is not expected to do the same as someone who is healthy.
2. The sick person must not be sick by choice. A malingerer or a hypochondriac is someone who tries to manipulate the sick role, rather than someone who is genuinely of it; the fact that the illness is voluntarily assumed breaks expectations and alters the obligations of others towards the sick person.
3. Though the sick role is an undesirable status, it is accepted as a legitimate one.
4. The sick person must seek help in an attempt to get better.[1]

Long-term incapacity occurs either when this pattern disrupts work and employability, or when the incapacitating condition is of a kind that is liable to produce such an effect. Long-term incapacity has two implications. One is that the sick role is eroded, and the allowances which are made for sickness cease to apply. The second is that the point of reference alters. Illness may impair a person's ability to do a task without necessarily preventing performance altogether: people who are unable to work in a role they previously filled may still be able to work in other roles. The distinction between short and long term incapacity was institutionalised in the British system for many years. From 1971 onwards, there was a distinction between Sickness Benefit, which covered the first six months, and Invalidity Benefit, which was reserved for longer-term illness. After the introduction of Statutory Sick Pay, the distinction remained. The choice of six months is entirely conventional; by contrast with Britain, transfer to an invalidity pension in France takes place formally after three years, the point when entitlement to earnings-related sickness benefits expires.

Long-term incapacity shades into disability because duration is one of the principal defining features of a disability. If there is a distinction, it is that there are limiting long-term illnesses which are not permanent, and to which the sick role can still validly be applied. Stroke (cerebro-vascular accident) is one of the principal causes of disability and incapacity in the UK for people of working age. Many victims of stroke, however, recover over time. Some benefits require that the disabling condition must have lasted for some time before the claim; others that the condition must be likely to last for a period after it. To receive Disability Living Allowance in Britain, claimants must have been disabled for three months before claiming, and the condition must be likely to last for at least six months. The total period of nine months excludes many strokes from which people are likely to recover. (Exemptions from this kind of provision are made for people who are diagnosed as being terminally ill.)

---

[1]    T Parsons (1958) 'Definitions of health and illness in the light of American values and social structure', in E G Jaco (ed) *Patients, physicians and illness,* Glencoe, IL: Free Press.

Disabled people may be encouraged, or expected, to work. Incapacity, by contrast, legitimates withdrawal from the labour market. More than half the claimants of Invalidity Benefit in a 1993 survey in Britain considered that they would not work again, or described themselves as retired.[2] (It is a response that current claimants would find it more difficult to make, because they could be jeopardising their entitlement if they did.) Although disability is a different issue, it may be true that perceptions of disability are affected by people's prospect of working. The 1988 UK survey on disability, when repeated in 1996/97, showed a striking increase in the numbers of people identified as disabled – from 6.2 million to 8.6 million disabled adults.[3] The bulk of the increase concerns self-identification of limitations in ability by older people; there is some foundation for an increase, because there are growing numbers of very elderly people, but the increase far exceeds what might be expected given the health of the population. The questions for the 1980s study were tested at the time for reliability and validity, and on the face of the matter it is difficult to see why large numbers of people should have begun to complain of problems of locomotion, bending, stretching and so forth. The most plausible explanation is that the responses reflect, to an unexpected degree, the economic circumstances of the respondents. During the 1990s, many unemployed people    more than a million – were reclassified as being incapacitated. Many were older people with little realistic prospect of regaining work in Britain's depressed economy. Such respondents may well legitimise their dependent position by reference to their incapacity.

## Benefits for incapacity

For most of the post-war period incapacity has been responded to through a combination of insurance-based and means-tested benefits: first Sickness Benefit or National Assistance, then Invalidity Benefit or Supplementary Benefit, then Incapacity Benefit or Income Support, and now Employment and Support Allowance, which has both contributory and means-tested elements.

The distinction between those who had made contributions and those who had not has been central until very recently. Most people who had no contributions would have had to claim Supplementary Benefit and then Income Support. A Non Contributory Invalidity Pension was introduced in 1975, and replaced by Severe Disablement Allowance in 1983. People who received NCIP or SDA while on low incomes would often have had them deducted from Supplementary Benefit and Income Support; the benefits were most important for people in different circumstances, notably those living in institutions (like some people

---

[2]  S Lonsdale, C Lessof and G Ferris (1993) *Invalidity benefit*, London: Department of Social Security.

[3]  R Berthoud (1998) *Disability benefits*, York: Joseph Rowntree Foundation.

with a learning disability) who would otherwise have been entitled to nothing. SDA was formally combined with Incapacity Benefit in 2001, and all were put together with Income Support for people with disabilities in 2008, to form the client group for the new Employment and Support Allowance.

Despite the obvious importance of means testing for people with incapacities, the benefits in the past that were specifically identified as dealing with incapacity have mainly been non-means tested. They have often been more generous than the alternatives – especially benefits for unemployment, which have not just been lower but also carried the requirement to be available for work. People who have become unemployed when they also had chronic illnesses – such as people with chronic mental illness – may reasonably have chosen to claim as incapacitated. Employment and Support Allowance represents a major shift away from this approach. The claimants who will lose out because of time limits on the contributory benefit will mainly be people whose partners work and those who retire sick with occupational pensions.

The crucial points about the benefits, I think, are these. First, the benefits have been defined in relationship to the world of work, not to illness or disability. Claimants are expected to be unable to work, which sits uncomfortably with policies that have increasingly focused on re-engaging people with work. There is a problem in defining the position of people who can work only for a limited time: there has been a long-standing exemption for people doing 'therapeutic work', allowing a small amount of paid employment while on benefit. The critical issues have been about withdrawal from, or engagement in, the labour market.

Second, the benefits for incapacity have not just been about incapacity. The benefits have been used to cover a range of circumstances, including disability and early retirement. About a third of Incapacity Benefit claimants, now being transferred to ESA, are over 55. (It has been suggested, too, that the benefits have been used to cover up unemployment. The Conservative government under John Major may have preferred to have had people classed as incapacitated rather than unemployed, leading to a surge in claims in the 1990s.) Many of the recipients of benefits report that they would prefer to work, if only they had the opportunity. Most of them – about 60% of new claimants – actually do return to work.[4] Third, the incapacity benefits are based, like benefits for people with disabilities, on a test of need. They have all the problems associated with selectivity and needs-testing.

## The Work Capability Assessment

Despite the myths propagated in the press, it has not been true for years that people would be signed off work solely on the strength of a doctor's note saying

---

[4]   Department for Work and Pensions (2006) *A new deal for welfare: Empowering people to work*, Cm 6730 (www.dwp.gov.uk/aboutus/welfarereform/).

they were unfit. That was the system under Invalidity Benefit, and it still applies to some private arrangements for long-term sick pay or early retirement. Since the introduction of Incapacity Benefit in 1995, however, a claimant would either need to have one of a specified series of conditions – for example, blindness, 80% disability, severe intellectual disability or terminal illness – or be subject to an assessment of their capacity for work. Incapacity Benefit was initially based on an 'all work' test. This was renamed the 'Personal Capability Assessment', and in the Employment and Support Allowance it has become a 'Work Capability Assessment'. The first of these names captures an important aspect of the test: people are not being asked whether they are too sick to continue in their job, but whether they can do any job.

---

### Box 17.1: The Work Capability Assessment

For the initial six months of sickness, the test is whether people are able to do their own work (the 'own occupation' test), but most people during that period will receive Statutory Sick Pay rather than Employment and Support Allowance. After that period, they are subject to assessment.

The Work Capability Assessment has three elements:

- a limited capability for work test;
- a limited capability for work-related activity; and
- a work-focused health-related assessment.

The first part is a test of disability. It is based on a points scheme, identifying physical and mental problems.

Physical problems include:

- walking on level ground
- standing and sitting
- bending or kneeling
- reaching
- picking up and moving things
- manual dexterity
- speech
- hearing
- vision
- continence, and
- consciousness

Mental problems include:

- completion of tasks
- awareness of hazards
- memory and concentration
- execution of tasks
- initiating and sustaining personal action
- coping with change
- getting about, and
- interaction with others.

Long-term illness, whether physical or mental, needs to be assessed in terms of its functional implications. Serious illness does not imply automatic disqualification from the labour market.

The second part of the assessment is not based on the points scheme: it is a judgement about whether or not people are selected for 'support' or for 'work-related activity'.

Despite the judgement that people are incapable of doing any work, more than 70% of claimants who pass the assessment are directed to work-related activity groups. Fewer people are being nominated for the 'support' group; it was intended for people with 'very severe' disabilities but is currently confined to very severe mental disorder, chemotherapy users, terminal illness and people who are unable to communicate at all.

The third part of the Work Capability Assessment is a medical assessment, done on behalf of the Department for Work and Pensions, which reviews future prospects and options. This element has been suspended until 2012, while the government consider how better to integrate the WCA with the new Work Programme.

The Work Capability Assessment has been represented as a way of toughening up the previous system, though that was also largely based on a points scheme. It is not obvious that the rules (as opposed to the practice) have actually become more restrictive. The expansion and clarification of mental capacity, in particular, has the potential to lead to a broader and greater range of claims. There are exemptions from the WCA, as there were to the Personal Capability Assessment before it; but whereas more than a third of claimants were previously exempt from the PCA, for example because of disability, blindness or mental illness, limiting the exemptions in the new scheme means that only about 10% of claimants (mainly pregnant women, people with terminal illnesses and those who are in-patients in hospital) will not now be put through the test. The loss of those exemptions is likely in principle to have more impact than any adjustment in the points.

There is, however, evidence that beyond this, the new scheme is being interpreted very restrictively. The Harrington report found 'that the system can be impersonal and mechanistic, that the process lacks transparency and that a lack of communication between the various parties involved contributes to poor decision making'.[5] Under the Incapacity Benefit rules, 37% of claimants who went through the assessment process were found to be fit to work. The Department for Work and Pensions's initial targets expected to put 51% of applicants into Employment and Support Allowance, in place of the previous 63%. In fact, only 32% have been passing scrutiny.[6] There are questions being raised about the accuracy of the medical examinations.[7] About a quarter of claimants who are found fit for work appeal against the decision, and 40% of them win their appeal.[8] The process has many weaknesses – excessive numbers of assessments, lack of reference to medical evidence and examinations that are

---

[5] M Harrington (2010) *Independent review of the Work Capability Assessment*, London: DWP.

[6] K Dryburgh (2010) *Unfit for purpose*, Edinburgh: Citizen's Advice Scotland; Harrington (2010) ch 5.

[7] For example, M Daly (2010) 'Who's cheating who?', BBC Scotland, 26 May.

[8] Department for Work and Pensions (2010) *Employment and Support Allowance: Work Capability Assessment official statistics*, April (http://research.dwp.gov.uk/asd/workingage/esa_wca/esa_wca_27042010.pdf).

driven by the demands of the computer rather than the assessor — but it seems to be particularly deficient in the assessment of fluctuating conditions and mental health issues.[9]

Incapacity Benefit was formally wound up in October 2010, but the process of transferring existing claimants from it to ESA is scheduled to take three years. Many of those claimants will not transfer, but will be required to claim Jobseeker's Allowance instead. The first indications are that, rather than being rejected, large numbers of claimants are dropping out of the assessment at some stage. 37% of claimants are disappearing before they are even assessed.[10] It may be true that the greater frequency of assessment, the impact of calling people in for tests and the general preference of claimants to work when they have the opportunity may combine to reduce the numbers of claimants. It is probably also true that Incapacity Benefit was used in the 1990s to legitimate the long-term unemployment of an ageing cohort of male manual workers; that cohort is now gradually retiring, and with the decline of manufacturing industry and heavy labour it is unlikely to be replenished.

## Responses to incapacity

Benefits for disabled and incapacitated people have tended to be developed together, but their aims and objectives are importantly different, and so is the pattern of responses that is appropriate to them. In the previous chapter I outlined a range of principles that explain why benefits for disability might be provided. The principles on which incapacity is provided for are related, but different. They include:

- *Social protection* The principle of social insurance is intended to cover changes of circumstance and needs that might arise. This extends to cover for medical care, the incurring of unexpected costs and income maintenance (the next item on this list).
- *Income maintenance* People wish to protect themselves from circumstances in which their income might be interrupted. This is sometimes done through social assistance but more typically it affects people who have previously been earning, and so it will be done through an insurance-related benefit.
- *Economic efficiency* Part of the rationale for incapacity benefits is based, not in the circumstances of the incapacitated worker, but in economic processes. Employers wish to maximise the productivity of the workforce. This is less likely to be achieved if workers are unable to function adequately — and less likely still if a worker with a short-term illness like influenza infects everyone else. Rules relating to short-term incapacity allow for restoration

---

[9] Dryburgh (2010); Harrington (2010).
[10] Dryburgh (2010).

of full capacity; rules relating to long-term incapacity allow for removal of less productive workers from the labour market. (Note that there is a potential tension between this principle and the desire, in relation to people with disabilities, to promote increased participation in the labour market.)

- *Early retirement* A scheme for incapacity benefits may become in effect a surrogate scheme for early retirement. Because it legitimates withdrawal from the labour market, it makes retirement possible for people who have not reached retirement age.[11]
- *The functioning of medical services* The balancing of medical priorities has been an important element in the administration of incapacity benefits: part of the purpose of sickness benefits has been to facilitate and encourage medical consultations, but the routine certification of sickness has proved burdensome and (in some systems) ineffective as a means of managing medical care.

Although there is some overlap between these principles and provision for disability, it mainly happens in so far as disability implies incapacity, or incapacity includes disability. A disability implies functional limitation of ordinary activity, and if the ordinary activity refers to the ability to work, the terms become equivalent. A person who is disabled does not need social protection or income maintenance solely on account of the disability. A person who is incapacitated without disability does need social protection, but is not necessarily disadvantaged in terms of equality of opportunity or participation in society.

## The reform of incapacity benefits

Benefits for incapacity have not attracted as much attention in the academic literature as they should, because academics and researchers have tended to focus on means-tested benefits. However, the arbitrariness of the rules, the problems of treating claimants according to their circumstances and the sheer number of people affected, make incapacity one of the problematic issues in the system.

The main thrust of the Labour government's Green Paper outlining the change to Employment and Support Allowance was about getting people on Incapacity Benefit back to work.[12] There were certainly people on the benefit who would prefer to work. But the arguments for the effectiveness of work-based measures were extremely weak. The pilot programme, *Pathways to Work*, had a very poor return on effort. The evaluation claimed that 'Pathways significantly increased

---

[11] P Alcock, C Beatty, S Fothergill, R Macmillan and S Yeandle (eds) (2003) *Work to welfare*, Cambridge: Cambridge University Press.

[12] DWP (2006).

the probability of being employed.'[13] That finding depended on some creative interpretation. The sample consisted of people thinking of claiming Incapacity Benefit rather than people claiming it. Being 'employed' was redefined to include any work of any length[14] – a position often permitted as 'therapeutic work' under the old system. That redefinition produced the only apparent gain from the programme, presented as the headline figure in the report's summary. The evaluation discarded evidence that gains from one cohort in the programme were not found in other cohorts[15] – a pattern that usually indicates that if there is a difference, it is not the programme that has made it. And, unbelievably, the conventional test of statistical significance was altered to claim that results were significant,[16] when no other study would have said they were. Even at that level, a later study had to conclude that there was no significant effect.[17] A DWP consultation in 2010 acknowledged the poor results, noting that 'when Pathways was extended to further Jobcentre Plus areas, no employment impact was found', and called for suggestions.[18] The National Audit Office's investigation found that while there was some gain from having earlier medical assessments, because they led to fewer people receiving the benefit in the first place, the scheme had little or no impact on employment prospects and offered 'poor value for money'[19] This is a disquieting episode. The analysis was designed to show the programme in the most favourable light, and it was directly misleading.

The core problem with the emphasis on work is that provision for incapacity is meant to legitimate long-term withdrawal from the labour market     that is what it is there for. There are two main circumstances in which people withdraw from the labour market. The first is that people are unable to do work which is appropriate to them personally. When people retire through sickness, the test applied for invalidity pensions in the independent sector is whether they are able to do their job, not whether they are able to do any job at all. People who have

---

[13] H Bewley, R Dorset and G Haile (2007) *The impact of Pathways to Work*, London: Department for Work and Pensions (http://research.dwp.gov.uk/asd/asd5/rports2007-2008/rrep435.pdf), p 2.

[14] Bewley, Dorset and Haile (2007), table 5.1.

[15] Bewley, Dorset and Haile (2007), pp 42, 43-4.

[16] Bewley, Dorset and Haile (2007), p 48 footnote.

[17] H Bewley, R Dorsett and S Salis (2009) *The impact of Pathways to Work on work, earnings and self-reported health in the April 2006 expansion areas*, DWP Research Report 601, London: Department for Work and Pensions (http://research.dwp.gov.uk/asd/asd5/rports2009-2010/rrep601.pdf).

[18] Department for Work and Pensions (2010) *Pathways to work policy review: Review of support for disabled customers and customers with a health condition* (www.dwp.gov.uk/docs/pathways-evidence-gathering-151209.pdf).

[19] National Audit Office (2010) *Support to incapacity benefit claimants through Pathways to Work*, HC21 2010-11, London: The Stationery Office.

trained as teachers or plumbers do not, as a general proposition, expect to have to work at a supermarket till; when they insure themselves against incapacity, or join social protection schemes, they do it on terms that mean they will not have to do much lower-paid jobs. This applies to large numbers of people currently receiving benefits for incapacity, but the system does not recognise their situation. Instead, they are supposed to be unable to do any work.

The other contingency covered by this kind of benefit happens when people who have functional impairments are unable to function or compete in the job market. Beatty and Fothergill comment: 'These men are hidden employed in that in a fully employed economy they could reasonably have been expected to be in work.'[20] When people with impairments withdraw from the job market, it is not necessarily because there is no job they might be interested in, but because there is not much point in looking for work. People suffering from intermittent schizophrenia, for example, are not unable to work for periods, but they are unlikely to function adequately in the labour market.

Three quarters of a million of the remaining claimants may be employable.[21] If someone is disabled, we do not in general assume that the disabled person should not work. What we say, instead, is that such a person should have the opportunity for appropriate work – facilitated, where possible, by training, equipment and measures to remove disadvantage in the labour market. On the face of the matter, people who are classified as having an incapacity are in the same position. If we plan to apply a different standard to people who are incapacitated and people who are disabled, there should be some rationale behind it. There does not seem to be.

The Labour government initially proposed to replace Incapacity Benefit with two benefits. 'Disability and Sickness Allowance' would have been for people with more severe disabling conditions. 'Rehabilitation and Support Allowance' would have been for people with more 'manageable' incapacities, who would be expected to make efforts to return to work.[22] In the Green Paper, this proposal was replaced by the Employment and Support Allowance, with a heavy emphasis on making efforts to find work. The government was right initially, I think, to be thinking in terms of disability and rehabilitation; they were also right to be thinking about breaking up Incapacity Benefit into its constituent parts. I am not convinced, however, that they ever identified the right parts.

---

[20] C Beatty and S Fothergill (2003) 'Incapacity Benefits and unemployment', in P Alcock, C Beatty, S Fothergill, R Macmillan and S Yeandle (eds) *Work to welfare*, Cambridge: Cambridge University Press.

[21] Beatty and Fothergill (2003), p 133.

[22] Jobcentre Plus (2005) *Reform of Incapacity Benefits to replace sickness culture with work focus* (www.jobcentreplus.gov.uk/cms.asp?TextOnly=True&Page=/Home/News/2618).

Incapacity Benefit mainly dealt with three different kinds of circumstances. The first was long-term sickness, where people who have been sick with longer-term problems (like stroke or mental illness) may need more than six months to recover their full capacities. The second was disability, where the most appropriate response may be to emphasise people's capabilities, rather than their incapacity. The third was early retirement through sickness. This has now been added to the issues of low income and special income needs that used to be dealt with under Income Support. Instead of a rationalised system, then, we have finished, instead, with another complex, portmanteau benefit, where a range of rules are supposed to apply across the piece, and where people who sit in the wrong category will be required to comply with rules intended for others in very different circumstances.

## QUESTIONS FOR DISCUSSION

Should we allow people to retire sick?
Should there be an 'all work' test?

# Chapter 18

# Children and families

Benefits are not usually given to children, but to parents. Child poverty can only be responded to, within this model, by enhancing family incomes. Following a series of reforms that have removed allowances for children from the basic benefits, the most important benefits for people with children are Child Benefit, Child Tax Credit and the Working Tax Credit. They have not, however, been sufficient to remove families from poverty.

## Benefits for children

The received wisdom at the time of the Beveridge report was that people relied on an income available to the household, and that interruptions to the breadwinner's earnings were fundamental.[1] The principle can be seen, for example, in the operation of survivors' benefits – benefits received by family members after the insured person has died (examples were given in Chapter 3). The idea of the family wage has been criticised by feminists because of the assumption in it that women were likely to be dependent. But there is another parallel assumption, which, even if it is more defensible, is hardly examined: that support for children also has to be done by supplementing the income of the household. Children generally live in families, and the provision that is made in social security goes to responsible adults, rather than to the child. Responses to the needs of children are based in support for their families, as people who are unemployed, lone parents, disabled or on low incomes, rather than support for children as such. Few benefits are either available to children in their own right, or treated as being intended for the child (as they are in French law[2]). It is possible in principle to offer distinct benefits where the child is considered to be the beneficiary, rather than the adult who receives the money. The Child Trust Fund, or 'baby bond', was like this, but when it was introduced in 2002, it carried the stipulation that no children would receive the benefit until they reached their majority. It is also possible to offer benefits that might be received directly by the child, as school meals and school health services used to be; among the few remaining benefits of this kind are

---

[1]  I Montari (2000) 'From family wage to marriage subsidy and child benefits', *Journal of European Social Policy*, vol 10, no 4, pp 307-33.

[2]  J Dupeyroux, M Borgetto and R Lafore (2008) *Droit de la sécurité sociale* (16th edn), Paris: Dalloz, ss 954-5.

free prescriptions for children, Healthy Start vitamins, generally distributed by health visitors, and free milk for children under five in day care.

In most cases, however, the principle is that the parents receive money, not that a person is receiving money to be used specifically for the child. The income is not the child's, and there is no requirement to use the benefit for the child's welfare. Children are a cost that has to be borne by the adults in the family. Child Benefit is treated as part of a 'family fund' in disputes about maintenance, and there is no presumption that the money will follow the child;[3] and if the money is paid to the wrong person, so that it never goes near the child, it cannot be paid again.[4] Until relatively recently, there used to be allowances for 'dependants', with additions for the costs of children being made to other benefits like Income Support. These have now largely been replaced by Child Benefit and Child Tax Credit, where the benefits go to the responsible parent. The Child Tax Credit allows all families a monthly payment, with extra to allow for the costs of formal childcare. The credit is withdrawn at higher levels of income. (A similar effect could be achieved in principle by making Child Benefit taxable, but this has been problematic, because people become liable to tax at very low incomes.) A third benefit, the Working Tax Credit, allows parents with children working for low wages to receive a supplement to those wages. In previous incarnations this was done through Family Income Supplement and Family Credit. And food vouchers are available to low-income families where children are under four, but effectively they offer a supplement to the family diet, not a guarantee of food to the child.

Maternity benefits, in the same way, are not benefits for children; what they cover is the interruption of earnings for women. This can be seen as an example of the principle of social protection – avoiding interruptions in the flow of income even if the circumstances where the benefits are needed are largely predictable. Given that focus, in most cases it has been possible for governments to replace the previous system of maternity payments with Statutory Maternity Pay (now supplemented with Statutory Paternity Pay and Statutory Adoption Pay). Women who do not have coverage from an employer may be entitled to Maternity Allowance, which is insurance based.

The insurance principle does not cover every case of maternity, and the effect of pregnancy, birth and child care can also lead to a significant drop in income for parents and families. Other minor benefits have been intended to cover the circumstances for childbirth, including the Health in Pregnancy Grant (abolished in January 2011), Healthy Start food vouchers for expectant mothers on low

---

[3]   J Mesher, P Wood, R Poynter, N Wikeley, D Bonner (2009) *Social security legislation 2009/10, volume II: Income Support, Jobseeker's Allowance, State Pensions Credit and the Social Fund*, London: Sweet and Maxwell, p 530.

[4]   M Rowland and R White (2009) *Social security legislation 2009/10, volume III: Administration, adjudication and the European dimension*, London: Sweet and Maxwell, p 42.

income benefits, and the even more clumsily named Sure Start Maternity Grant, a lump sum given to recipients of other benefits, confined to the first child after 2011. (The 'Sure Start' programme was an attempt to present various child welfare measures, including this benefit, as an integrated programme.[5] In Scotland Sure Start has been replaced by the Early Years Framework.) Even before the 2010 budget, which cut away half the provision, these benefits were worth far less than equivalent benefits in some other European countries; childbirth has not been thought of in the UK as a major contingency requiring statutory provision.

Probably the most important effect of aggregating resources for children with the rest of the household has been that, for much of the post-war period, support for children disappeared into the general allowances made for households. The rules of the basic means-tested benefits meant that any increase in support for children – like child benefit or maintenance – was deducted from the family's benefits, leaving no net gain to the poorest people. Following rules introduced in April 2004, families on the basic means-tested benefits no longer receive allowances for children as part of those benefits; instead they receive Child Benefit and Child Tax Credit. In the same way, Child Support (that is, maintenance paid for a child from an absent parent) has in the past been largely deducted from the basic means-tested benefits, which means that it carries only a limited benefit for the poorest families. That position has only recently come to an end – Child Support ceased to be counted as income set against the basic means-tested benefits from April 2010.[6] For the first time since the system was established, the basic income-replacement benefits no longer make provision for children, and children are dealt with through other systems. Although the reforms passed almost unnoticed at the time, this may well have been the most important social security measure introduced in the course of the Labour government. It has left it open to governments in the future to increase (or reduce) support for children without affecting the operation of other benefits. And the consequence of this change has been seen in a significant change in the composition of family incomes. The combined effect of Child Benefit and Child Tax Credit may well mean that families with children get higher incomes than adult families of the same size.

## Education benefits

The main exception to the proposition that children do not receive benefits can be found in the special case of education benefits. Children do not usually claim the benefits, but they do receive them personally. Free school meals used to be of considerable importance because all schools provided meals at lunch times and

---

5   K Broadhurst, C Mason and C Grover (2007) 'Sure Start and the re-authorization of section 47 child protection policies', *Critical Social Policy*, vol 27, no 4, pp 443-61.
6   Child Poverty Action Group (2010) *Welfare benefits and tax credits handbook 2010/2011*, London: CPAG, p 775.

they were conceived as part of the provision of basic nutritional requirements. However, the effectiveness of school meals provision was always mixed. Many parents did not claim for their children; many children did not take school meals anyway; and those children who did receive free school meals sometimes felt singled out.[7]   In 1980, the government removed the obligation on local authorities to provide school meals, with the exception of free school meals for children of families on means-tested benefits. The separate and independent schemes formerly run by local authorities have been scrapped. School meals are now largely confined to children whose parents are entitled by virtue of claiming other means-tested benefits, but some local authorities have virtually suspended the provision of meals in schools anyway. (Scotland, however, is in the process of reintroducing school meals for younger primary children, and the government in England is reviewing provision for young children in low income families.)

School uniform and clothing grants have also declined in importance, partly because school uniform is much less often required than it was in the past, and partly because the discretionary schemes run by local authorities have been the victims of economies. Some schools still run their own discretionary schemes.

Third, there is the Education Maintenance Allowance for pupils who stay on at school after the age of 16. Introduced in 1944, the benefit was largely within the discretion of local authorities, but over the course of the last twenty years it had gradually been disappearing, the victim of progressive economies. The Labour government revived it as a national scheme, with some pilots being rolled out in 1999, and a national scheme in 2004. The benefit was, uniquely, paid directly into the bank account of the school pupil. It was announced shortly after in the 2010 Spending Review that EMA would be discontinued in its present form and that a more restrictive, discretionary scheme would be run instead by local authorities.

## Benefits and child poverty

The calculation of how much a child costs relative to an adult is referred to as the problem of 'equivalence'. The most generally used scales used to assess child poverty currently are based on the assumptions that a child under 14 costs less than two thirds of what an adult costs, and a child over 14 costs the same as an adult. As a general proposition, however, children cost more as they get older, and teenage children cost more than adults (because they eat the same but have higher needs for clothing replacement). The position is further complicated because younger families tend to be poorer. In part, it happens because the mothers of children under school age are unable to work, but it also reflects the lower income and resources of people who have not been able to gather all the resources that an

---

[7]   L Bissett and J Coussins (1982) *Badge of poverty: A new look at the stigma attached to free school meals*, London: Child Poverty Action Group.

older household can muster. This is an argument for smoothing out variations according to age, and that is largely what the benefit rates do.

For much of the period since the Second World War, benefits for children have been notoriously inadequate, and that was largely attributed to the inadequacy of the allowances made for them. Piachaud, in *The cost of a child*, put together a budget to show that benefit rates were inadequate to meet the subsistence of a child.[8]  Mack and Lansley argued that serious deprivations began, for most people, when incomes fell below 150% of the Supplementary Benefit level.[9] A particularly shocking piece of research into SB in the 1980s showed that half the families on benefit ran out of money most weeks.[10] That meant that most families would find themselves, at the end of the week, with no money for food. Later studies differ as to the level of deprivation which might be experienced through living long term on benefits,[11] because they apply different tests about the minima, but it was clear that the Income Support rates for many years were effectively lower than SB was for many families. In the data for the annual Families and Children Study in 2002, most IS claimants had run out of money

## Timeline: benefits for children and families

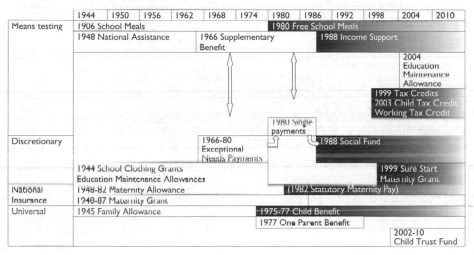

---

[8]  D Piachaud (1979) *The cost of a child*, London: Child Poverty Action Group.

[9]  J Mack and S Lansley (1985) *Poor Britain*, London: Allen & Unwin.

[10]  Policy Studies Institute (1984) *The reform of Supplementary Benefit*, Working Papers, London: PSI.

[11]  S Stitt and D Grant (1993) *Poverty: Rowntree revisited*, Aldershot: Avebury; J Bradshaw (1993) *Household budgets and living standards*, York: Joseph Rowntree Foundation.

before the end of the week at some point, and over a fifth said that they always ran out of money.[12]

The reforms of allowances for dependants are important, but they have not been enough to avoid the problems of inadequate income in families overall. There is no effective way of protecting resources for children, and if benefits are inadequate for the household, they will also be inadequate for a child living in that household. According to official estimates, 2.2 million children are living in low-income households and suffering material deprivation.[13] Most of these children (about 60%) are in households where no-one works.[14] Getting children out of poverty has been seen, then, as a combination of getting people into work, and making sure that people who are working are receiving adequate incomes.

The Labour government believed that the combined effects of a minimum wage, Tax Credits and a push towards greater employment would at least make a difference to working families with low incomes. This proved less effective than they had hoped. The minimum wage was never a major issue in family poverty: most of the people benefiting from it would be young people without families or second earners. Although the coverage of the Tax Credit system has been better than might have been expected, it still fails to reach one person in six, and the administrative problems have still to be overcome. Overall, as families have moved into work, the balance has shifted: children are still poor, but they are more likely to be in families where someone is working.[15]

## QUESTIONS FOR DISCUSSION

Can the situation of children be separated from the position of families? Should there be benefits for children in their own right?

---

[12] N Finch and P Kemp (2004) *The use of the Social Fund by families with children*, DWP In-house Report 139, London: Social Research Division, Department for Work and Pensions.

[13] Department for Work and Pensions (2010) *Households below average income: An analysis of the income distribution 1994/95-2008/09*, table 4.5tr.

[14] DWP (2010), table 4.3.

[15] P Kenway (2008) *Addressing in-work poverty*, York: Joseph Rowntree Foundation.

# Chapter 19

# Lone parents

Lone parents are particularly vulnerable to low income. Some important benefits for lone parents have been abolished, reflecting their lack of political support, but there are still different rules for lone parents on the basic means-tested benefits, Housing Benefit and Tax Credits. Other rules reflect the distinctive position of lone parents. Wherever there are specific benefits for lone parents, there has to be a cohabitation rule. Most lone parents become so through family breakdown, and Child Support is also a major issue.

Lone parents include unmarried mothers, divorcees (male and female) and widows and widowers (who are covered by National Insurance). 23% of all the families in Britain are one-parent families, and a considerable majority of them − over 97% − are headed by a female.[1] The largest category, over half the total, consists of people who are unmarried; that reflects increasing numbers of parents who have cohabited without being formally married. Overwhelmingly, children subsequently live with their mother rather than their father.

Lone parents are vulnerable to low income for three main reasons. First, their income from earnings tends to be low, because having two incomes in a household is fairly important to living standards, and because most of them are women. Second, lone parents are vulnerable to unemployment − like any other worker − and because they are also responsible for child care they also have to be able to make arrangements to make it possible to work. Although the number of one-parent families has generally been increasing, the numbers receiving earnings replacement benefits have grown disproportionately. This is partly because of the vulnerability of lone parents to a lack of resources, but mainly it reflects the growth of long-term unemployment; the growth is not simply in the numbers of lone parents, but of unemployed lone parents. Third, there are issues around the support of children, considered in the previous chapter.

Lone parents occupy a special place in the demonology of welfare. Opposition to providing for them is attributable in part to a residual view, which holds that parents should be responsible for children; in part, to moral disapproval of lone parents, especially unmarried mothers; and in part because of the general English distaste for children, who no respectable adult would wish to be associated with. There is a great deal of myth-mongering (like the wholly imaginary 'automatic

---

[1]  Office for National Statistics (2010) *General Lifestyle Survey 2008: Overview report* (www. statistics.gov.uk/downloads/theme_compendia/GLF08/GLFoverview2008.pdf).

right' of lone parents to have a council house[2]), and there have been some wildly irresponsible generalisations (the Social Exclusion Unit report on teenage pregnancy slid between talking about parents under 16, parents under 20 and parents under 25 as if they were all evidence of the same issue[3]). It is possible to take a diametrically opposed position: that the needs of children and families are institutional, and everyone is likely to be subject to them; that moral disapproval is an unhealthy basis on which to found a welfare system; and that Britain needs to produce more children if it hopes to have a future.

The classification of 'lone parents' as a group requiring social protection is potentially contentious. You might reasonably ask: do lone parents require any protection that is not available to other families? and recent governments answering that question seem to have taken the view that they do not. Although children of lone parents are more likely to be disadvantaged, all children, and all families, are vulnerable to some degree. A similar argument applies more forcefully to other disadvantaged families: younger families, large families or people in minority ethnic groups. The reason for looking at lone parents, and not at these other groups, is not just that their circumstances give grounds for concern, but that they have been the subject of a series of distinctive provision, and this book is about the British social security system, not the circumstances of families in general. There used to be special benefits for lone parents, including One Parent Benefit and the single parent premium on Income Support. These benefits were removed by the Labour government in 1997, which had undertaken to implement the policy introduced by the previous Conservative government. The remaining provisions are less visible, but they still rely on distinguishing lone parents from other types of benefit claimant. They include:

- the rules for Child Support;
- special provisions for the circumstances of lone parents, like special earnings disregards in Income Support and Housing Benefit; and
- rules that allow the needs of lone parents to be treated as if they were couples, for example in the calculation of Housing Benefit or Tax Credits.

## What is a lone parent?

At the most basic level, a lone parent is someone who is responsible for a child but who is not living with another parent. People's lives are complicated, however, and the arrangements are not always easy to classify. Rowlingson and McKay identify five common patterns:

---

[2]  J Sherman and J Prynn (1994) 'Lone mothers lose priority in housing queue', *The Times*, 19 July.

[3]  Social Exclusion Unit (1999) *Teenage pregnancy*, Cm 4342, London: The Stationery Office, p 17.

- people living with a partner, in the same home;
- people who live apart, but who identify themselves as a couple;
- people who live together, but identify themselves as having separate lives;
- people who have their own homes but who often stay in each other's homes; and
- people who live without a partner.[4]

Benefits for lone parents are intrinsically problematic, because before it is possible to give them, one has to distinguish one-parent families from two-parent families. Every benefit for lone parents has, then, to have a 'cohabitation rule' – a rule that means that two adults living together as if they were a couple are treated in the same way as any other couple. There would not be a problem if couples were always in the same position as two individuals, but they aren't. The resources of couples are aggregated – treated as if they were a single income. This used to be the case for adult children, too, in the days of the pre-war means test, but now it only applies to couples. If there were no cohabitation rule, every family could claim, and if the benefit was for people on low incomes, then any member of a couple who did not have an income could claim, irrespective of the income of their partner.

Cohabitation rules have a bad name; for the most part, it is deserved. Formally, whether or not a couple is cohabiting depends on a number of factors: whether they are members of the same household, whether they share household expenses, how they present their general relationship, whether the relationship is stable and whether they have children. But the benefit system allows mothers and daughters, brothers and sisters or friends to claim independently. The difference between a cohabiting couple and these other types of couple is, bluntly, about sex – where couples are able to show they do not have a sexual relationship, there is an initial presumption that they are not cohabiting.[5] Despite that, investigating officers are not allowed to ask about sex. There are difficulties for claimants in understanding their position, and myths abound – like the often-repeated, fictitious, belief that cohabitation only happens if someone stays three nights a week. (This is obviously wrong: a married couple where the man is working away from home is still cohabiting, even though they see each other only for short breaks.) Odd as it may sound to people who have never been in this position, lone parents do not always know whether they are single or not. During separation, people often cannot tell if their position is permanent. During the process of forming a new relationship, they often do not know whether or not their situation has stabilised. Life is rarely as clear-cut as the rules suppose.

---

4  K Rowlingson and S Mackay (2002) *Lone parent families*, Harlow: Pearson Education, p 67.
5  CIS/87/1993, cited J Mesher, P Wood, R Poynter, N Wikeley, D Bonner (2009) *Social security legislation 2009/10, volume II: Income Support, Jobseeker's Allowance, State Pensions Credit and the Social Fund*, London: Sweet and Maxwell, p 207.

Cohabitation rules have some perverse implications. Phillips argues that a cohabitation rule discourages people from forming permanent relationships: temporary relationships carry no financial penalty, but permanent relationships do. It penalises people for having children within a relationship, because that implies permanency. It discourages claimants from allowing people not on benefit to live with the household.[6] It assumes that someone who is not a parent takes on, by virtue of a sexual relationship, the responsibility to support their sexual partner and that partner's family. That assumption seems increasingly questionable in circumstances where children, even in established second families, are usually supported by the absent parent.

These are, however, principally implications for equity, rather than the behaviour of families – there is no conclusive evidence that any of these factors affects people's family structures at all.[7] The main issue about cohabitation rules is that they treat certain families inappropriately. The alternative is, however, not to have benefits for lone parents at all. There are various ways the issues could be managed instead – to treat each person in a household as a separate individual; to direct benefits to children; to give benefits to households rather than to individuals. The problem with all of them is that they fail to address the specific disadvantage of one-parent families. There seems to be little choice.

## The growth in lone parenthood

When Beveridge wrote his report, lone parenthood was hardly considered. Apart from the circumstances of widows, it was very much a marginal problem; divorce, Beveridge considered, was not an insurable risk. In subsequent years, society has changed beyond recognition. In 1950, fewer than three couples in every 1,000 divorced; by the 1990s, more than four times as many did, and the rate of divorce has been similar since then.[8] Living together without being married is also important. 70% of couples who marry have lived together first, a trend that seems to stem from a cultural change in the 1970s.[9] Many couples do not marry, and so when they separate they do not divorce. They may, however, have children. In 1964, a quarter of children born outside marriage were registered by both parents; in 2008, 86% were, and 65% were to two parents living at the same address.[10] The point at which a woman becomes a lone parent is often not

---

[6] M Phillips (1981) 'Favourable family impact as an object of means support policy', in P.G Brown et al (eds) *Income support*, Totowa, NJ: Rowman and Littlefield.

[7] B Stafford and S Roberts (2009) *The impact of financial incentives in welfare systems of family structure*, London: Department for Work and Pensions.

[8] Office for National Statistics (2010) *Social Trends 40*, Basingstoke: Palgrave Macmillan, p 22.

[9] H Land and J Lewis (1997) *The emergence of lone motherhood as a problem in late twentieth century Britain*, London: London School of Economics/STICERD.

[10] Office for National Statistics (2010) p 24.

when she has a child, but when cohabitation breaks down. The crude figures do not give the full sense of the complexity of the issues: many people have had children while cohabiting outside marriage, or will have passed through a series of formal statuses.

There are strong links between marital dissolution and unemployment, whether the unemployment precedes the marriage or happens during the marriage.[11] Cohabiting parents are likely to be on very low incomes,[12] and cohabiting fathers are particularly likely to have been unemployed.[13] The link between economic insecurity and instability in marital relationships has been confirmed in cross-national research in the UK, the Netherlands, Italy, France, Denmark and Spain.[14] People are brought into contact with social security precisely because of their economic vulnerability. The same vulnerability means that they are more likely to experience family breakdown or to have children outside stable family relationships.

There have also been increasing numbers of children born to people who are not married, though a large part of this relates to cohabitation rather than unplanned pregnancy. Unmarried mothers tend to be younger than others, because with or without children older women are more likely to be separated or divorced. Despite the preconceptions of government,[15] this has very little to do with sex education. Figures from the United States show that women who are poor for a period prior to pregnancy are much more likely to have children when they are not married.[16] Children are born to unmarried women not simply because unmarried women get pregnant, but because women are choosing to have the baby without marrying. They have the options of terminating the pregnancy, or of marrying. The figures on termination are very striking. Middle-class girls, like poor girls, also get pregnant. There is, however, a huge differential in the decision about whether or not to have an abortion.[17] Poor young women have much less chance of higher education, and they do not have many career prospects. They are likely to think that if they do get pregnant, they wanted eventually to have a baby, and they may as well have a baby now as later. Having a baby

---

[11] R Lampard (1994) 'An examination of the relationship between marital dissolution and unemployment', in D Gallie, C Marsh and C Vogler (eds) *Social change and the experience of unemployment*, Oxford: Oxford University Press.

[12] K Kiernan and G Mueller (1998) *The divorced and who divorces?*, London: London School of Economics and Political Science.

[13] K Kiernan and V Estaugh (1993) 'Parents who cohabit poorer than those who marry', *The Guardian*, 1 June, p 4.

[14] S Paugam (1996) 'Poverty and social disqualification', *Journal of European Social Policy*, vol 6, no 4, pp 287-303.

[15] Social Exclusion Unit (1999).

[16] C S Fischer, M Hout, M Jankowski, S Lucas, A Swidler and K Voss (1996) *Inequality by design*, Princeton, NJ: Princeton University Press, p 94.

[17] B Gillam (1997) *The facts about teenage pregnancies*, London: Cassell.

in these circumstances is a positive choice.[18] The decision not to marry can be explained as a rational assessment of economic interest. Several analyses have explained this pattern in terms of the relative economic position of men and women.[19] The economic pressure on lone parents is to separate from partners who are unable to support them or pay their own way. It is possible to see poverty as the consequence of unmarried motherhood; the effect of having a child on education, employment and the establishment of material possessions is considerable. But it is also possible to see the growth of lone parenthood as a consequence of poverty.

## Child Support

Because lone parenthood often stems from a breakdown in relationships, child support has become one of the central issues. Child support is financial support by an absent parent, typically the father. For most of the post-war period, it has been paid through maintenance agreements, either made voluntarily or through court orders. Although maintenance was supposed to meet the financial needs of dependent children, maintenance orders were often low relative to the father's salary, and they were liable to be paid intermittently if at all. Prior to the reform of the system, there was a general fall in the numbers of families on low incomes where the mother received any maintenance. In 1979, half the lone parents on benefit received maintenance; by 1991, it was down to a quarter. The decline reflects an increase in the number of unmarried and never-married mothers, as well as the increasing likelihood that the man would be unemployed and less able to make a meaningful financial contribution. Government policy in the 1990s has emphasised the responsibility of the absent parent, and the Child Support Act was passed in 1991, in an attempt to reverse the trend.

The reforms were ill judged, and spectacularly ineffective. There were several contributory factors. First, the initial calculation was extremely complex. It had to take into account the circumstances, income and liabilities of both parents, and the calculation was based on the difference between the net incomes of the two parents, adjusted for their liabilities. Means tests are difficult to administer at the best of times; the effect of multiple calculations generated confusion and disputes. Second, the Child Support system was aimed at people on Income Support, with the main intention of saving money. There was no benefit to either parent. This has to be seen in the context of relationship breakdowns, where many women do not want contact with their previous partner. Third, the measures generated a sense of

---

[18] I Allen and S Dowling (1998) *Teenage mothers: Decisions and outcomes*, London: Policy Studies Institute.

[19] H Rodman (1971) *Lower class families: The culture of poverty in Negro Trinidad*, London: Oxford University Press; W Wilson (1987) *The truly disadvantaged*, Chicago, IL: University of Chicago Press.

injustice, both from couples who had made financial agreements, including 'clean break' settlements, and particularly from fathers, many of whom are deliberately denied contact with their children by their former wives. A government White Paper suggests that 40% of women admit to thwarting their partner's attempts to keep contact, and not altogether coincidentally, 40% of fathers lose contact with their children after two years.[20] The Child Support Agency, which was appointed to do the calculations, rapidly fell behind; this exacerbated the problems, where fathers were presented retrospectively with bills for thousands of pounds. The system was reformed in 2001, with the substitution of a more comprehensible formula: absent parents were to pay 15% of their income after tax for one child, 20% for two and 25% for three or more. Like all such formulas, it represented rough justice: some people have responsibilities for second families, some are being denied contact with their children and some are not able to pay. The Child Maintenance and Enforcement Commission formally replaced the CSA in 2008, while carrying over many of the cases and calculations. Its functions currently are being absorbed back into the DWP, but it is estimated that it will be 2014 or 2015 before the revised procedures are fully implemented. Probably the most significant change is the simplest: couples will now have the option of negotiating voluntary agreements, rather than using the statutory system. Because many divorced couples already have such an agreement, that should remove much of the workload rapidly.

## Benefits for lone parents

Lone parents tend to be on low incomes. That means they are more likely than others to claim benefits, but the main issue is not about numbers: it is whether lone parents can be dealt with under the same rules as couples. There may be one less person to feed and clothe, but lone parents still have the expense of running the household. Benefits for lone parents have attempted to remove some of the disadvantage experienced by one-parent households, by ensuring that the qualifying levels of benefit for lone parents are the same as for a couple. This is the rule on Working Tax Credit, where the allowance for a lone parent is the same as the allowance for a couple; it is almost (but not quite) true of the calculation of Housing Benefit, where the calculation for lone parents includes a 'premium' to bridge the gap.

The issues of unemployment among lone parents has not been addressed very clearly. Many lone parents do work, but unlike most other unemployed claimants, lone parents are not required to make themselves available for work. After 1997, lone parents were encouraged to take part in the New Deal, with an emphasis on employment; this seems to have had some impact above the

---

[20] Department of Social Security (1999) *A new contract for welfare: Children's rights and parents' responsibilities*, Cm 4349, London: The Stationery Office.

generally favourable employment conditions.[21] A more aggressive policy is now being rolled out in much less propitious circumstances. Policy makers have been ambivalent about the desirability of enforcing rules about work in the way as they are enforced in the United States, but there is an increasing stress on 'activation' for work. The Freud report suggested that lone parents should be required to be available for work after their youngest child reaches 12, and that as childcare becomes more available, the age should fall.[22] In the event, the requirement to be available for work has now been implemented for lone parents whose youngest child is over 7.

Income Support has special rules allowing lone parents to keep more than others when they do work (up to £20). Housing Benefit allows lone parents up to £25. By comparison with couples, then, the rules are slightly favourable to lone parents. However, the principal benefits that used to be available for lone parents are no longer there. Over 30 years ago, the Finer Report proposed the establishment of a Guaranteed Maintenance Allowance for one-parent families.[23] This never happened, but the Labour government did introduce Child Benefit Increase, a small addition to Child Benefit made for one-parent families; it was renamed One Parent Benefit in 1981. The case for One Parent Benefit was that it was universal, non-means tested and that it recognised that one-parent families have extra income needs. The case against was that, like Child Benefit, it was not worth claiming for lone parents on Income Support; take-up was poor, possibly because it was not worth claiming; and that it was very uncertain whether a benefit which picks out a stigmatised group can avoid being stigmatised itself. The benefit proved politically very vulnerable to criticism, and it has now been scrapped. Similarly, the premium for lone parents on Income Support has also been removed. The imposition of liability of the absent parent has effectively replaced this approach altogether.

## QUESTIONS FOR DISCUSSION

Should the benefits for lone parents be restored?
Should lone parents be expected to work?

---

[21] T Knijn, C Martin and J Millar (2007) 'Activation as a common framework for social policies towards lone parents', *Social Policy and Administration*, vol 48, no 6, pp 638-52.

[22] D Freud (2007) *Reducing dependency, increasing opportunity,* London: DWP, p 91.

[23] Cmnd 5629 (1974) *Report of the Committee on One-Parent Families,* London: HMSO.

# Chapter 20

# Unemployed people

Provision for unemployed people has been driven by myths about 'incentives to work' and the belief that unemployment is a matter of individual choice. After the virtual collapse of the National Insurance system for unemployed people, provision for unemployment has shifted to a means-tested system with a heavy emphasis on preparation for work and the personal responsibility of the claimant.

## Unemployment

Benefits for unemployed people have generally been provided in a two-tier structure, either insurance based or means tested. These structures are now combined in one benefit, Jobseeker's Allowance. One of the most striking developments in social security policy in the last twenty years has been the collapse of the National Insurance system as it applied to unemployment. By the time Unemployment Benefit was reformed in 1996, only 8% of unemployed people had any National Insurance entitlement.

Part of this reflected the changing pattern of unemployment. Beveridge outlined several kinds of unemployment:[1]

- *Technical* People become unemployed because their skills are made redundant, or because work is replaced by machines. Unemployment has fallen disproportionately on people in social classes IV and V.
- *Cyclical* Industry relies on demand from consumers to keep going; in a slump, this demand is not there. Primary producing industries – like heavy engineering or energy – are affected first; consumer industries follow.
- *Casual* This is less important now than in Beveridge's day; it referred to people who looked for work day by day (like dockers) or week by week.
- *Strikes and lockouts* These are not treated as 'unemployment' officially; they may lead to benefit claims, but entitlements are restricted.
- *Seasonal* Certain trades, like building and hotels, take on people at some times of year and drop them at others.
- *Voluntary* Voluntary unemployment is when a person is unwilling to work at the market wage.
- *Frictional* This refers to people changing jobs.

---

[1] W Beveridge (1944) *Full employment in a free society*, London: Allen & Unwin.

The Beveridge scheme was principally concerned with casual, seasonal and frictional unemployment; for the rest, he had assumed full employment. The National Insurance scheme's Unemployment Benefit was designed to deal with short-term interruptions in employment. People could gain benefit, for example, for some days in the week, if they were working short time or casually; if they worked seasonally, they would re-establish their entitlement to benefit for future years during the time when they worked, but Unemployment Benefit stopped after a year. National Insurance was never intended to cope with long-term unemployment. Indeed, the Minister of National Insurance who brought in the Beveridge plan in 1946 commented: 'If we were − God forbid that we should − to allow ourselves to drift back to the mass unemployment of the inter-war years, this scheme would be sunk.'[2]

Long-term unemployment accelerated in the slump of the 1980s, as Britain's manufacturing industries went into terminal decline. It increased dramatically over the period up to 1988, and again, less dramatically from 1994 − though the slower pace at that point may have disguised a no less dramatic rise in the numbers of unemployed people classified as incapacitated. The growth in long-term unemployment takes place at a different speed from the growth in unemployment overall. Unemployment can be seen as a reverse queue; the shorter the time you have waited, the more likely you are to be re-employed. The image, if it helps, is like filling a balloon from a tap: most of the water runs out the neck, but the balloon gets slowly largely and larger as some of it stays. While general unemployment was increasing, long-term unemployment − initially counted as people out of work for six months, and then for a year − increased far more. Changes in the basis of the unemployment count tended to reduce the apparent totals: they included, for example, the removal from the count of people who were registered for work but not claiming benefit, and rises in figures for lone parents, disabled people and incapacity. Benefit entitlement is crucial to whether and how people register, which is why more men than women are recorded as being long-term unemployed.[3]

As unemployment increased in the 1990s, relatively few unemployed people were being covered by National Insurance. This lay behind the change to Jobseeker's Allowance in late 1996. JSA still has an element relating to insurance, nominally covering the first six months. This element is not means tested and is not affected by capital − like redundancy payments − or income that is not from earnings, though earnings indicate that a person is not unemployed.

---

[2] *Hansard*, 6 February 1946, cited in A B Atkinson (1988) *Income maintenance for the unemployed in Britain and the response to high unemployment*, London: Suntory Toyota International Centre for Economics and Related Disciplines, p 2.

[3] National Statistics (2010) *Labour Force Survey: Unemployment by age and duration* (www.statistics.gov.uk/STATBASE/xsdataset.asp?More=Y&vlnk=1385&All=Y&B2.x=77&B2.y=9).

The means-tested element, however, dominates. The rules for income-related JSA were inherited directly from Income Support.

## The economic implications of unemployment benefits

Unemployment benefits protect people, at least to some degree, from the vicissitudes of unemployment. Some economists see this as way of supporting the economy. The effect of provision for unemployment is to act as an economic regulator: when production falls, the amount paid in benefits increases, and this helps to shore up aggregate demand and protect the economy.[4] It has been more common, however, for economists to view unemployment benefit as a wage for not working, limiting the wage for which people are willing to work.[5] This has the effect of reducing the supply of labour at lower wages. The Conservative government in the 1990s believed that benefits force wage rates up and that this increases unemployment because employers then cannot afford to take people on. When they were in opposition, they used the same model to argue that a minimum wage would increase unemployment; it did not, and they later recanted.

There are three main reasons why benefits for unemployed people do not adversely affect unemployment. The first is that there are countervailing economic pressures: employment also depends on the level of demand in the economy, growth and productivity, and forcing down wages does not necessarily help any of these. Second, unemployment benefits are so very far below the level of wages available that they have minimal impacts on the choice of economic behaviour for employed people. Third, unemployment benefits simply don't work that way. Atkinson points to five common assumptions in the economic literature:

(a) the benefit is paid irrespective of the reasons for entry into unemployment
(b) there are no contribution conditions related to past employment
(c) the benefit is not related to past earnings in employment, and is usually assumed to be a constant flat-rate amount
(d) the benefit is paid independently of the recipient's efforts to search for new work, or of availability for work
(e) the benefit is paid for an unlimited duration.

'Real world benefits', he notes, 'do not satisfy these assumptions.'[6]

---

[4] See, for example, J Richardson (1960) *Economic and financial aspects of social security*, London: George Allen & Unwin, pp 215 ff.
[5] Cited in A Atkinson (1990) *Institutional features of unemployment insurance and the working of the labour market*, London: Suntory-Toyota Centre for Economics and Related Disciplines.
[6] Atkinson (1990), p 2.

The coalition government has been concerned with the impact of the benefits system on incentives to work. 'The benefits system as it stands often provides incentives to stay on benefits rather than take on a job.'[7] In the government's view, the benefits which are available to people out of work have fostered long-term dependency – 1.4 million claimants out of 5 million are receiving out of work benefits. That figure relies heavily on a classification of people with incapacity or severe disabilities as if they were part of the labour market.

Unemployed people are said to have an 'incentive to work' if they stand to gain financially from working. The process of 'incentives' can be understood in two very different ways. The first is the view that the way people behave in aggregate is directly affected by the balance of costs and benefits they experience. Economics is about aggregate behaviour – not what each person does, but what more or fewer people do in responding to influences. A demand function, for example, is a description of the behaviour of everyone taken together, illustrating the impact of changes in price and availability on the quantities that will be consumed under specified conditions. Quantities can be affected either by changes in price (moving along the demand function) or changes in basic conditions (shifting the demand function). There is no assumption or implication in economic theory that an inducement will generally lead to a particular individual response, or even that it will lead to a uniform aggregate response. That depends on aggregate responsiveness, or 'elasticity'. Where functions are inelastic, changes in price may make little or no difference.

The economic approach could be used consistently with the government's view – the argument would be that dependency is produced cumulatively by incentive effects – but that is not where the emphasis tends to fall. When people comment on the impact of benefits on 'incentives to work', they are usually concerned not with aggregate behaviour – about which there is surprisingly little good evidence – but the circumstances of individuals. The second and more common view of incentives is that they are about rewards and punishments, rather than economic behaviour. People who receive benefits are being given a disincentive to work, presumably in the same way as people who receive assistance with funerals are being given a disincentive to stay alive. Charles Murray's book *Losing ground* begins with three premises:

1. People respond to incentives and disincentives. Sticks and carrots work.
2. People are not inherently hard working or moral. In the absence of countervailing influences, people will avoid work and be amoral.
3. People must be held responsible for their actions. ...[8]

---

[7]  Cm 7913 (2010) *21st century welfare,* London: DWP, p 2.

[8]  C Murray (1984) *Losing ground*, New York: Basic Books, p 146.

Murray presents his work as an example of 'rational choice', which is about the behaviour of the average individual, but there is nothing in these three assumptions that relates to the way that either a 'rational' person would behave, or that real people might. The statement that 'sticks and carrots work' is based in behaviourism, the psychology of stimulus and response. If a stimulus is present, the argument runs, then a response should follow. This may or may not be true, but it has very little to do with economic argument. Aggregate decisions depend on aggregate preferences, and Murray is not interested in preferences. Rational decisions depend on the balance between costs and benefits, and Murray is not looking at either the non-economic costs or at the opportunity costs of not working.

The second assumption, that people will avoid work given the chance, is an empirical statement, but one that bears only limited resemblance to real life.[9] People work for all kinds of reasons, including money, but also including status, social contact, individual priorities and personal fulfilment. (If someone says, for example, that they work because 'I just need to get out of the house', they are referring to a non-financial motive.) The third statement really gives it away. More important than any theory of behaviour is that this view of rewards and punishments reflects a set of moral judgements. The sticks and carrots are there not because they work, but because some people think that is how donkeys should be treated.

## Box 20.1: Jobseeker's Allowance

Jobseeker's Allowance is a combination of different schemes. The larger part of JSA is a basic means-tested benefit, on the pattern described in Chapter 8. There is also, however, a contribution-based benefit, which works on the principles outlined in Chapter 7.

To claim JSA, claimants must be unemployed; if the claim is for contribution-based JSA and they have a partner, the partner must also be workless. There is a three-day waiting period, and some people move in and out of work; in those circumstances there are 'linking rules' so that periods of unemployment are linked together and treated as one claim.

While claimants are receiving Jobseeker's Allowance they have to be 'available for work', which means being willing and able to take up work immediately, and they have to be 'actively seeking work', taking three or more steps each week to find a job. 'Steps' include things like applying for jobs, preparing a CV or getting advice. What claimants actually have to do depends on the 'Jobseeker's Agreement' they have to make – it is possible that the agreement means that they cannot take steps in a particular

---

[9]   See, for example, R Gebauer and G Vobruba (2003) 'The open unemployment trap', *Journal of Social Policy*, vol 32, no 4, pp 571–87.

week[10] — and they can make some reasonable restrictions on the basis of child care or physical limitations. There are penalties for refusing suitable offers of employment; for voluntary unemployment, including leaving a job without good cause; and for being fired for misconduct.

## The unemployment trap

Much concern has been expressed that people are 'better off on the dole' and that this will undermine incentives to work. It has been called the 'unemployment trap'. *The Daily Express* reported in September 2008, for example: 'YOU ARE BETTER OFF ON BENEFITS. Millions of benefits claimants are better off living on handouts than getting a job, a government report confirmed yesterday.'[11] The 'government report' in question was the *Tax benefit model tables*,[12] a series of hypothetical calculations used to examine possible permutations of benefits and income. The highest possible 'replacement ratio' shown in those tables was for a married couple living in social housing with no children on £100 per week (about half the minimum wage for a full-time week); they would get 95% of their income in work while on benefits. In other words, the 'government report' showed no such thing. Benefit rates in the UK are spectacularly lower than wages. It is possible for people to be worse off in work than on the dole, because people who work may have expenses like travel and childcare that people on benefits do not have, but it is unusual: much more typically, people in work find themselves only a little better off after tax and work costs are taken into account.

Jobcentre Plus offices offer 'in work calculations' for claimants, so that they can see what the implications of taking employment will be. These calculations are difficult and sometimes inconsistent,[13] but there is little indication they make much difference. The incentive for any individual to work depends on that individual's earning power, not on the lowest wage paid anywhere. It is true, for example, that people with mortgages on Jobseeker's Allowance can get assistance after several months that brings their income above some people on low wages. However, almost all these people have taken a massive cut in income; they would not have got a mortgage otherwise. It is unlikely that people will actually be worse off, but the difference, after work expenses, may be very limited. Some people may be worse off if they have substantial expenses in work — typically expenses

---

[10] J Mesher, P Wood, R Poynter, N Wikeley, D Bonner (2009) *Social security legislation 2009/10, volume II: Income Support, Jobseeker's Allowance, State Pensions Credit and the Social Fund*, London: Sweet and Maxwell, pp 63-4.

[11] M Hall (2008) 'You are better off on benefits', *Daily Express*, 26 September.

[12] Department for Work and Pensions (2008) *Tax benefit model tables*, April (http://research. dwp.gov.uk/asd/asd1/tbm/TBMT_2008.pdf).

[13] House of Commons Work and Pensions Committee (2007) *Benefits simplification*, HC 461, London: The Stationery Office, ch 3.

relating to travel or childcare. There may also be specific liabilities incurred as a result of moving back to work.

The main response to this has been the combination of the minimum wage, with the benefits available to people in work: Child Benefit, Housing Benefit and Tax Credits. Several bonuses have been used to remove financial obstacles to returning to work. They include:

- a back-to-work bonus, discontinued in October 2004, and a lone parent run-on, for single parents in a similar position;
- a mortgage interest run-on, or extended payments of Housing Benefit, for people with liabilities for housing payments;
- a child maintenance bonus, for people who would incur increased liabilities for child maintenance on a return to work;
- Job Grant, a lump sum for returning to work.

A 'better off in work credit' is due for introduction in January 2011, but it is not really consistent with the coalition's commitment to improve incentives by simplifying benefits. A consultation paper published in July 2010 argues for a more integrated system, bringing together out of work benefits and Tax Credits, where the marginal rate of deduction - the 'poverty trap' - can be limited to 75%.[14]

One of the key weaknesses in all these approaches is the assumption that the calculation that people make when they return to work is principally based on relative levels of income. It is questionable whether that is really what people focus on. The question that people want answered is often 'what happens if ...?', not 'how much will I get?' Research for the Joseph Rowntree Foundation comments that 'employment of the "wrong sort" – low paid and insecure – could in some cases be worse than no employment at all because of the instability it brings to a family's finances.'[15] The labour market is often unstable, particularly in the lower income ranges, and the perceived stability of future income and employment is at least as important as the financial amount.

## Workfare and welfare to work

The belief that unemployed people are unemployed through idleness and personal choice goes back a long way. It remains influential in several cultures, most notably the liberal, English-speaking regimes of the United States, Australia and the UK. The idea of 'Workfare' developed in the US as a way of requiring

---

[14] Cm 7913 (2010).
[15] C Goulden (2010) *Cycles of poverty, unemployment and low pay*, York: Joseph Rowntree Foundation.

unemployed people to work as a condition of receiving benefit.[16] At the time, most beneficiaries in the US were on the federal program of Aid to Families with Dependent Children, a benefit aimed principally at lone parents. (AFDC has now been replaced by Temporary Aid to Needy Families.) Workfare made it a condition of receiving benefits that people should work for their benefit — a principle which harks back to the Poor Law, with its combination of 'setting the poor on work' and deterrent hardship. The influence of US models on the UK is hard to explain rationally — the economies and social systems have little in common, and the US is a notorious welfare laggard — but there was certainly a reflection of US ideas in the British 'New Deal'[17] (ironically, a term which in the past was associated in the US with public job creation and publicly sponsored economic development) and the current emphasis on individualised employability programmes. However, there is also a European influence: the Scandinavian system of 'activation' aims to re-engage unemployed people in the labour market through a programme of activity, job search and training.[18] The New Deal was essentially an activation programme rather than a system of Workfare,[19] seeking to engage people, including lone parents and people with disabilities, in the labour market. The New Deal for Young People, for example, offered four options for claimants: subsidised employment, education, environmental work or voluntary work. Young people do not have the option of non-participation.

Welfare to work takes in a wide range of programmes and policies, going well beyond social security. Alex Bryson lists nine categories of programme:

- Assistance with job searches
- Training provision (such as Modern Apprenticeships)
- Job sampling (for example, work trials, options for employers to test the water etc)
- 'Make work' schemes (the Environment Task Force)
- Systems of review, which are considered later in this chapter
- Assistance to employers (like wage subsidies)
- 'Making work pay', through the National Minimum Wage and benefits to support people in work
- Community-based initiatives, like Employment Zones and Action Teams for Jobs, and

---

[16] S Miller and J Markle (2002) 'Social policy in the US: workfare and the American low-wage labour market', in P Townsend and D Gordon (eds) *World poverty*, Bristol: The Policy Press.

[17] A Daguerre (2004) 'Importing workfare', *Social Policy and Administration*, vol 38, no 1, pp 41-56.

[18] N Gilbert and R van Voorhuis (eds) (2001) *Activating the unemployed*, New Brunswick, NJ: Transaction.

[19] S Wright (2002) 'Activating the unemployed: the street-level implementation of UK policy', in J Clasen (ed) *What future for social security?*, Bristol: The Policy Press.

- Assistance with caring responsibilities (for example, parental leave and Tax Credits).[20]

The government is in the process of replacing many of these measures. For the first year of unemployment, most claimants will begin with support from Jobcentre Plus. Those who have been claiming for a year, along with others in certain specially vulnerable categories like ex-prisoners and homeless people, will be put on a single Work Programme, offering a personalised response to unemployed claimants.[21] No programme aimed at several million people can offer a uniform response; whatever the shape of the reform, it is in the nature of the exercise that it will incorporate some, and possibly all, of the kinds of measure listed here.

Much of this provision will be made by commissioning private sector firms to deliver the service. The approach has not been seriously evaluated. The Office for Government Commerce found that:

> the DWP's commercial strategies have been 'consistently inconsistent'; contracts have not always been sufficiently outcome-focused. DWP are aware of these legacy issues and are making plans to address them. However, it is not clear DWP currently has the commercial capacity, the management information or the appropriate organisational structure in place to manage providers and markets successfully.[22]

In the case of employment support for incapacity benefits, the National Audit Office commented that 'aspects of the Department's contracting practice for Pathways were undesirable and in other circumstances should not be repeated'. The performance of private contractors was worse than Jobcentre Plus staff; there were inadequate controls over sub-contractors; and the contractors had seriously underestimated the difficulty of dealing with the client group.[23] The Work Programme will pay contractors by results, but it still leaves the DWP with little effective control over the type or quality of work done.

The conditions of work programmes are separable from the rules relating to the benefits themselves. If we focus more specifically on the rules of unemployment benefits, we can see that people have been formally encouraged to seek work in several ways:

---

[20] A Bryson (2003) 'Permanent revolution', *Benefits*, vol 11, no 1, pp 11-17.

[21] Conservative Party (2010) *Invitation to join the government of Britain*, London: Conservative Party, p 16.

[22] Office of Government Commerce (2007) *Procurement Capability Review Programme*, London: The Stationery Office, p 9.

[23] National Audit Office (2010) *Support to incapacity benefit claimants through Pathways to Work*, HC21 2010-11, London: The Stationery Office, pp 10-11.

- Benefits for unemployment are stopped for up to 26 weeks for people who have refused a suitable job, become unemployed 'voluntarily' or through 'misconduct'. The 26 week period has too often been seen as the norm, and the Social Security Commissioners, who heard most appeals before the reform of the tribunal system, were critical: 'The 26 week period is not a starting point. It is a maximum.'[24] The Conservative Party manifesto of 2010 proposed that 'people who refuse to accept reasonable job offers could forfeit their benefit for up to three years';[25] the specific pledge is not, however, in the Coalition's programme for government.[26]

- Claimants are asked to attend interviews to discuss their efforts in seeking work. Many claimants subsequently cease to claim. This began with the system of 'Unemployment Review', and was later superseded by 'Restart', then 'Jobseeker's Interview' and 'ONE', which was the pilot scheme for Jobcentre Plus. New claimants are required to sign a Jobseeker's Agreement.

- Claimants are required to be 'actively seeking work'. They have to give evidence that they have taken more than two 'steps' towards employment in every week they are unemployed. A 'step' can be a range of actions, including job applications, getting information about jobs, preparing a CV or investigating a career opening. Claimants who fail to comply can be subject to a 'jobseeker's direction' – effectively an instruction to take steps, such as an order to apply for a particular job, to attend a training course, or even to change one's appearance. There are sanctions for failure to comply, for being violent or abusive, and for making oneself less employable.

- 'Full-time' work has been redefined as being 16 hours a week. This means anyone working for at least this will be able to claim Tax Credits rather than Jobseeker's Allowance. At the same time, there are certain disincentives to part-time employment: a claimant found to be working part time can be assumed to be employed and have benefit stopped, and an unemployed person who earns while on JSA loses all income over £5. A person in part-time employment whose spouse loses work may have to give up virtually all the income.

- Several training and work-based schemes have effectively been compulsory, because claimants will have benefits stopped for not participating. Examples for young people have included the New Deal for Young People, Gateway to Work and the Community Task Force. For older people and the long-term unemployed there have been the Flexible New

---

[24] Commissioner Levenson, cited in Mesher, Wood, Poynter, Wikeley, Bonner (2009), p 94.

[25] Conservative Party (2010) *Invitation to join the government of Britain*, London: Conservative Party, p 16.

[26] HM Government (2010) *The coalition: Our programme for government*, London: Cabinet Office, p 23.

Deal and Employment Zone programmes. The Welfare Reform Act 2009 made provision for a scheme based on workfare in the United States, and for mandatory work trials for people who have been on JSA for six months.

- From 2013, Housing Benefit for Jobseeker's Allowance claimants will be cut by 10% after one year, to encourage people to look for work and housing elsewhere.

The main reservation to make about all provision of this sort is that it seems to be centred on the idea that unemployment is an individual situation and a matter of personal choice. Effective employment policy depends on the demand for labour as well as willingness to work, and there are large swathes of the UK where there is no work for people without specialised skills (and little enough for those who have them). There was once a time when governments were committed to the maintenance of full employment. Keynes had argued that paying people to do useful jobs may be wiser than paying them benefits to do nothing.[27] This was the position of both Labour and Conservative governments after 1944. It was not abandoned until 1970, when concerns about other economic objectives (principally the control of inflation and promotion of growth) seemed more pressing to the government of the day. Governments do know how to avoid unemployment – they did it for nearly thirty years – but the issue of unemployment is no longer considered to have priority over other economic objectives. That discussion, however, would take us beyond the bounds of social security policy.

## QUESTIONS FOR DISCUSSION

Why work?
What would happen if there were no benefits for unemployment?

---

[27] J M Keynes (1936) *The general theory of employment, interest and money*, London: Macmillan, p 129.

# Chapter 21

# Benefits for the poor

A small number of benefits are aimed at people who are 'poor', in a different way to the contingency-based benefits considered up to this point. These are not necessarily means-tested benefits, but rather benefits that have been constructed to respond to different understandings of poverty. They include benefits for people who fall below minimum income standards, earnings replacement benefits, benefits for people in material need and benefits for people who are socially excluded.

The idea of poverty is much broader than the issue of social security, and there are many potential aspects of a discussion of poverty that would not belong in this book.[1] Poverty is important for consideration of social security in two ways. The first is that the relief of poverty is often seen, rightly or wrongly, as a central aim of the social security system – one of the key tests of whether or not social security is operating effectively is whether people continue to be poor after benefits are paid. That issue is dealt with in the course of Part V. In the context of this part of the book, the reason for considering poverty is rather more specific: some benefits are benefits for poor people, in the same way as there are benefits for 'old people' or 'people with disabilities'.

A focus on 'the poor' is potentially controversial. It seems to undermine the institutional aspirations of the benefits system. There is a risk that defining people as 'the poor' treats them in some sense as an alien population – it 'others' them.[2] Beyond that, there are concerns that a disproportionate focus on a mythical underclass is distorting policy, justifying an emphasis on conditionality and disciplinary interventions. At the same time, there are categories of benefit that may need to be understood in terms of responding to the circumstances of people who are poor. They include:

- benefits for people falling below a *minimum income standard*, such as Income Support;
- benefits for people who are *dependent*, notably the earnings replacement benefits represented by Jobseeker's Allowance, the Employment and Support Allowance and the Guarantee Credit for pensioners;
- benefits for people in *material need*, such as the Social Fund;

---

[1] See P Spicker (2007) *The idea of poverty*, Bristol: The Policy Press.
[2] R Lister (2004) *Poverty*, Cambridge: Polity.

- benefits for people who are *socially excluded*, such as the cash payments made to families, by social workers or the provision of support to people with disabilities through the recently closed Independent Living Fund.

## Poverty and the minimum income threshold

Poverty is not the same thing as a minimum income.[3] When poverty is discussed in the context of social security benefits, however, it tends to be identified with income below a particular threshold. The association of the two stems from research at the end of the 19th century. When Charles Booth undertook his monumental study of poverty in London, he clearly had a broad understanding of what poverty was, and what kind of problems might need to be considered.[4] Booth was not especially concerned with benefits or the Poor Law; his enquiry took into account family, housing, work, educational issues and 'spiritual' needs. In the course of his research, however, one of his ideas was to have a particular influence on the development of policy. Booth suggested there was a 'poverty line' – a general range of income (not a threshold) where people started to be poor, generally associated with the difference between full-time workers and others. This was received dismissively: Booth suggested that people started to be poor on less than 18 to 21 shillings a week, when one of his critics suggested it was perfectly possible to live on 5 shillings a week. That, Booth retorted, may well be true; they might live on 5 shillings a week, but they would be poor if they did. In the course of the argument, Booth took the crucial step of trying to explain how people spent their household budgets, and offered some general illustrations. The household budgets became the centre of the political debate – poor people who spent money on extravagances like a cup of tea were considered profligate – and this was the germ for the work of Seebohm Rowntree.

Rowntree felt that Booth had been insufficiently precise, and he wanted to put the numbers of people in poverty beyond dispute. To do this he defined a minimal household budget – a budget that would be impossible to live on in real life, but which would represent an irreducible, unarguable minimum standard.[5] This was Rowntree's measure of 'primary poverty'.[6] The household budgets used in Rowntree's research were the basis for much of the research that followed, and when Beveridge came to devise a standard for social security, it was Rowntree's budgets that he turned to. The National Assistance rates in

---

[3] P Spicker (2007) 'Definitions of poverty: twelve clusters of meaning', in P Spicker, S Alvarez Leguizamon and D Gordon (eds) *Poverty: An international glossary*, London: Zed.

[4] P Spicker (1990) 'Charles Booth: the examination of poverty', *Social Policy and Administration*, vol 24, no 1, pp 21-38.

[5] B S Rowntree (1901) *Poverty: A study of town life*, Bristol: The Policy Press, 2000.

[6] J Veit Wilson (1986) 'Paradigms of poverty: rehabilitation of B.S Rowntree', *Journal of Social Policy*, vol 15, no 1, pp 69-99.

1948 were based, more or less, on Rowntree's 1938 budgets.[7] It was generally considered that benefits provided in some sense an adequate minimum benefit. In an important sense, the idea that benefits were going to eradicate the problem of poverty was 'built in' to the system.

The benefit rates started, however, with some initial differences from Rowntree's budgets. Over time, the erratic process of uprating, altering and trimming came to mean that they bore less and less relationship to the minimum subsistence level that Rowntree had intended.

- Beveridge used lower figures than Rowntree.[8]
- The figures were based on 1938, and no allowance was made for inflation.
- The government made adjustments, because of free school meals, which cut the rates for children.
- Later upratings took the rates away from the initial figures. Governments came to accept that benefits should cover more than minimal subsistence: the Macmillan government stated, in 1959, that 'the time has come when it is right to move to a higher standard, so giving them a share in increasing national prosperity.'[9] Through the 1970s, benefits for long-term claimants increased by prices or wages, whichever was greater; this magnified the difference between long-term claimants and others. After this link was broken, later upratings became increasingly politicised and subject to small but incremental alterations.[10]
- Inflation was measured by the general increase in prices, not the items used by Rowntree. Since the 1980s, upratings have been based on a modified version of the Retail Price Index, the 'Rossi Index', which initially excluded housing costs and Council Tax but later had to be modified to take into account costs that claimants continued to be liable for.[11] (After 2010 upratings were geared to a different 'Consumer Price Index', which produces a consistently lower measure of inflation.[12])
- No direct account has been taken of the continued availability or non-availability of 'poverty goods' – second-hand items, cheap foodstuffs, etc.

---

[7] J Veit Wilson (1992) 'Muddle or mendacity? The Beveridge Committee and the poverty line', *Journal of Social Policy*, vol 21, no 3, pp 269-302.

[8] F Field (1985) *What price a child?*, London: Policy Studies Institute.

[9] Ministry of Pension and National Insurance (1959) cited in A B Atkinson (1990) *A national minimum?*, London: Suntory-Toyota International Centre for Economics and Related Disciplines, p 14.

[10] J Bradshaw and T Lynes (1995) *Benefit uprating policy and living standards*, York: Social Policy Research Unit.

[11] Bradshaw and Lynes (1995), pp 17-18.

[12] J Browne and P Levell (2010) *The distributional effect of tax and benefit reforms to be introduced between June 2010 and April 2014*, London: Institute for Fiscal Studies, pp 16-17

- The allowances for dependants were altered in 1980, all the basic rates were restructured in 1988 and there were major revisions in 2000. After 2004, allowances for children were replaced by a different system, the Child Tax Credit.

Although the identification of benefits with low income is most directly linked with means-tested benefits, they are not the same. One reason is that the idea of benefits as providing a minimum subsistence influenced the rates of non-means-tested benefits as much as it did means-tested ones. The rates of National Insurance for basic benefits like Retirement Pension, Unemployment Benefit and Sickness Benefit were supposed to represent a minimally adequate level, and that meant that for most of the early period of the Beveridge scheme – well into the 1970s – the rates broadly speaking tracked the levels of National Assistance and Supplementary Benefit with only minor variations. This arrangement was not enough to mean that people receiving National Insurance benefits did not need to claim means-tested benefits: apart from people with deficient contributions, people who received help with housing costs and people with additional needs also received more from means-tested benefits, implying that their weekly income was less than adequate. The other reason for questioning the link is that means-tested benefits have increasingly been introduced, not to provide a basic minimum, but in the form of thresholds and tapers – a process which began with Rate Rebate in the 1960s and which has gradually extended across a wide range of benefits, including Housing Benefit and Tax Credits.

*The poor and the poorest*[13] was a seminal work in the 'rediscovery' of the poverty people believed had been abolished by the welfare state. Abel Smith and Townsend used the minimum standards set for National Assistance as their basic test of adequacy, and a further test of those rates plus 40% (partly to allow for housing costs, but also partly to emphasise how close many people were to the minimum). In the forty years that have followed, the identification of basic benefit rates with minimum income standards has become increasingly questionable. Despite the protestation that benefits are designed to provide a basic minimum income, the link between benefit rates and minimum standards was always tenuous, and there is no mechanism by which benefit rates can be related to expenditure needs. Most independent research in the intervening period has suggested that benefit rates are not enough to live on.[14]

There is a crucial problem in discussing poverty in terms of benefit rates. Quite simply, putting benefits up defines more people as being 'poor', and putting

---

[13] B Abel-Smith and P Townsend (1965) *The poor and the poorest*, London: Bell.
[14] See, for example, J Bradshaw (2001) 'Child poverty under labour', in G Fimister (ed) *Tackling child poverty in the UK: An end in sight?*, London: Child Poverty Action Group.

them down implies that fewer are. John Veit Wilson has suggested that we should talk about benefit rates not in terms of a standard of 'poverty', but rather of the 'minimum income standard' that governments consider acceptable.[15]

## Benefits and dependency

The idea of dependency, which I referred to at the start of this part of the book, is contentious. Dependency means that people are drawing resources from the state, but we do not say that people who use public roads or who call the police are 'dependent'. 'Dependency' certainly conveys the idea that people need a service, but it also carries some negative implications, suggesting that people are draining resources from others without putting anything back. The idea of 'social protection' also refers to people in need, but it has not come (yet) to carry to same stigma; it covers earned entitlements through insurance, as well as solidaristic and redistributive payments. The characteristic mode of social protection is 'horizontal' redistribution – that is, redistribution between groups, based on their general circumstances rather than low income. The principle of social protection is widely supported: people accept that people in some circumstances need protection, and sometimes they recognise that they may fall into the groups themselves.

Dependency is linked with poverty because, in many people's understanding of the terms, being poor and being on benefits boils down to much the same thing. The sociologist Georg Simmel argued that 'the poor person, sociologically speaking, is the individual who receives assistance because of the lack of means.'[16] There is a circularity here: benefits are for the poor, so people who get benefits must be poor. It does not make much sense when it is looked at closely, but it has been hugely influential: there tends to be the assumption, in the press and in political discourse, that this is both how things are, and how they ought to be. I have written critically about this discourse elsewhere,[17] but in this rather specific context I am concerned only with the way that this is expressed in the structure of benefits. The answer to that rests in the idea of the 'earnings replacement' benefit. There are certain contingencies in which people become dependent; people who are in work do not need such benefits.

Earnings replacement benefits are those benefits that are designed to pay people who are unable to earn through employment. They include Jobseeker's Allowance, Employment and Support Allowance, Carer's Allowance, maternity benefits and pensions. People cannot receive more than one earnings replacement benefit at a time; they are expected not to work while receiving the benefits; if they are found to be working, even if they are not actually being paid, the

---

[15] J Veit Wilson (1998) *Setting adequacy standards*, Bristol: The Policy Press.
[16] G Simmel (1908) 'The poor', *Social problems*, 1965, vol 13, pp 118-39.
[17] P Spicker (2007) *The idea of poverty*, Bristol: The Policy Press, ch 9.

investigators are entitled to assume that the work is remunerative. Earnings replacement is a sort of social protection, rather than poor relief, but it is a very limited sort. It does not protect people from radical interruptions in their incomes, or from financial need. It seems, rather, to be based on the principle that where people do not have a source of income, a source of income must be provided. In many cases, that is done through insurance-based or non-contributory benefits – that is, without reference to the level of income as opposed to the source. The issue is not, apparently, whether people are in work, or whether they are on low incomes, but whether they are deemed to be in the sort of circumstances where people are dependent. There is a line drawn between people in certain circumstances (like unemployment) and others (like being in higher education), where the first group are presumed to be dependent in a way that the second group is not. A 19-year-old living with parents in a family where everyone else is working is entitled, but a 19-year-old who leaves school to get married to someone who is working is not. The rationale for this is based partly on conditionality (the insistence that benefits should be confined to those available for work) and partly on the peculiar distinction between couples and other family members, but the overall effect is that it becomes difficult to see any consistent principle in the structure and function of these benefits.

## Material need

A third category of benefits for the 'poor' is concerned with examples of specific material need. The Social Fund and the benefits that preceded it – such as the provision of 'Exceptional Needs Payments' and 'Exceptional Circumstances Additions' on Supplementary Benefit – are examples, as are special provisions like hardship payments within Jobseeker's Allowance. The hardship payments cover the gaps left in certain circumstances – people who are waiting for benefits to be paid, and people who have had their benefit suspended. Another example might be some benefits in kind, like free school meals and income-based free prescriptions. If we want to understand a benefit like the Sure Start Maternity Grant (technically a part of the Social Fund) or Healthy Start food vouchers, it helps to think of them as benefits targeted not just at expectant mothers but at *poor* expectant mothers – which is why they include people in receipt of JSA, Working Tax Credit and Child Tax Credit at some rates and not others.

These examples are specific and relatively minor, which tends to suggest that this is not an important principle. That is not altogether true: they may not play a large role in social security benefits, but they do play a major part in a range of other services, including housing (provision for homeless families) and social care (community care assessments). Looked at again, the examples in the preceding paragraph – school meals, prescriptions and support for maternity – can be taken to be about health or education rather than income support. The reason why this kind of provision does not feature more prominently in social security is, I think, that it is not really consistent with the way that social security is delivered. Where people are in need, social security responds not by providing them with the goods in question, but with income; and with very few exceptions (like the food vouchers formerly used for asylum seekers), claimants are then given money to spend, rather than the goods. (Vouchers suffer notoriously from the problem that people will trade them for non-voucher items.[18] Usually the trade is to the disadvantage of the poor person.) The issue is not, then, that there are no services for people in material need, but that it is done by other services in other ways.

## Benefits for socially excluded people

The fourth category of benefits for the poor, like the third, is relatively little used in social security in Britain. In Britain the idea of social inclusion has come to stand for a distinct set of issues, related to problematic or persistent poverty. The Labour government presented it as:

> a short hand label for what can happen when individuals or areas suffer from a combination of linked problems such as unemployment, poor skills, low incomes, poor housing, high crime environments, bad health and family breakdown.[19]

The identification of exclusion as equivalent to either multiple deprivation or area deprivation is questionable.[20] That does not stop it, however, from being a motive force in policy. The kind of issues considered by the Labour government's Social Exclusion Unit included teenage pregnancy, rough sleeping, children in care, mental health and the problems of poor areas. Although any of these has some relationship to benefits, benefits tend to have been seen as tangential. The main exception was the case of rough sleepers, who were formerly the object of the Resettlement Agency in the Department for Work and Pensions. Their functions were absorbed into the Rough Sleepers Unit and subsequently into Homelessness Directorate of the Department for Communities and Local Government, who have responsibility for 'Supporting People', the programme offering support in housing of a kind once funded through social security.

The idea of exclusion does also have a broader meaning. The term originated in France, where initially it referred to people who were not covered by the existing insurance-based provisions, in the main because they had not been employed and so were unable to contribute.[21] It came to refer more generally

---

[18] For example, P Kelso (1999) 'Parents "exchanging milk tokens for alcohol"', *The Guardian*, 20 October (www.guardian.co.uk/uk/1999/oct/20/paulkelso).

[19] A Blair (1997) cited in *Hansard*, HL Deb 09 December 1997 vol 584 cc20-2WA.

[20] P Spicker (2002) *Poverty and the welfare state*, London: Catalyst.

[21] R Lenoir (1974) *Les exclus*, Paris: Editions de Scuil.

to people who are unable to participate in society, and in that form the principle was enshrined in successive European Union treaties.[22] In both senses, it could be argued that the British social security system already had provision for those who were excluded. The British system was always intended to be comprehensive and all-inclusive. National Assistance was there to cover people who the insurance scheme left out, and the progressive development of the benefits system for other marginalised groups, like the introduction of non-contributory benefits for people with disabilities, served to fill in gaps when they were found. An example might be the Severe Disablement Allowance, discussed in Chapter 16: it became the principal benefit for people with disabilities living in institutional care, but was absorbed into Incapacity Benefit in 2001. The equivalent benefit for disabled people in France, introduced in 1975, was directly justified in terms of '*insertion*', or social inclusion of excluded people.[23]

The key initiative in France was the introduction of the *Revenu minimum d'insertion*.[24] As a condition of receiving benefit, people are engaged in a contract with society. The contract has two elements: one is made between the benefit recipient and the agency (the *Commission Locale d'Insertion*), for engagement in society, whether through jobs or through some patterns of social work. The second element is a set of contracts made between the agency and other local agencies to develop social opportunities, including jobs, training places, educational courses and engagement in social support.[25] The French model has been imitated in a number of other countries, including Portugal,[26] northern Spain[27] and in Italy.[28] However, subsequent reforms have pushed the French system in the same direction as Britain, with provision for the exclusion of people who are not actively seeking work and a new stress on personalised direction of unemployed people.[29]

---

[22] P Spicker (1997) 'Exclusion', *Journal of Common Market Studies*, vol 35, no 1, pp 133–43.

[23] P Maclouf (1992) 'L'insertion, un nouveau concept opératoire des politiques sociales?', in R Castel and J-F Lae (eds) *Le Revenu minimum d'insertion: Une dette sociale*, Paris: Editions L'Harmattan, pp 123-4.

[24] Commission Nationale d'Evaluation du Revenu Minimum d'Insertion (1992) *RMI: Le pari de l'insertion*, Paris: La documentation française.

[25] P Spicker (1995) 'Inserting the excluded: the impact of the Revenu Minimum d'Insertion on poverty in France', *Social Work in Europe*, vol 22, pp 8-14.

[26] M Coutinho (1998) 'Guaranteed minimum income in Portugal and social projects', *Social Services Research*, no 2, pp 1-10.

[27] L Ayala (1994) 'Social needs, inequality and the welfare state in Spain', *Journal of European Social Policy*, vol 4, no 3, pp 159-79.

[28] MISEP (European Commission Employment Observatory) (1998) *Policies*, no 64, Winter, pp 23-4.

[29] J Dupeyroux, M Borgetto and R Lafore (2008) *Droit de la sécurité sociale* (16th edn), Paris: Dalloz, ss 1705-9.

The British 'Jobseeker's Agreement' can be seen nominally as a reflection of the influence of the French model, but it is a pale shadow of the original – the emphasis in the Jobseeker's Agreement has fallen on the obligations of the unemployed person rather than the mutual undertakings made by different parties. The idea of social inclusion is reflected more effectively in some of the community-based programmes used in welfare to work measures: examples are the Environment Task Forces, New Deal for Communities or linking activation with the national childcare strategy. If we are looking for examples of 'insertion' in Britain, however, the best examples are found in some of the marginal systems offering specialised care and support. One example is the use of direct payments in social work,[30] which can be used in conjunction with the process of social work to offer payments to clients as part of a series of measures intended to integrate a person with society. Another example was the work of the Independent Living Fund, which negotiated packages of support individually tailored to the needs of disabled people who want to be able to live in the community.[31] This shares with the French model the principle of offering individually negotiated support to promote participation in society.

## QUESTIONS FOR DISCUSSION

Is means testing the best way to get support to poor people?
Can benefits alone promote social inclusion?

---

[30] See Scottish Executive (2003) *Direct Payments: Social Work (Scotland) Act 1968: Sections 12b and 12c, Policy and practice guidance* (www.scotland.gov.uk/Publications/2003/06/17612/23018).

[31] Independent Living Fund (2010) (www.ilf.org.uk/home/index.html).

# Part V

## Issues in social security policy

The evaluation of the impact of social policy usually depends on its aims. That is difficult to do for social security. Social security does not have a single set of aims, or aims that tend in a particular direction; there are many, and in the context of particular benefits, conflicting objectives often jockey together for priority.

This part of the book focuses, instead, on a limited but important range of evaluative criteria, principally concerned with the question of whether the system offers value for money. It discusses the costs of social security, and how the money is spent. A focus on value for money points to some of the tests by which social security can be evaluated:

- cost;
- effectiveness, including whether social security reaches the people it is intended for, and whether it goes to others who it is not intended for;
- the impact on poverty; and
- the redistributive impact of benefits.

It concludes by considering lessons from other countries.

# Chapter 22

# The cost of social security

Expenditure on social security is massive, and attempts to economise have driven many reforms, not always to best effect. Costs have been increasing because of the growing number of pensioners and the extension of their entitlements, the impact of unemployment, and the recognition of the position of people with disabilities. Governments cannot easily control the numbers of pensioners, children or unemployed people, and many benefits are based in established entitlements, which have limited the scope for governments to reduce spending.

Spending on social security constitutes the largest single part of government spending, more than double the cost of any other service. The Department for Work and Pensions's figures for expenditure for 2009-10 are shown in Table 22.1.

The amounts of money are staggering, and it takes most of us a little while to make the mental adjustment to think about these figures sensibly. It has become normal to use the term 'billion' to refer to a thousand million (£1,000,000,000), so another way of saying this is that social security costs about £150 billion. Governments often represent savings of several million pounds as significant. They sometimes seem like a drop in the bucket. For example, there are over 12.4 million pensioners. That means that £1 on the pension costs over £12 million per week, or about £645 million pounds per year.

The figures that governments use are not always reliable. The basis on which figures are produced tends to shift – for example, the figures for long-term illness and incapacity have been reviewed retrospectively to put Income Support receipt together with incapacity benefits, and recently statistics have been modified to refer to people of 'working age' rather than 'people under 60'. There are some approximations - the Department for Work and Pensions estimates receipt of several benefits by sample survey, rather than by keeping a current tally – but the most important benefits are now being fully recorded. It takes some months to confirm the out-turn. Discrepancies in official accounting of £10 billion or more were common in the 1990s, but the worst inconsistencies have now been brought under control, and figures produced by different departments are now normally close to each other.

It can be arbitrary to decide what is 'social security expenditure', and what is not. Free school meals are on the education budget, and free prescriptions are on the health budget. Payments for Housing Benefit can be treated as spending on housing instead, and they have wobbled in and out of the figures over the years. Tax Credits are not treated in the accounts as part of social security expenditure, and Child Benefit, which used to be on the figures, is no longer there. Comparable figures from HM Revenue & Customs are not available, but it seems likely that expenditure on Child Benefit will be in the region of £12 billion.[1] Child Tax Credit and Working Tax Credit cost £27.3 billion.[2] It follows that the total headline expenditure on benefits can reasonably be presented as being about £190 billion.

**Table 22.1: Expenditure on social security, 2009-10[3]**

| Benefit | Expenditure (£m) | No. of beneficiaries (000s) |
|---|---|---|
| *National insurance* | | |
| State pension | 67,391 | 12,417 |
| Pension Credit | 8,229 | 2,742 |
| Widows and bereavement | 649 | 115 |
| Jobseeker's Allowance – contributory | 1,089 | 297 |
| Incapacity Benefit and ESA | 6,692 | 1,362 |
| Industrial injuries benefits | 844 | 269 |
| *Non-contributory benefits* | | |
| Disability Living Allowance | 11,796 | 3,108 |
| Attendance Allowance | 5,256 | 1,605 |
| *Means-tested benefits* | | |
| Income Support | 8,344 | 1,923 |
| Jobseeker's Allowance – income based | 3,601 | 1,116 |
| Carers Allowance | 1,499 | 526 |
| Housing Benefit | 19,978 | 3,547 |
| Council Tax Benefit | 4,698 | 5,602 |
| ESA – income based | 687 | 199 |
| *Universal benefits* | | |
| Winter Fuel payments | 2,735 | 12,625 |
| Category D universal pension | 49 | 27 |
| Over 75s TV licence | 549 | 4,128 |
| *Discretionary benefits* | | |
| Social Fund | 749 | n.a. |
| Independent Living Funds | 339 | 21 |
| **Total benefit expenditure (DWP)** | 147,768 | |

---

[1] HM Treasury (2010) 'Chancellor announces reforms to the benefits system', Press release 48/10 (www.hm-treasury.gov.uk/press_48_10.htm).

[2] National Audit Office (2010) *HM Revenue & Customs 2009-10 Accounts: Report by the Comptroller and Auditor-General*, London: NAO, para 17.

[3] Department for Work and Pensions (2010) *Benefit expenditure tables* (http://statistics. dwp.gov.uk/asd/asd4/alltables_budget2010.xls).

Beyond the problem of classification, it is also debatable what part of this figure should be thought of as 'spending'. In the first place, some of the expenditure in the accounts is notional – such as Council Tax Benefit, which is a way of reducing a bill rather than increasing income, or over £5 billion in Tax Credits that comes in tax reductions rather than payments. Second, income from social security provision, through National Insurance contributions, is not offset against expenditure; the National Insurance system brings in a surplus, and currently National Insurance contributions pay for about half the cost of DWP benefits. Third, more generally, it could be argued that much social security spending should be presented differently from other kinds of expenditure; paying for pensions is not the same kind of activity as equipping an aircraft carrier. In economic analysis, social security represents a 'transfer payment', where money is moved from one set of people to another; it would be possible to present part of the accounts in that form.

## Trends in expenditure

Expenditure on social security has risen as a proportion of gross domestic product from under 5% in the 1950s to over 10% now; at its highest, in the mid-1990s, it passed 12%.[4] This rise of expenditure as a proportion of GDP may give the impression that benefits have improved more than national income, but that is not really what has happened. The number of claimants has increased, and although benefits have been uprated in line with inflation, this has not necessarily kept pace with relative prices. The current proportion of GDP spent on social security is not very different from the early 1980s, when there was mass unemployment; reductions in the number of unemployed people have been offset by increasing numbers of pensioners.

The growth in demand has many elements, but three are most important. They are:

- The growth in the elderly population, who have retired earlier and lived longer than previous generations, but who have established rights. Pensions and provision for older people account for more than half of all expenditure on social security in Britain, and two thirds of the spending by the Department for Work and Pensions. Even minor benefits for pensioners, like the Winter Fuel Payments, are liable to be expensive, because of the large number of recipients. Pensioners also receive a substantial proportion of benefits like Housing Benefit, Council Tax Benefit and Disability Living Allowance, where over £4 billion goes to people past working age. Overall, pensioners account for nearly £97 billion of spending on

---

[4] Department for Work and Pensions (2003) *The abstract of statistics: 2003 edition*, chart A (www.dss.gov.uk/asd/asd1/abstract/Abstract2003.pdf)

benefits, about two-thirds of the budget of the DWP. The spending is difficult to control. Governments are unable to reduce the numbers of entitled elderly people, and find it difficult to renege effectively on previous undertakings.

- The problem of unemployment, which is also reflected in the increasing numbers of other non-employed groups, including people with incapacity and lone parents. Alcock et al write of the 'detachment' of large numbers of older males from the labour market, through a combination of redundancy, ill health and early retirement.[5]
- The recognition of the needs of people with disabilities. Three benefits recorded here – Attendance Allowance, Carer's Allowance and Disability Living Allowance – come to over 12% of the budget, and the incapacity benefits, which include substantial support for disabilities, account for another 5%. These benefits did not exist when the first national research on disability was done in the 1960s. Most people who now claim Employment and Support Allowance would at that time have had to claim Sickness Benefit or Unemployment Benefit, but people claiming the other benefits mentioned would not have found an effective substitute. There is nothing inevitable about having to meet need when claims are made, but governments have found themselves trapped by a combination on one side of a disparate but effective campaigning force, and on the other by the dawning realisation that if millions of people who are disadvantaged financially are also physically disabled, then once the basis of provision has been established, it is very difficult to deny the validity of their claims. Many subsequent reforms have been a rearguard action by governments trying to limit the financial damage.

There are two other factors that may have contributed to the growth of expenditure, though their effect is more limited:

- There has been an increase in the relative generosity of benefits for long-term claimants, particularly pensions and disability benefits.
- Some benefits have been created because of an effective shift of responsibility between government departments. Housing Benefit exists because governments withdrew the general subsidy from public housing; Council Tax Benefit has had to reflect the reduction of central government finance for local government; the concealed payment of mortgage interest, buried in the Income Support figures, has been pushed up by the loss of the former subsidy to owner-occupiers for mortgage interest relief; and Child Benefit conceals an effective transfer of resources from the amount formerly given in tax relief to families with children. These examples have all added to

---

[5]    P Alcock, C Beatty, S Fothergill, R Macmillan and S Yeandle (2003) *Work to welfare*, Cambridge: Cambridge University Press.

the social security budget, but that should be balanced against some other factors which formerly were part of the social security budget, and have been moved elsewhere. Payments for residential care for elderly people, and for rental charges related to supported accommodation, were formerly part of the social security budget and have been shifted to the budget for community care; and the cost of support for people in work has been eased by the introduction of a minimum wage and by moves to improve women's wages.

## The control of public expenditure

Social security policy for much of the last thirty years has been dominated by attempts to curb the growth in expenditure. Public expenditure is largely controlled through the Treasury. The Treasury used to be a very traditional department, heavily dominated by people with an education in classics rather than economics; in the 1970s, its style was compared to that of an exclusive gentleman's club.[6] Writing in the 1990s, Deakin and Parry described the social policy of the Treasury as dominated by several long-running themes. These include:

- preserving its right to intervene when cost implications arise;
- reserving the sole 'proprietorship' of budgetary matters, like tax and National Insurance;
- crude economics (for example, work incentives or public sector pay);
- crude social philosophy (for example, on whether women should work, educational opportunity or the role of private savings); and
- selectivity (represented as 'targeting').[7]

These themes are still present, but the style of operation is markedly different.

The system of control developed in the 1960s and 1970s was effective for most social services – expenditure on health, for example, has been strictly controlled and scrutinised for most of the last thirty years – but control of social security went beyond the scope of that system, partly because of difficulties in controlling unemployment, and partly because many established rights had to be taken as given. Although the constraints imposed could be traced back to economic management – such as the idea of reforming Supplementary Benefit, in 1980, at no cost, or the attempt in the Fowler Reviews to limit future expenditure on pensions – the mechanisms did not exist for direct control. The only cash-limited benefit is the Social Fund, introduced in 1988. Since then, however, there have been moves to bring the system more directly under the aegis of the Treasury.

6    H Heclo and A Wildavsky (1974) *The private government of public money*, London: Macmillan.
7    N Deakin and R Parry (1993) 'Does the Treasury have a social policy?', in N Deakin and R Page (eds) *The costs of welfare*, Aldershot: Avebury.

Tax Credits have brought major functions related to benefit delivery under the direct control of the Treasury. They also offer a means of delivering benefits where the entitlements can vary according to economic circumstances; the scheme has already undergone at least two major structural reforms. In administrative terms, the Treasury has an increasingly direct role in the management of social security: the annual report of each government department is now coordinated with the budget and the government's expenditure plans. Departments have to negotiate with the Treasury to produce a Public Service Agreement and a Service Delivery Agreement. Carmel and Papadopoulos write: 'The policy objectives themselves, how policies are delivered, and how that delivery is to be measured are all now subject to Treasury approval and monitoring.'[8] From announcements in various budgets, it seems that departmental staffing and administration is also now under the control of the Chancellor.

## How to save money

Governments have made periodic attempts over the years either to reduce public spending on social security or at least to limit the growth of expenditure. The scale of the operation means that minor cuts are easily made; failing to increase Child Benefit by 20p saves £125 million pounds per year, and limiting the increase in pensions (which used to rise in line with average wages) has saved billions. The three-year freeze in Child Benefit announced in the 2010 budget was intended to save nearly £3 billion over four years.[9]

Social security spending is difficult to control, because governments cannot easily determine the number of pensioners, children or unemployed people. They can only seek to reduce the level of benefits. The Fowler Reviews in the 1980s were one of the most substantial attempts to cut back the scope of benefits: they led to the termination of SERPs (after nearly 20 years), pruning of minor benefits like Maternity Grants and Death Grants and changes in rules to limit the growth of Exceptional Payments. More typically, attempts to economise usually lead to progressive tightening of rules. In the case of unemployment, for example, this has included alterations in the qualification period, loss of earnings-related benefits and changes in the basis of payment (which used to allow for days of unemployment).

The kinds of savings that governments have tended to concentrate on have been attempts to rein back on benefit expenditure: paying less for disability, reducing fraud, reclassifying people as unemployed rather than as long-term sick and limiting Housing Benefit. Most of these measures are marginal. For example, limiting the Sure Start Maternity Grant to the first child will save £75 million a year; and

---

[8]   E Carmel and T Papadopoulous (2003) 'The new governance of social security in Britain', in J Millar (ed) *Understanding social security*, Bristol: The Policy Press, p 43.

[9]   HM Treasury (2010) *Budget 2010*, HC 61, London: The Stationery Office, p 41

while the effect of reducing Housing Benefit to long-term unemployed people could be very serious for those people, the actual saving will only be about £110 million of a £20 billion budget.[10] Measures against fraud, the subject of Chapter 24, are similarly unlikely to yield major savings.

The Institute for Fiscal Studies has suggested a series of rather more trenchant cuts;[11] any of them could have happened in the 2010 Budget or Spending Review, but few did. They include:

- *Means testing Child Benefit* This could save large amounts of money; limiting eligibility to half the population would probably save half the money, because the costs of administration would be met by reduced take-up; but it is a terrible idea. It would largely destroy the point of Child Benefit, which provides a stable and predictable income; the take-up and coverage would inevitably be worse; the administrative problems are obvious; and as we already have a general means-tested benefit for families with children, creating a second one makes no sense at all.

- *Scrapping marginal benefits* Reducing benefits for pensioners, including winter fuel payments and TV license exemptions, would save £1.4 billion if there was compensation to people on the means-tested Pension Credit.

- *Limiting disability benefits* Means testing Attendance Allowance and Disability Living Allowance might save a proportion of the cost, though the low income of many people with disabilities makes this uncertain.

- *Time-limiting contributory benefits* The rationale for this is that contributory benefits are a form of insurance, and what insurance buys can sensibly be related to what is contributed. There was a precedent for this in the time-limiting of unemployment benefits, and it has been implemented in small part through time-limiting the contributory Employment and Support Allowance.

- *Increasing the tapers of means-tested benefits* – withdrawing benefits more rapidly as income increases. The amount saved would depend on how fierce the taper was.

- *Making benefits taxable* Taxes are only paid when people's income goes above a specified threshold; the effect is similar to means testing, but in administrative terms it is much simpler. Taxing benefits reduces their value to people on higher incomes, while preserving the structure of benefits. One option is to make Child Benefit taxable.[12] This has been done before – it was known as 'clawback' – and it is simple to do; however, it is unpopular and 'churning' money, paying with one hand and taking it back with

---

[10] HM Treasury (2010) p 40.

[11] M Brewer, J Browne, A Leicester and H Miller (2010) 'Options for fiscal tightening: tax increases and benefit cuts', in R Chote, C Emmerson and J Shaw (eds) *The IFS Green Budget: February 2010*, London: Institute for Fiscal Studies.

[12] T Clark and J McRae (1998) *Taxing Child Benefit*, London: Institute for Fiscal Studies.

another, is likely to be seen as wasteful.[13] Tax rates are, however, much lower than the tapers on means-tested benefits, so it would save less money than means testing the benefit would.[14] Making Attendance Allowance and DLA taxable would also be feasible, but because most of their recipients are on very low incomes it would yield less than £1 billion.

Making savings on a larger scale calls for a basic rethink of the contingencies that benefits provide for. Here are some examples:

- *Raising the pension age* If pensioners retired at 70 rather than 65, reducing the number of pensioners by over 2.5 million, it should save a fifth of the cost of pensions and at the same time prolong the period when people pay tax and contributions. However, some people would be unemployed or invalided, so they would become dependent on other benefits instead; set against this, many of those denied retirement would make contributions.

- *Reducing the entitlements of young people* Raising the school leaving age to 18 would have only a limited effect, because most entitlements to under-18s have already been restricted, but as more young people move into education post 18, there may be scope to extend the normal period of education, and dependency on parents, to 21. Another idea floated by Frank Field has been to end Child Benefit at 13, on the basis that low income is focused far more in families with younger children.[15] That would have saved more than a quarter of the cost.

- *Privatising social protection* This does not reduce social expenditure at all – most private pensions tend to be more generous, and incur greater costs – but it would reduce government expenditure, which is what most governments seem to care about.

- *Moving back to full employment* Creating enough jobs could remove not only a million unemployed people, but many people of working age receiving other benefits.

- *Offering services in place of benefits* It is possible in theory to restore public services that have been removed, and which imposed burdens on the benefit system instead. The need for Council Tax Benefit reflects the transfer of financial burdens from central to local government; the removal of general housing subsidies made Housing Benefit necessary. Conversely, it would be possible to offer public services that would reduce the demand for benefits, like universal childcare in place of the element of Working Tax Credit offered for people with childcare expenses.

---

[13] J Kincaid (1973) *Poverty and equality in Britain*, Harmondsworth: Penguin, pp 69-70.

[14] Brewer, Browne, Leicester and Miller (2010), p 172.

[15] J Sherman and R Bennett (2010) 'Millions may lose out in reform of child benefits', *The Times*, 11 June, p 1.

These options may seem far-fetched and unrealistic, but they have all been done before:

- *Raising the pension age* Governments are increasing the pension age; by 2020, men and women will retire at 66. (I write 'governments' because a decision initially made by the Conservatives was taken forward by Labour; there is no political divide on the issue.) Between 2024 and 2046 the pension age for men and women will rise to 68.
- *Reducing the entitlements of young people* The Heath government raised the school leaving age from 15 to 16, and the effects of benefit entitlement and unemployment figures were virtually invisible within two years. The Fowler Reviews in the 1980s treated young people under 25 differently, on the basis that few of them had independent households at the time; that difference still appears in the basic benefit rates.
- *Privatisation* There has been no attempt to privatise the social security system, a trend pioneered by the dictatorship in Chile,[16] but bits of the system have been moved to the private sector: the strongest examples are the transfer of Sick Pay to employers, and the growth of occupational pensions in place of National Insurance.
- *Full employment* Governments do not seem to believe in full employment any more, but it was government policy in Britain from 1944 to 1970. Full employment was maintained during that period, it did represent a major transition from the inter-war years and it did have the effect of taking a generation of people off benefits.
- *Public services* The fifth option was one of the major implications of the introduction of the welfare state: the effect of the National Health Service meant that people did not have to pay for medical insurance or receive Poor Law assistance.

## QUESTIONS FOR DISCUSSION

Does it matter if social security spending is high, if the costs are covered?
If there was to be a major increase in funding, what should it be spent on?

---

[16]  H Glennerster and J Midgley (eds) (1991) *The radical right and the welfare state*, Harvester Wheatsheaf.

# Chapter 23

# Targeting

The question of 'targeting', or whether the money goes where it should, is central. Targeting does not mean only that benefits go to the poor, but rather that they should reach the peoply they are meant to reach. It is not at all clear that focusing the system more narrowly, or making it more selective, would be more effective or efficient: selectivity is expensive, and the system already fails to provide for many people who are supposed to be entitled. It is important to ensure that people are not excluded inappropriately.

Targeting is concerned with the allocation and distribution of resources and services: services are targeted when they are aimed at a particular client group. The term is used confusingly in the literature. For some writers, targeting is pretty much equivalent to selectivity and means testing,[1] but this is a muddle and it needs to be unravelled. The first strand is the assumption that targeting works by selection. Services are selective when people in the target group are picked out and treated differently from the rest. It is perfectly possible to target poor people without making any deliberate selection. For example, a soup kitchen or canteen is aimed at homeless people, but the service is delivered without a test; the people who want it select themselves. The same principle is widely used in developing countries, where the practical problems of identifying individual recipients are considerable. Cornia and Stewart consider the effectiveness of food subsidies in helping poorer people. They are not concerned with precise measurement, but with the way the benefits relate to the circumstances of poorer groups.[2] Poor people often eat different foods from rich people. Food subsidies can work for poor people if the foods that are subsidised are the foods that poor people eat. The World Bank has argued for broad-based 'indicator targeting', picking on regions, age groups, gender or other kinds of common characteristic.[3] We have used this principle in Britain when providing benefits for vulnerable groups, like pensioners and one-parent families.

---

[1] For example, D Mitchell, A Harding, A Gruen and F Gruen (1994) 'Targeting welfare', *The Economic Record*, vol 70, no 210, pp 315-40; P Whiteford (1997) 'Targeting welfare: a comment', *The Economic Record*, vol 73, no 220, pp 45-50.

[2] G Cornia and F Stewart (1995) 'Food subsidies: two errors of targeting', in F Stewart, *Adjustment and poverty*, London: Routledge.

[3] World Bank (1990) *World development report*, Oxford: Oxford University Press.

The second assumption is that selection is done by means testing. Means testing is only one option. In Britain, targeting the poor was often done in the 1970s by targeting elderly people; now, it is often done by trying to move people from benefits to work, rather than focusing on their income. In the context of developing countries, Coady et al suggest that some methods, including means testing, geographic targeting and work-based programmes, tend to be more effective in redistributing resources, while those based on receiving bids from communities and targeting to elderly people tend to be less effective, and even regressive.[4]

The third assumption is that targeting is principally concerned with getting services to the poor. It is a much broader concept. Social policies have to affect someone, and any attempt to identify a client group specifically can be referred to as 'targeting'. Policies may be focused on a range of different groups: individuals, households, families, communities and blocs or categories of people.[5] This process is basic to service delivery. There is no intrinsic reason why the target should be the needs of poor individuals; it may be possible, for example, to attribute needs to broader categories of people, such as lone parents or residents of particular neighbourhoods.[6] Nor does a policy even have to be aimed at the person who is intended to benefit. The disadvantage of women can be addressed by targeting men, as has happened recently in the extension of paternity leave in the European Union. Equally, targeting does not necessarily call for targeting of benefits; it may imply targeting of costs or disincentives (there have been proposals, for example, to cut benefits to people involved in anti-social behaviour). Programmes that focus on particular types of social issue, like teenage pregnancy, drug use or people suffering from HIV, need to address the issues of effectiveness, efficiency and allocation that the debate on targeting is concerned with.

## Fairness and efficiency

The key arguments for targeting are fairness and efficiency. Targeting is fair if it redresses disadvantage – either by redistributing benefits or by redistributing burdens (such as tax loads). It is efficient if it yields the greatest benefit possible for each unit of cost, and it does that by concentrating the benefit where it ought to go. Targeting does not need to be exact, but if it is going to make a difference it will be because it gets resources to where they ought to go.

---

[4] D Coady, M Grosh and J Hoddinott (2003) *Targeting outcomes redux*, Washington: World Bank, p 38.

[5] P Spicker (2008) *Social policy: Themes and approaches*, Bristol: The Policy Press.

[6] N Gilbert, H Specht and P Terrell (1993) *Dimensions of social welfare policy*, (3rd edn), Englewood Cliffs, NJ: Prentice Hall, pp 84–5.

The language of 'efficiency' is often identified, misleadingly, with cutting costs. One of the primary justifications for targeting has been the belief that it is a way to save money.[7] 'Should the growth in total welfare spending be constrained by moving from universal programs to more targeted ones?'[8] There are several implicit assumptions in this question. The first is that targeting means cutting back — a confusion that comes about because targeting has often been emphasised in that context.[9] Cuts to services can be done in many ways — for example, through deterrence, conditionality, delay and restricted access. Targeting new services to cover gaps is likely to cost more money, not less. The second assumption is that targeted programmes cost less because they focus on fewer people: if targeting leads to lower costs, it is largely because it might save money by denying services to people who are not part of the focus of policy. Whether this works depends on the balance between the costs of targeting (mainly administration) and the impact of the policy measure. The third assumption is that universal programmes are intrinsically expensive because they deal with more people. That is not necessarily true. The costs of a service are determined by many factors, including the overall resources that are committed, the conditions that it addresses and the terms on which it addresses them. Coverage is one factor to consider; other factors to set against this include lower average unit costs, administrative savings and economies of scale.

At different times, governments have attempted to tighten up the specifications and conditions attached to benefits in the expectation that this would define the target group more precisely. Another example is the development of Incapacity Benefit in 1995. Incapacity Benefit was intended to be much more tightly defined than Invalidity Benefit, which preceded it. The Conservative government which introduced Incapacity Benefit in 1995 had been informed, quite wrongly, that the effect of introducing explicit, firm rules in place of medical discretion would be to greatly limit the number of claims. (The advice of the civil servants was, unusually, recorded and broadcast in a television documentary.[10]) Bonner et al record:

---

[7]  M Andries (1996) 'The politics of targeting: the Belgian case', *Journal of European Social Policy*, vol 6, no 3, pp 209-23; M Ferrara (1998) 'Targeting welfare in a "soft" state: Italy's winding road to selectivity', International Social Security Association, 2nd International Research Conference on Social Security, Jerusalem; P Keizer (1998) 'Recent trends in targeting social welfare in the Netherlands', International Social Security Association, 2nd International Research Conference on Social Security, Jerusalem.

[8]  D Besharov (1998) 'Social welfare's twin dilemmas: universalism versus targeting and support versus dependency', International Social Security Association, 2nd International Research Conference on Social Security, Jerusalem.

[9]  Andries (1996).

[10]  P Dale (1996) 'The system', broadcast on BBC2.

> It was estimated that the switch to the 'all work' test (*now the Work Capability Assessment*) would mean that over the first two years after its introduction some 220,000 existing recipients would be denied benefit ... while some 55,000 new claimants ... would be ruled out.[11]

What happened was quite different. The statistical record is complicated by people claiming for credits and people receiving Invalidity Benefit after retirement, but if we look only at the figures for incapacity benefits in payment for people of working age, there were 1,611,000 claims for Invalidity Benefit in 1994/95. Incapacity Benefit was introduced in April 1995. For 1995/96, there were 1,638,000 benefits in payment; for the year after, the number was 1,622,000.[12] There is not much evidence, then, to suggest that the stricter rules did anything to reduce the number of claimants. Numbers did gradually fall in later years − by 2007/08, they were down to 1,412,000 − but that was probably for other reasons, either the fall in unemployment over this period or the gradual retirement of former manual workers who had become long-term disabled.

A clue to what has happened here is provided by another example. The definition of single payments in 1980 was supposed to save money by offering clearly and more precise rules. It had the opposite effect, with an initial fall in the number of claims being followed by a massive increase.[13] The effect of defining the rules and benefits more precisely was to make claimants aware that they might be entitled, and to reduce the discretion to refuse them. The effect of redefining categories and benefit rules is not necessarily an incremental change from the existing situation: it changes the terms on which benefits are delivered. (In economic terms, shifting the supply function can have the effect of shifting the demand function.) In both these examples, defining the rules worked not so much to prevent access to benefits as to redefine people's entitlements. The lesson is that measures to improve targeting may do just that − and better targeting is not the same thing as saving money.

## Problems of targeting

If targeting works, then no-one should be excluded who is meant to be included, and no-one should be included who is meant to be excluded. (These are sometimes referred to as 'type 1 errors', for false negatives, and 'type 2

---

[11] D Bonner, I Hooker and R White (2003) *Social security legislation 2003: Non means tested benefits*, London: Sweet and Maxwell, pp 31-2.

[12] Department for Work and Pensions (2010) *Benefits* (http://research.dwp.gov.uk/asd/asd4/Alltables_budget2010.xls).

[13] R Cohen and M Tarpey (1988) *Single payments: The disappearing safety net*, London: Child Poverty Action Group.

errors', for false positives.[14] These terms are drawn from statistical method, but there is no general agreement about what they mean in practice, and they are not universally applied in this context.)

People are excluded inappropriately if they are in the target group, but are nevertheless left out. An example of this is the case of people on very low incomes who are not entitled to benefit, for example because they are under the age of 18 (where benefit payment becomes discretionary), or because they have been excluded from benefit by the threat of prosecution. Decisions about targeting are often approximate: one effect of the reforms of Supplementary Benefit in 1988 was to make a distinction between people over and under 25 in place of the previous distinction of householders and non-householders. The government argued that as 90% of people under 25 were non-householders, this would not cause hardship. (In subsequent years, people over 18 came increasingly to form their own households, invalidating the argument; the reduced support for under-25-year-olds has been retained nevertheless.)

The main reason for inappropriate exclusion seems to be the problem of take-up and access to benefits. However, low take-up is not quite the same thing as failure to reach the target group. The rules of benefits are often approximate, and Atkinson points out that it does not follow, because people are entitled, that they were really within the intended target group.[15] The tolerance of low take-up, and the assertion that its value and implications are small, suggests that as a matter of policy low take-up is not considered materially to compromise the effectiveness of the benefits system. That is questionable: low take-up also implies that services are failing to reach people.

False positives tend to excite more attention, particularly in the popular press. There are several ways of including people who are meant to be left out. The definitions or categories that are used sometimes include people who are not part of the target group, because it is difficult administratively to leave them out. One example of unintended inclusion is *deadweight*, where people receive a service or benefit but their circumstances are not materially changed by it. For example, because most unemployed people will move from benefit to jobs regardless of policy, 'welfare to work' policies always carry deadweight. To take a different kind of example, giving Tax Credits to people formerly on Income Support does not make a material difference to outcomes; it simply changes which fund the income is paid from. Another form of inappropriate inclusion stems from *spillovers*. People are sometimes helped because the categories are drawn more widely than the target group: policies for pensioners which are not income-tested almost invariably draw in some people who are not on low incomes and whose

---

[14] For example, in A B Atkinson (1991) *The social safety net*, London: Suntory-Toyota International Centre for Economics and Related Disciplines.

[15] A B Atkinson (1989) 'The take-up of social security benefits', in A B Atkinson, *Poverty and social security*, Brighton: Harvester Wheatsheaf.

income flow has not been interrupted. To complicate the matter further, some people may be helped who it was intended to include, but they may get more help than was strictly speaking necessary. The effect of basing some benefits on previous income, or previous tax years, inevitably implies overpayment for some.

The main concern that has been expressed in this area relates to overpayments, which occur either through fraud or through error. The issue of fraud and abuse is considered in the next chapter. Error, whether administrative error or based in mistaken information, is actually a larger element of the benefits system numerically: the principal cause is the complexity of the rules, which in conditions where entitlements fluctuate make it difficult to determine either that people are receiving the benefits they are entitled to or that they are not receiving benefits they are not entitled to.

In so far as targeting is concerned with effectiveness rather than efficiency, inappropriate inclusion is less important than inappropriate exclusion. Deadweight and spillovers can be tolerated, but low take-up tends to imply that a measure will fail to meet its goals. The high administrative costs associated with curbing overpayments also argues for some tolerance of inefficiencies if they would otherwise compromise effectiveness.

## QUESTIONS FOR DISCUSSION

Who should benefits be targeted on?
How can inappropriate exclusions be avoided?

# Chapter 24

# Fraud and abuse

The idea that large sums of money are wasted through fraud and abuse is exaggerated. Official estimates, based on survey evidence, combine figures for fraud, claimant error and official error; overpayments attributable to claimants tend to reflect the complexity of the benefits system as much as any deliberate action. However, the pursuit of fraud has had a major effect on the way that the system operates.

One of the factors that is most often identified as the reason for inflated costs is the problem of abuse. Fraud is, in the terms of social science, a myth:[1] that is, it may or may not be true, but what is really happening is probably less important for policy than what people believe is happening. There is some evidence to show fraud, even if most of the survey evidence is confined to a limited part of the benefit system, focusing on unemployment, disability and lone parents. There is very little evidence to suggest that fraud is a major problem in either pensions or Child Benefit, and together they constitute half the costs of the system. Irrespective of the evidence, however, there is a widespread belief that the system is riddled with fraud. This belief is shared by the press, the public, politicians and administrators of the system. The effect of the belief is powerful enough to change the way the system as a whole operates.

## How much fraud is there?

The concern with fraud in the benefit system is very long-standing, but it revived in the 1970s. The political right picked up the issue after the publication of an anonymous exposé by a benefits officer, Robin Page, who was subsequently identified and sacked. Page's subsequent book, *The benefits racket*,[2] crystallised concern, and the press latched on to the issue. A government inquiry into the subject in 1973 focused the attention of benefits administrators on the issue.[3] The

---

[1]   G Sorel (1961) *Reflections on violence,* New York: Collier-Macmillan.
[2]   R Page (1971) *The benefits racket,* London: Temple Smith.
[3]   Cmnd 5228 (1973) *Report of the Committee on abuse of social security benefits,* London: HMSO.

press gave increasing attention to fraud cases, notably the Deevy case in 1976,[4] and coverage and concern escalated, although official estimates were that fraud was tiny – about £2.6 million in 1975. The Conservative government which came into power in 1979 greatly increased both the numbers of investigators and the estimated levels of fraud, raising the official estimate from £4 million to £200 million.[5] The government's justification for this increase was that the previous figure was based in detected, irrecoverable fraud; the £200 million represented what might be happening.[6] They argued that about 1% of all funds were claimed fraudulently. The basis for this figure was explained in Parliament by Reg Prentice, the minister responsible:

> There is no need to ring around department stores to know that they, and other large commercial organisations, assume a loss through fraud of 1 or 2 per cent in their operations. Applying that to the DHSS, with its expenditure of £20 billion a year, leads to an estimated figure of £200 million.[7]

There are perhaps some differences between the administration of benefits and department stores: Jobcentre Plus does not lay the money out on display and invite people to walk round and handle it. But Prentice's rough guess has been the basis for much of the work done subsequently. When a 1998 Green Paper recorded that 2% of fraud was 'confirmed', it did not mean that it was established, discovered, detected or even based on evidence; it meant that the figure was generally accepted to be true.

The estimates of benefit fraud were frequently revised upwards throughout the next twenty years. A study in 1981 by Sir Derek Rayner suggested that 8% of unemployed people (in one location) were working while claiming benefit.[8] The claim was described by the permanent head of the DHSS as 'speculation in the absence of hard evidence'.[9] In the 1990s, Benefit Reviews suggested levels of fraud, varying according to benefit, of up to 12.2%. The argument was made not that fraud had risen proportionately as expenditure on social security increased, but that it had mushroomed, outstripping the growth in benefits. That was certainly the view of the former Chief Executive of the Benefits Agency, in

---

[4]  P Golding and S Middleton (1978) 'Why is the press so obsessed with welfare scroungers?', *New Society*, 26 October; P Golding and S Middleton (1982) *Images of welfare*, Basingstoke: Macmillan.

[5]  F Field (1979) 'The myth of the social security scrounger', *New Statesman*, 16 November.

[6]  L Chalker (1979) 'Reply to Field', *New Statesman*, 7 December.

[7]  *Hansard* (1980) HC Deb.981-1156, 25 March.

[8]  D Rayner (1981) *Payment of benefits to unemployed people*, London: Department of Employment, Department of Health and Social Security.

[9]  Cited in R Smith (1985) 'Who's fiddling? Fraud and abuse', in S Ward (ed) *DHSS in crisis*, London: Child Poverty Action Group.

his evidence to the Public Accounts Committee: 'We always took the view that fraud was increasing through social security.'[10] The 1998 Green Paper was more graphic: 'our budget is under attack.'[11]

Some of the estimates have been unreliable to the point of being irresponsible. The Green Paper estimated fraud at 7% of total benefit costs. This was made up of 2% 'confirmed fraud', 3% 'high suspicion' and 2% 'low suspicion'. These figures were inflated at every turn − in the initial assumptions, the acceptance of suspicion as fact, exaggerated estimates of the cost of fraud, the inclusion of further material on 'low suspicion', the extension of assumptions to benefits that have not been investigated and a liberal rounding up of all the totals. Following public criticism in 2002, the government reduced the estimates from £7 billion to about £2 billion. This figure was more securely founded, because there was some survey evidence to back it up, but it was still based substantially on the assumptions that suspicions raised are justified and that where fraud is happening, it happens for long periods.

The Department for Work and Pensions currently estimates figures for 'fraud and error' in the benefit system. Some benefits are 'continuously reviewed': Income Support, Jobseeker's Allowance, Employment and Support Allowance, Pension Credit and Housing Benefit. Most other benefits are reviewed only intermittently, and some are either too small to bother with or, like Council Tax Benefit, are assumed to follow the pattern of other benefits. The headline figures for fraud and error are:

- 5.5%, or £640 million, on Income Support and Jobseeker's Allowance;
- 4.9%, or £840 million, on Housing Benefit;
- 5.1%, or £390 million, on Pension Credit;
- 3.4%, or £220 million, on Incapacity Benefit.

The estimate for the total loss through fraud and error is £3,000 million.[12] Those figures are substantial, and consistent with the (lower) previous estimates, but they still need to be treated with some caution. They bring together three different types of estimate: assessments of fraud, overpayments through customer error and overpayments through official error. The total on the five benefits listed in the headline figures is £2,090 million. Without official error, that figure becomes £1,510 million. The estimate of fraud on its own for these five benefits is £770 million, and the total estimate for fraud across the whole system is consequently

---

[10] House of Commons (1998) *Select Committee on Public Accounts: 58th Report, Minutes of evidence*, HC 570, London: The Stationery Office

[11] Department of Social Security (1998) *Beating fraud is everyone's business*, Cm 4012, London: The Stationery Office, para 2.2.

[12] Department for Work and Pensions Information Directorate (2009) *Fraud and error in the benefit system: April 2008 to March 2009*, London: DWP (http://research.dwp.gov.uk/asd/asd2/fem/fem_apr08_mar09.pdf).

£1,100 million.[13]   This is less than one sixth of what was supposed to be true in 1998.

Other recent figures estimate the level of fraud for the DWP at £1 billion and fraud for Tax Credits at £0.6 billion. A further £2.6 billion is attributed to customer error, of which £1.5 billion is attributed to Tax Credits.[14]   HMRC has in the meantime undertaken to deliver £8 billion of savings from fraud and error in tax credits by 2014-15,[15] which appears to be nearly all the money lost. The commitment seems unrealistic.

## The prevention of fraud

The strategy for dealing with fraud commits the agencies to 'prevent, detect, correct, punish and deter'.[16]   The principal forms of fraud are claiming benefit while working, cohabitation, feigning disability and having access to undeclared resources. They mainly affect benefits for people of working age, which is why measures to deal with fraud have concentrated principally on those groups. The system of unemployment review, now an established part of the response to unemployment, invites unemployed people for interview, at which point many people sign off. This could be taken as an indication they were not really entitled, though as many unemployed people sign off anyway in the normal course of events, it is difficult to be certain.

In relation to unemployment, certainly, the shift to a casualised and ephemeral labour market among low-paid workers creates both the opportunity and the motive for abuse of the system. The directions to fraud officers are to consider unemployed people as possibly fraudulent if they have:

- a suspiciously high standard of living
- a skill or trade that should be employable
- past self-employment
- good health and fitness.

Working while employed also depends on the collusion of employers, and the Fraud Investigation Service conducts special operations in relation to certain sectors (such as building, catering and taxi services) where irregular employment is common.

Lone parents are suspected of cohabiting if:

- they are in debt
- they refuse to get a maintenance order

---

[13] DWP Information Directorate (2009) table 2.1.

[14] HMRC and DWP (2010) Tackling fraud and error in the benefits and tax credit systems, www.dwp.gov.uk/docs/tackling-fraud-and-error.pdf, p 12.

[15] Cm 7942 (2010) Spending Review 2010, London: HM Treasury, p 71.

[16] HMRC/DWP (2010) p 7.

- they have been deserted
- there are signs of a male presence.

The main form of fraud by pensioners is failure to declare capital resources. Prosecution is rare, but a claim may be made against the estate when the pensioner dies.

Besides the detection of fraud through the process of review, fraud has been the subject of national campaigns.[17] There is a National Benefit Fraud Hotline, which is widely advertised and receives over 17,000 calls a month. Informing on friends, neighbours and relatives is a popular pastime, but overwhelmingly the helpful citizens who make these calls turn out to be mistaken. Recent requests for information have not been answered informatively,[18] so I have to rely on earlier material. According to a Parliamentary statement, 205,999 calls were received in 2001-02 concerning 161,052 cases of alleged fraud. Of these, 6,385 people had their benefit altered: the statement notes that these figures 'include increases and decreases and can relate either to fraud, client error or official error' In other words, the vast majority of calls were misconceived, and some of the reports of fraud were so very mistaken that the people investigated had their benefit increased as a result. Only 768 cases, fewer than 1 in 200, led to prosecution.[19]

## Why has fraud been so difficult to eradicate?

There is a widespread suspicion that the social security system has failed to deal with fraud effectively. Despite repeated, often severe crackdowns, the level of fraud seems to remain high – and may, if the figures are to be believed, be rather higher than when the crackdowns started. The Comptroller and Auditor General, who is responsible for monitoring the accounts of the DWP, has for several years 'qualified' the accounts, which means that he has refused to approve them while a large black hole continues to appear in them.

It seems appropriate to ask why nearly forty years of crackdowns on fraud seem to have little effect, or even the reverse effect from that intended. Partly, it may be because the obsessive pursuit of abusive claimants has poisoned the water; the constant harping on fraud generates secretiveness and alienation from the system. Dean and Melrose classify four groups among fraudulent claimants. Some are 'subversive', justifying their action; some are unprincipled, seeing no need to justify what they are doing; some are 'fatalistic', finding it difficult to justify what

---

[17] S Connor (2007) 'We're on to you', *Critical Social Policy*, vol 27, no 2, pp 231-52.

[18] *Hansard* (2009) www.publications.parliament.uk/pa/cm200809/cmhansrd/cm090127/text/90127w0037.htm; see also Ipswich Unemployed Action (2010) www.intensiveactivity.com/government-hides-false-disability-benefit-fraud-allegations/fraud-referral-and-intervention-management-system-0913,1257,351,37.html.

[19] *Hansard* (2002) col 1143W, reproduced in *Benefits* (2002) vol 10, no 3, p 244.

they do and feeling guilty about it; and some are 'desperate', feeling they have been forced into it.[20]

Arguably, there may be a problem because the rules on fraud are trying to eradicate behaviour which is normal, reasonable and desirable. For many single parents, forming a new partnership is crucial to moving off benefits; creating obstacles to the process may not help. In situations where people have no regular income, taking the opportunity to earn some extra money is not necessarily something to be disapproved: on the contrary, it may be just the sort of engagement in society that the benefits system wants to encourage. (Insurance benefits often allow for some earnings, such as the allowance for 'therapeutic work' in Incapacity Benefit.)

In part, too, the lack of success may be because the circumstances in which people claim benefits illegitimately are built in to the benefits system. The benefits rules create their own problems: if people have changing circumstances, rules relating to income, part-time earnings and domestic arrangements inevitably catch some people out. As the rules have been tightened, and as benefits have become increasingly residual and conditional, it becomes more difficult to conform to them. A claimant comments:

> You always think you're doing wrong .... I think I'm doing wrong every time because I don't know what I can have. That thing [the fraud warning] frightens you to death.[21]

## Fraud, error and overpayments

There is a persistent blurring in official statements of the distinction between fraud – deliberate misrepresentation – and claimant error. Fraud generally implies an overpayment – that people receive money they are not entitled to. Genuine errors can lead to underpayment as well as overpayment, but in many cases an error which leads to people claiming too little (for example, by not getting a disability premium) will be classed as non-take-up rather than error. That means that the figures for error are biased towards overpayment. Despite that, the Department for Work and Pensions estimates that £1,200 million was underpaid through claimant or administrative error in 2008-09[22] – the £700 million not claimed through claimant error should be set against the £1,100 million overclaimed.

---

[20] H Dean and M Melrose (1996) 'Manageable discord', *Social Policy and Administration*, vol 31, no 2, pp 103–18.

[21] Claimant, cited in C Walker (1987) 'Reforming social security – despite the claimant', in A Walker and C Walker (eds) *The growing divide*, London: Child Poverty Action Group, p 104.

[22] DWP Information Directorate (2009).

---

There is some inconsistency in an official strategy which recognises that errors are produced by the muddles generated by the benefits system, but at the same time emphasises punishment and deterrent policies.[23] The fundamental problems here are the complexity of the system and the complexities of people's lives. What is classed as 'fraud' is not necessarily equivalent to the kind of rapacious and dishonest attempts to denude the system that are commonly reported in the press. Apparently the highest levels of fraud in the system are from lone parents who are cohabiting and who do not declare their situation. But the cohabitation rule is not clear-cut, and it is far from certain that the lone parents who are affected would recognise that they are in breach of the rules, or that the men who they are cohabiting with would recognise a financial responsibility to support them or their children. One example of a case meriting 'high suspicion' given in a DWP report was that of a lone parent who is visited, who denies that she is living with her boyfriend, but who comes in the day afterward to sign off benefit because she is living with her boyfriend.[24] This could have been dishonest, but it could also be that the lone parent in question did not think of herself as cohabiting until the process of review pushed her and her boyfriend into thinking about their relationship and where it had got to. Those who have been through the process of forming a long-term relationship may well recognise the hesitation and uncertainty involved.

If the problems of the benefit system are intractable, the fault lies in the structure of the system. We know that benefits which are not means tested, do not rely on identification of specific need and relate to long-term circumstances, are much less vulnerable to fraud and error than other benefits. The estimates for Pension Credit suggest that overpayment through fraud stands at 1.5%, customer error at 1.5% and official error at 2.1%, making 5.1% altogether. By contrast, the equivalent figures for Retirement Pension − a benefit delivered to much the same client group − are 0.0%, 0.1% and 0.0%. The government's conviction that a means-tested, frequently adjusted Universal Credit will reduce fraud and error [25] is hard to reconcile with this picture. If we want to make benefits more controllable and less prone to error, we have to reduce their responsiveness to individual circumstances and their complexities.

## QUESTIONS FOR DISCUSSION

Does fraud matter?
How can it be reduced?

---

[23] HMRC/DWP (2010).

[24] Department for Work and Pensions (2002) *The results of the area benefit review and the Quality Support Team from April 2000 to March 2001*, London: DWP.

[25] Cm 7942 (2010) p 7.

# Chapter 25

# Responding to poverty

The relief of poverty is only one aim of the social security system among many others. Poverty is a complex set of issues, and the performance of the benefit system is mixed. Overall, benefits provide for many of the contingencies that are likely to make people poor, but some benefits are inadequate, there are important gaps in provision for unemployment, disability and lone parenthood, and not all needs are met.

There is not much agreement about the idea of poverty, and commentators on the subject tend to express themselves in very different terms. For some, poverty is the inability to obtain the essentials of life; for others, a matter of low income; for others again, a problem of social inequality. There are at least twelve different clusters of meaning, overlapping but separable nevertheless. They include, first, definitions that are concerned with people's material conditions:

- *Need*, understood as a lack of the material goods or services, such as food, clothing, fuel or shelter, that people require in order to live and function in society.
- *A pattern of deprivation* This refers to circumstances in which people suffer from a constellation of deprivations associated with limited resources experienced over a period of time. Poverty is not defined, on this account, by any specific need (like hunger or homelessness), but on the existence of a pattern of deprivation.
- *Limited resources* Poverty can be taken to refer to circumstances in which people lack the income, wealth or resources to acquire the things they need.

Second, there are definitions concerned with people's economic circumstances:

- *Standard of living* Poverty is taken to refer to a general standard of living, or pattern of consumption, below the norm.
- *Inequality in resources* People may be held to be poor because they have less than others in society. Researchers have argued that poverty is defined by people's inability to use resources which are available to others, creating an 'economic distance' from the rest of society.[1]

---

[1] M O'Higgins and S Jenkins (1990) 'Poverty in the EC: 1975, 1980, 1985', in R Teekens and B van Praag (eds) *Analysing poverty in the European Community* (*Eurostat News* Special Edition 1-1990), Luxembourg: European Communities.

- *Economic position* Many commentators argue that people's economic position is stratified, and so that economic position shapes their life chances and opportunities. This is also a question of inequality, but the inequalities are defined in terms of economic relationships and long-term trends.

This shades, third, into ideas of poverty based on social relationships:

- *Social class* Poverty constitutes a class either when it establishes distinct categories of social relationship (like exclusion or dependency), or when the situation of poor people is identifiably distinguishable from others.
- *Lack of basic security* Charles Booth referred to poor people as 'living under a struggle to obtain the necessaries of life and make both ends meet'.[2] Poverty can be understood in terms of security rather than actual resources. The idea of basic security has been influential in international organisations: it has been defined in terms directly equivalent to need and it may also be seen in terms of vulnerability.
- *Exclusion* Poverty can be seen as a set of social relationships in which people are excluded from participation in the normal pattern of social life. The idea of exclusion extends beyond the experience of deprivation to include problems that result from stigmatisation and social rejection. The European Community has defined poverty as exclusion resulting from limited resources:

  > The poor shall be taken as to mean persons, families and groups of persons whose resources (material, cultural and social) are so limited as to exclude them from the minimum acceptable way of life in the Member State in which they live.[3]

- *Lack of entitlement* It has been argued both that deprivation and lack of resources reflect lack of entitlements rather than the absence of essential items in themselves. Homelessness results from lack of access to housing or land, not from lack of housing; famines, Sen and Drèze argue, result not from lack of food, but from people's inability to buy the food that exists.[4] Poverty can also, then, be described in terms of a lack of social rights.
- *Dependency* Poor people are sometimes taken to be those who receive social benefits in consequence of their lack of means.

---

2  C Booth (1902) *Life and labour of the people in London*, First Series: Poverty, vol 1, London: Macmillan.

3  European Community (1985) 'On specific Community action to combat poverty (Council Decision of 19.2.84)', 85/8/EEC, *Official Journal of the EEC*, 2/24.

4  J Drèze and A Sen (1989) *Hunger and public action*, Oxford: Clarendon Press.

Lastly, there is a moral view of poverty:

- *Serious hardship* Poverty consists of serious deprivation, and people are held to be poor when their material circumstances are deemed to be morally unacceptable.

The root of disagreements about poverty is not just a matter of definition: it is that poverty is a moral concept. When we say that someone is poor, we are saying that there are serious hardships, and implying that something ought to be done about them. That is one reason why the Conservative government in the early 1990s denied that poverty existed in Britain, and sought to remove the term from government reports. They were not saying that people did not have low incomes, or that they were not in need; they did not think that the problems were so serious as to demand a change of policy. 'These people', a Conservative minister famously argued against the poverty lobby, 'would find poverty in paradise.'[5]

Is anyone really poor in Britain? It is true enough that there is no mass starvation here. However, the supposition that mass starvation is representative of poverty elsewhere in the world is just as mistaken. Poverty in developing countries may involve a lack of basic necessities, but it involves many other things, too. The World Bank has commissioned an extensive number of studies. *Voices of the poor* summarises responses from over 20,000 poor people in 23 countries.[6] Poverty is treated as a multidimensional issue. The researchers focus on ten interlocking dimensions of poverty: precarious livelihoods, excluded locations, physical problems, gender relations, problems in social relationships, lack of security, abuse by those in power, disempowering institutions, weak community organisations and limitations on the capabilities of the poor. There are certainly important differences between the experience of poverty in Britain and in developing countries. It is striking, for example, how far in developing countries the organisations of the state, and in particular the police, are seen as part of the problems of poverty. But what is apparent in much of this research is how far poverty is about other things apart from physical subsistence. From the perspective of people who are poor in developing countries, poverty is not just about food; it is about personal security, rights, social relationships and the lack of power. The same is true in Britain.

## Measuring poverty

The central problem of identifying who is poor is that there is so little agreement about the basic problems we are trying to define. There are no indisputable

---

[5]  J Moore (1989) *The end of the line for poverty*, London: Conservative Political Centre.

[6]  D Narayan, R Chambers, M Shah and P Petesch (2000) *Voices of the poor: Crying out for change*, New York: World Bank/Oxford University Press.

'facts'; there are only hints, pointers and half-truths. Measuring complex problems is usually done, in social science, through the use of 'indicators'. The term 'indicators' was chosen to emphasise that the kinds of official statistic produced for this sort of exercise were not conclusive proof of anything; they were signposts. Indicators do not have to be precise, but they have to point the way; over time, it should be possible at least to say whether problems are getting better, worse or staying about the same. They need to be accessible, reasonably comprehensible and persuasive.

There are three main types of headline indicator that are used to discuss poverty. The first is the number of people who are receiving basic benefits. Because means-tested benefits are aimed at people on low incomes, and because they have been held to a very low level, entitlement to benefit is a good indication of people living on very low incomes. There are nearly five million claimants receiving the basic means-tested benefits – Guarantee Credit, Income Support or income-related Jobseeker's Allowance (see Chapter 8). The figures are reasonably reliable (though, as explained in Chapter 22, they are not as precise as they might at first appear). They can also be misleading. For one thing, the rates that are used to gauge entitlement are different for different groups: pensioners are rather more generously treated. For another, the figures relate only to the number of people who receive benefit, which is rather lower than the number of people on similarly low incomes.

A second commonly used indicator is based on low income. There is no official measure of poverty in the UK, but the standard generally used in the European Union relates poverty to median income, identifying people as poor if they live on less than 60% of median average income after income tax, social security contributions and benefits. The median income is the level of income where half the population are above the figure, and half are below it. This represents, in the view of the researchers who developed the measure, a useful indicator of 'economic distance', or the adequacy of income relative to other social standards.[7] Official statistics in the UK for some time referred to 50% of the mean average, not the median. The mean is a moving target; unlike the mean, the median does not change if the incomes of relatively poor people, or relatively rich people, go up or down. This was not the test that was being used in the rest of the EU, and it seems likely that the mean was being used by mistake. Converting to 50% of the median, the figure the government should have used at first, would have defined fewer people as being in poverty while excluding many people just above the 50% level, so the figures were converted to 60% of the median as the nearest equivalent.

---

[7]   M O'Higgins and S Jenkins (1990) 'Poverty in the EC: 1975, 1980, 1985', in R Teekens and B van Praag (eds) *Analysing poverty in the European Community*, Luxembourg: European Communities.

Median income is found, in general, in the lower part of the earnings distribution. That happens because the lowest part of the income distribution tends to be occupied by people who rely on social benefits rather than earnings. As a very broad generalisation, state support is the main source of income in the bottom 20% of the income distribution, while earnings are the main source of income in the remaining 80%.[8] As long as benefits are lower than wages, it must be true that the larger the section of the population is who receive benefits, the further down in the earnings distribution is the median found. The median income is higher than the lowest parts of the earnings distribution, but not so much higher that it is wholly immune from the problems of low pay; and among those problems seems to be the exposure of lower paid workers to insecure, unstable and precarious employment. The basic position seems to be, then, that people are considered to be poor only if their position is markedly worse than those who live on modest but potentially insecure incomes.

The UK series appears annually under the title *Households below average income*. The figures are equivalised for different sizes of household. *HBAI* reviews a range of different calculations – 50%, 60% and 70% of the median, both before and after housing costs.[9] The headline figures usually refer to 60% of the median after housing costs; the figures before housing costs show more people with children in poverty. The figure before housing costs is more meaningful. If the purpose of using the median is to point to economic distance, housing is one of the principal elements to consider: unlike the costs of food or fuel, housing costs are determined relatively, in competition with others. In 2007/08, 18% of the population lived on less than 60% of the median income.[10]

The third test is the examination of deprivation. The work of Peter Townsend, and subsequent studies for the *Breadline Britain* programmes, have sought to identify poverty in terms of people's access to essential goods, services and amenities.[11] The approach attempts to gauge what people think of as essential, and to see how many people are unable to afford those things. A related survey for the Joseph Rowntree Foundation estimates that 26% of the population (approximately 14.5 million people) are poor. The findings suggest that roughly 9.5 million people in Britain today cannot afford adequate housing conditions. About 8 million cannot afford one or more essential household goods. Almost 7.5 million people are too poor to engage in common social activities considered necessary by the majority of the population. About 2 million British children

---

[8]  Department for Work and Pensions (2010) *Households below average income: An analysis of the income distribution 1994/95-2008/09*, London: DWP, table 2.2.

[9]  DWP (2010).

[10]  DWP (2010), table 3.5.

[11]  P Townsend (1979) *Poverty in the United Kingdom*, Harmondsworth: Penguin; J Mack and S Lansley (1985) *Poor Britain*, London: Allen & Unwin; D Gordon and C Pantazis (eds) (1997) *Breadline Britain in the 1990s*, London: Avebury.

go without at least two things they need. About 6.5 million adults go without essential clothing. Around 4 million are not properly fed by today's standards. Over 10.5 million suffer from financial insecurity.[12]

Bradshaw and Finch have examined the overlap between poverty on three different dimensions: a measure of deprivation, a test of low income and a sense of 'subjective' poverty, where people feel they are poor. People who are poor on all three criteria tend to be in greater poverty than others, and of course there are smaller numbers on all three than on one or the other. The surprising finding is not that poverty is more intense in those circumstances, which might be expected, but that it seems to be different in character. The people who were poor by all three measures were far more likely not to be working, not to be receiving essential public services and not to be engaging and participating in society.[13]

The indicators reviewed here suggest that up to a quarter of the UK population may be poor, depending on how the figures are calculated. We can say that the people on the lowest incomes in the UK are unlikely to be engaged in the labour market. This is the basis for the government's emphasis on work as the principal means of escaping poverty. (The main reservation is that people on benefit do not necessarily have the option of working.) The largest categories of people who are vulnerable to poverty are young single people who are not working, families with young children, female lone parents, people with disabilities and older pensioners. The prevalence of poverty in different households has changed radically in the last thirty years. In the 1960s and 1970s, the largest category of poor people were pensioners.[14] The position of pensioners has improved steadily since that time, but the situation of families with children has not improved, and in the 1990s there was a very marked deterioration. Currently, 2.8 million children − about a third of all children − live below 60% of median income.[15] Most of these children are in families without work, but nearly half live in families with low earnings, where the main earner is in the bottom quartile of the earnings distribution.[16]

Although these groups are more vulnerable, it is not clear that any group is immune to poverty. Most of the population is likely to have been on a low income for at least some time in the last few years. According to official statistics, 58% of the population spent at least one year below the threshold of 60% of the median

---

[12] D Gordon et al (2000) *Poverty and social exclusion in Britain*, York: Joseph Rowntree Foundation.

[13] J Bradshaw and N Finch (2003) 'Overlaps in dimensions of poverty', *Journal of Social Policy*, vol 32, no 4, pp 513-25.

[14] R Layard, D Piachaud and M Stewart (1978) *The causes of poverty*, Royal Commission on the Distribution of Income and Wealth Background Paper no 5, London: HMSO.

[15] DWP (2010), table 4.3tr.

[16] P Gregg, S Harkness and S Machin (1999) 'Poor kids: trends in child poverty in Britain 1968-96', *Fiscal Studies*, vol 20, no 2, pp 163-87.

income between 1991 and 2002, and 67% spent at least one year in the bottom 30% of the income distribution.[17] This information was dropped from the tables after 2004, but as the prevalence of low income has not much changed,[18] and DWP statistics show that poor people are now less likely to be below the 60% threshold for long periods,[19] it seems to follow that more people, not fewer, must be passing through low income transiently. Most of the population is liable to be on a low income for some time in the next few years.

## The relief of poverty

Many of the deficiencies in the system have been covered at earlier stages in this book, so part of the task at this stage is simply to summarise. The largest class of cases where social security has failed to protect people from poverty are those that were left out of the Beveridge plan. The most important of these were:

- *unemployment*, because full employment had been assumed;
- *disability,* because people with disabilities were unable to work;
- *lone parenthood*, because of the growth of divorce, cultural change and the return of mass unemployment; and
- *low pay*.

Low wages have not usually been seen as a major cause of poverty because benefits levels are so much lower, but ensuring an adequate standard of living for people in work requires some consideration of income levels and of expenses. Beveridge assumed full employment and child allowances, but he took it for granted that once people were employed, they would have enough money. This was not necessarily true, because for most of the post-war period Britain did not have a minimum wage, unlike most other countries in the European Union. Support for low pay workers was introduced in the 1970s through means-tested benefits, from 1971 in the form of Family Income Supplement and Family Credit (now the Working Tax Credit), and from 1972 in the form of Rent Rebate (now Housing Benefit). The minimum wage was introduced only in 1999.

The second class concerned circumstances where benefits were inadequate. This has been generally true, but it was avoidable in at least two cases:

- *old age*, where many deficiencies have been largely rectified for the next generation, because the pensions were not minimally adequate, and
- *children*, because allowances for dependants were low.

---

[17] ONS (Office for National Statistics) (2005) *Households below average income 1994/5-2003/4*, London: The Stationery Office, table 7.5
[18] DWP (2010), table 3.1tr.
[19] DWP (2010) ch 7.

There were also specific deficiencies in benefit adequacy. There are several examples, because increased bills in any area − like water, fuel or transport − might lead overall to a shortage of income. Two examples, however, are particularly important, because of their relative scale and because of their direct effect on benefits. These are housing costs and liability to tax. Housing expenses used to be taken into account directly on National Assistance and Supplementary Benefit: tenants had their rent treated as part of the assessment of need, and owner-occupiers had mortgage interest paid. Many pensioners in particular received Supplementary Benefit for housing costs alone. There have been significant changes in this position. First, council housing − at its peak, a third of all households in Britain received a general subsidy, meaning that rents were kept low. Housing Benefit was introduced (as Rent Rebate) because the government decided, as a matter of policy, to withdraw this general subsidy. Rents trebled, and most tenants were not able to pay the increased costs without receiving benefit. For owner-occupiers, the biggest change came in the 1990s, when the protection for mortgages was reduced − it now only becomes available after a six-month wait − and they were encouraged to get private insurance instead.

People on benefits were unlikely in the immediate post-war period to be substantially liable to tax. This is no longer the case. One important change, for people on very low incomes, was the introduction of Value Added Tax, which makes poor people liable for tax on expenditure on a range of goods, including adult clothing, domestic energy and household goods. (The exemption of food, which is a higher proportion of the expenditure of poor people than rich ones, helps to make the pattern of VAT more progressive overall.) Another change was the introduction of the Community Charge and then the Council Tax, where the government argued that even poor people had to have some liability for payment. Thirdly, there is also the effect of deterrent taxation, particularly on cigarettes. People on lower incomes tend to pay a much higher proportion of their income on cigarettes than people on higher incomes; penal taxation has had major public health benefits, but it also leads to the disturbing position where people on low incomes may go without food to be able to smoke.

## Benefits and poverty

One of the main tests that is made of social security systems is whether they leave people with enough income to be able to participate in society − the test of 'economic distance' used in the European Union. By comparison with other systems, the British system has tended to be inclusive, reaching a high proportion of people on low incomes, but in general it has provided them with benefits at a very low level. Despite its coverage, then, social security in Britain has often not done enough to prevent people from becoming poor.

The social security system in Britain was not intended to deal with poverty. Poverty had been the province of the Poor Law, and the social security system in the welfare state was going to be different. Despite that, the social security system continues to deal with issues of poverty. In principle, the social security system was intended to deal with all the main contingencies, leaving only a small residuum that would be mopped up by social assistance. In practice, the deficiencies of the National Insurance system were large, and they led to many people relying on residual provision for support.

In Chapter 21, I discussed benefits that are aimed directly at poverty – not, as some might have it, the means-tested benefits, but benefits that relate to different understandings of poverty, like material need, dependency and exclusion. Poverty is a much broader concept than lack of income alone, and although income maintenance can help to relieve some social problems, like social exclusion and a lack of material goods, it is not necessarily a complete answer. Responding to poverty can be done in many ways besides income maintenance – for example, through economic development, the provision of services or the development of social participation. Social security is important for action against poverty, however, because income maintenance is often enough to relieve poverty, and because even when it is not, it may be a prerequisite for other action.

## QUESTIONS FOR DISCUSSION

Should benefits be high enough to avoid low-income poverty altogether?
What would raising benefits not achieve?

# Chapter 26

# Social security and redistribution

Social security redistributes money in several directions – not only between rich and poor, but between age groups, different types of households and people with different types of need. Overall, the system has a progressive redistributive effect. The system might become more redistributive with greater means testing, but the aims of benefits depend on many other principles, and progressive redistribution is not the only test.

A measure is redistributive if the people who receive goods or services from a measure are not the same as the people who pay. All welfare provision is, by definition, redistributive in some way. Redistribution is conventionally classified as vertical or horizontal. Vertical redistribution may be progressive (from rich to poor) or regressive (from poor to rich). Horizontal redistribution goes from one kind of group to another – from men to women, households without children to families with children, tenants to owner-occupiers. Pensions are typically benefits that go from people of working age to people who are older. This is a horizontal redistribution: pensioners may be poorer than people of working age, but they are not necessarily poorer, and the system can be better understood as a transfer across generations.

Part of the issue of redistribution was considered in chapter 25, in the examination of the implications of social security for people on low incomes. This is 'vertical' redistribution. Much of the literature tends to take the aim of vertical redistribution for granted: it is assumed that benefits are intended for the relief of poverty, and the test of whether or not a benefit works is whether it gets resources to people on low incomes. When we are looking at redistribution through social security benefits, however, it is usual to look not just at the vertical movement, but also to consider horizontal shifts. Barr makes a general analysis of pensions. Pensions redistribute resources:

- from young to old;
- from rich to poor, in so far as the ratio of benefits to contributions is greater for people on lower incomes;
- from poor to rich, in so far as richer people live longer;
- from men to women, because women live longer and have earlier retirement.[1]

---

[1]  N Barr (2004) *The economics of the welfare state*, Oxford: Oxford University Press, pp 199–201.

Another example might be Child Benefit. The redistribution is horizontal, not vertical. There are three main directions of movement:

- from people without children to people with children. Families without children include both younger people (who tend to earn less) and older earners (who tend to earn more).
- from people with smaller households to people with larger households (someone with three children receives more in Child Benefit than someone with two). The families that are most vulnerable to low income are those with young children under five – these families are likely to be younger, which is associated with lower wages, but more importantly very young children stop one parent, usually the mother, from going out to work. Despite preconceptions to the contrary, larger families in the UK tend not to be on lower incomes. This is because larger families tend to be older (it takes time to have children) and older workers tend to earn more. The main exception to this are large families where the ages of the children prevent the mother working for long periods.
- from men to women. This has been one of the main arguments in favour of Child Benefit.[2]

Child Benefit is modestly progressive because households with children currently tend to be on lower incomes than households without them. This is a relatively recent development, partly because of a change in the relative distribution of household income during the 1990s, but mainly because until April 2004 Child Benefit did not give any net income to families on Income Support. Before that date, the pattern of redistribution was slightly regressive. The distributive effects are not, then, characteristic of family allowances in general – they are contingent, and specific to the system in Britain. By contrast, the complex system of family allowances in France is more progressive, because:

- some of the benefits are means tested, and so available only to families on lower incomes;
- they are linked to an extensive system of childcare, which means that women can return to work; and
- some benefits are specifically concentrated on children under the age of three.

In principle, the distributive impact of benefits requires detailed calculation. Economists model the effects of changes in benefits either using illustrative, typical households[3] or on the basis of survey evidence (like the regular *Expenditure and*

---

[2]  A Walsh and R Lister (1985) *Mother's life line*, London: Child Poverty Action Group.
[3]  For example, H Sutherland, T Sefton and D Piachaud (2003) *Poverty in Britain*, York: Joseph Rowntree Foundation

*Food Survey*).[4]   In situations where the effectiveness and impact of benefits rests on take-up and personal circumstances, it is difficult to predict the likely effect without detailed calculation. There is still a role, however, for commonsense evaluations. It does not take any great mathematical competence to anticipate that if benefits to older people go up, younger people have to pay, or that lowering the threshold for National Insurance contributions without raising the ceiling would leave lower-paid workers relatively worse off.

## How to redistribute more to people on lower incomes

Redistribution to people on lower incomes is often represented as an aim of social security.  Before we consider how benefits could redistribute more to people on lower incomes, we ought to hesitate for a moment, and ask whether that is what we really want to do.  Many benefits are intended to do other things entirely − like benefits for people with disabilities, which are based in different understandings of need, compensation and earned entitlement, as well as concepts like social protection and solidarity.

Redistribution to people on lower incomes takes three main forms.[5]   One approach is 'maximin' − maximising the minimum, or raising the floor, so that everyone on higher incomes contributes to improve the situation of people at the bottom. This is the general principle behind taxation in the UK: nearly all workers contribute to taxation, even if they are on low pay, and benefits provide a low-level income for those who cannot work.  However, the distribution of income for those who are poorest has been worsening: the ratio between the median income of the poorest fifth and the median income of the population currently stands at about 1:2.5.[6]   Second, we might alter the ratio of inequality, taking more from people on higher incomes, less from people on middling incomes, and distributing some money to people on lower incomes, and most money to people on very low incomes. This is, more or less, is the idea behind Tax Credits. Once again, the current trend is that inequality in these terms is increasing − there is greater dispersion, though more of this dispersion is attributable to the deterioration of the position of the people on lower incomes than it is to increases in higher incomes.[7]  A third approach is to reduce the range of inequality, taking money from people at the top and moving it to people at the bottom. This is the 'Robin Hood' approach: despite popular belief to the contrary, it has never been policy.

---

[4]   T Clark, C Giles and J Hall (1999) *Does Council Tax Benefit work?*, London: Institute for Fiscal Studies.

[5]   See D Rae (1981) *Equalities*, Cambridge, MA: Harvard University Press.

[6]   T Macinnes, T Kenway and A Parekh (2009) *Monitoring poverty and social exclusion*, York: Joseph Rowntree Foundation, pp 21–2.

[7]   Macinnes, Kenway and Parekh (2009), p 19.

All three approaches – maximin, ratio and range – can, if taken to extremes, lead to the same distributive outcomes. They are, however, very different in practice. Maximin can be achieved through universal benefits, like Child Benefit or Basic Income, paid for out of taxation, though it could also be achieved by a minimum income guarantee, which would be means tested. Changing the ratio, the second approach, is done through a combination of progressive taxation and means testing. Reducing the range would be achieved through a combination of highly progressive taxation, like 'super tax' or wealth tax, and strictly selective residual benefits. Ironically, given the resistance to means testing of many commentators on the political left, this is probably the most directly effective means of redistributing resources to the poor.

## Who benefits?

The overall effect of redistribution through taxes and benefits is substantially to equalise the distribution of resources in the UK. Table 26.1 comes from a controversial series that used to figure in the annual report *Social Trends* but has now been relegated to supplementary publications. Initial income starts off very unequal; the original income of the top fifth is 15 times the income of the bottom fifth. Benefits change the balance markedly, so that people in the bottom fifth have about a sixth of the income of people in the top fifth. When other welfare

**Table 26.1: Redistribution of income through taxes and benefits (£ pa, UK, 2007-08)**

|  | Quintile group of households | | | | | All households | Approx. ratio of top to bottom fifth |
|---|---|---|---|---|---|---|---|
|  | Bottom fifth | Next fifth | Middle fifth | Next fifth | Top fifth |  |  |
| Average income per household |  | | | | | | |
| Original income | 4,651 | 12,574 | 23,640 | 38,505 | 72,581 | 30,390 | 16:1 |
| *plus* cash benefits | 6,453 | 7,131 | 5,309 | 3,311 | 1,666 | 4,774 | |
| Gross income | 11,105 | 19,705 | 28,949 | 41,816 | 74,247 | 35,164 | 7:1 |
| *less* direct taxes and National Insurance contributions | 1,202 | 2,770 | 5,393 | 9,096 | 18,517 | 7,396 | |
| Disposable income | 9,903 | 16,936 | 23,556 | 32,720 | 55,729 | 27,769 | 6:1 |
| *less* indirect taxes | 3,100 | 3,672 | 4,615 | 5,723 | 7,408 | 4,904 | |
| Post tax income | 6,803 | 13,264 | 18,941 | 26,997 | 48,321 | 22,865 | 7:1 |
| *plus* benefits in kind | 7,494 | 6,602 | 6,206 | 5,591 | 4,040 | 5,989 | |
| Final income | 14,297 | 19,866 | 25,147 | 32,588 | 52,371 | 28,854 | 4:1 |

services are taken into account, the final figures are much more equal than many people imagine: people in the bottom fifth have about a quarter the income of people in the top fifth.[8]

These general observations need to be treated with some caution. In the first place, the distribution of income by household depends a great deal on age and family structure.[9] Second, the distribution of income does not reveal the distribution of income by class. There may be class inequalities concealed by the broad averages. Third, the figures are sometimes debatable: Evandrou et al, using a different statistical base, argue that the approach underestimates the value of education to people in higher income brackets.[10] Finally, income is only one of the criteria by which welfare is judged. Wealth is important; so is command over resources, which is the ability to draw on resources when in need.

Having said this, the figures in the table do seem to show that the distribution of income is more equal than it is commonly thought to be, and that it is benefits, rather than taxation, which make the difference. Using the Gini coefficient, a widely used measure of inequality, the National Equality Panel suggests that 'while cash benefits reduce inequality in the distribution of household income, the overall effect of the tax system as a whole ... is small (apart, of course, from financing the benefits).'[11] In Table 26.1, the ratio of the bottom fifth to the top fifth is much the same before and after tax. Much of the difference is made by cash benefits, but a significant contribution is also made by benefits in kind, notably health and education, which provide nearly half the annual income of the households on the lowest income.

Social security is only part of the pattern of redistribution; roughly half of the income gained through social security transfers disappears through taxation. Unless the tax system was to be reformed, it would require a major increase in social security expenditure to make a significant difference in the resources available to the households in the lowest part of the income distribution.

[8]   Office for National Statistics (2010) *Effects of taxes and benefits on household income* (www.statistics.gov.uk/statbase/product.asp?vlnk=10336).

[9]   Department for Work and Pensions (2010) *Households below average income: an analysis of the income distribution 1994/95-2008/09*, London: DWP, table 3.1

[10]  M Evandrou, J Falkingham, J Hills and J Le Grand (1992) *The distribution of welfare benefits in kind*, London: Suntory-Toyota International Centre for Economics and Related Disciplines.

[11]  National Equality Panel (2010) *An anatomy of economic inequality in the UK*, London: Government Equalities Office/London School of Economics and Political Science, p 50.

## QUESTIONS FOR DISCUSSION

Who should benefit from social security?
What changes to social security and taxation would redistribute resources in the best way?

# Chapter 27

# How social security in Britain compares to other countries

Social security systems have been compared in three main ways: models of idealised welfare regimes, reviewing the rules and structures of benefits and looking at the combined effect of benefits on final income. It is difficult to generalise, because what is true for one part of a system is not necessarily true of others, but the relative performance of the UK tends to be mixed, and some way from the model of the 'welfare state'. Policy cannot be easily transferred from other countries, but comparisons can at least draw attention to a broader range of methods and mechanisms.

Much of the literature in social policy is interested in how policies in one country compare with others. The idea of the 'Welfare State' tends to give the impression that social security in Britain can be understood in systematic terms, as a coherent whole. Part of the problem with that assumption is that there are too many principles, policies and approaches being applied for it to be possible to sum up the system in a neat formula. Equally, there are many ways of doing things, and many of the countries we might reasonably think of as 'welfare states' – countries like Sweden, France or Germany – approach the problems differently.

Comparative social policy has tended to focus on the operation of welfare states as a whole. Social scientists who want to be able to generalise about policy can do it most effectively by looking at patterns across a range of different national experiences. The distinction between residual and institutional welfare has been the starting point for a wide range of classifications and typologies of welfare states. Titmuss distinguished a residual system like that in the United States from an 'institutional-redistributive' model, possibly influenced by Sweden, and a third 'industrial achievement/performance' model that may have been based on Germany, where social policy was traditionally subordinate to economic development.[1] Gøsta Esping-Andersen modified Titmuss's model to make a distinction between 'liberal' regimes, such as the UK and the US; 'conservative/corporatist' regimes, like Germany and France; and 'social democratic' regimes, like Sweden and Finland.[2] Stephan Leibfried describes four characteristic welfare regimes in developed countries, including 'Scandinavian welfare states', chiefly represented by Sweden, Norway, Denmark and Finland, where

[1]   R Titmuss (1974) *Social policy: An introduction*, London: Allen & Unwin.
[2]   G Esping-Andersen (1990) *The three worlds of welfare capitalism*, Cambridge: Polity Press.

welfare is most highly developed; the 'Bismarck' countries, Germany and Austria (the term is explained in Chapter 7); the 'Anglo-Saxon countries', including the UK, US, Australia and New Zealand, where welfare is residual and individualised; and the 'Latin Rim', covering Spain, Portugal, Greece, Italy and perhaps France, where welfare is 'rudimentary'.[3]

The models offer a useful shorthand, but they should not be taken too literally. They tend, necessarily, to rely on broad-brush interpretations. All of them misrepresent the countries they are describing – in the same way as Britain is not well described as 'Beveridgean', comprehensive or uniform, the US is too varied to be thought of simply as 'liberal' or individualist,[4] Sweden is much too much influenced by occupational status, and too reliant on residual benefits, to be either egalitarian or citizenship-based,[5] and France has a patchwork quilt of services that are not easily described by any formula.[6] In every case, the rules that apply to one group of people (such as pensioners) will probably not be the same as those that apply to another (like unemployed people).[7] The generalisations that these studies rely on tend to be, at one and the same time, too narrow to capture the range of policies that apply in any country, and too vague to give any direct clue as to how policies work in practice. We cannot tell, from a description of social security as 'institutional' or 'rights-based', what benefits will actually be like. Beyond that, the models give very little sense of what different policies mean in the context where they apply. Cass and Freeland object, for example, to the characterisation of the Australian system as 'liberal' or residual, just because it relies heavily on means testing; in their view, it is 'radically redistributive'.[8]

## Comparing the performance of different systems

The policies and methods used in one country do not necessarily work the same way in another. For example, it is difficult to make sense of benefits for people with disabilities without knowing more about the context where it is delivered. The structure of labour markets makes a difference to people with disabilities

[3]   S Leibfried (1991) *Towards a European welfare state?*, Bremen: Zentrum für Sozialpolitik.
[4]   T Marmor, J Mashaw and P Harvey (1990) *America's misunderstood welfare state*, New York: Basic Books.
[5]   V Timonen (2001) 'Earning welfare citizenship', in P Taylor-Gooby (ed) *Welfare states under pressure*, London: Sage Publications.
[6]   J Dupeyroux, M Borgetto and R Lafore (2008) *Droit de la sécurité sociale* (16th edn), Paris: Dalloz.
[7]   D Mabbett and H Bolderson (1999) 'Theories and methods in comparative social policy', in J Clasen (ed) *Comparative social policy: Concepts, theories and methods*, Oxford: Blackwell.
[8]   B Cass and J Freeland (1994) 'Social security and full employment in Australia', in J Hills, J Ditch and H Glennerster (eds) *Beveridge and social security*, Oxford: Clarendon Press.

and to their carers. It matters what services are available (such as medical care or domiciliary support); social security is principally concerned with income and resources, but the resources that people need depend on what other resources they have. It matters what further benefits there may be. Sometimes benefits for disabled people are delivered in countries with virtually no unemployment benefit, long-term sickness benefits or carer's allowance, so that they are the only income open to a family with a disabled member. It is fairly common that schemes fail to distinguish adequately between disability and incapacity, so that people with one set of problems have to present themselves in terms of a different set. The same kind of problems are reflected in almost any category of benefit: provision for unemployment, maternity, family benefits or old age depends heavily on the economic and social context and resources and services that are otherwise available.

The main way that social protection systems used to be compared was by looking in detail at the range of benefits and services they provided.[9] One of the principal sources of material, the US Social Security Administration's *Social security programs throughout the world*,[10] is primarily based in this approach. For each principal client group, like pensioners or children, it identifies a range of policies, entitlements and methods of delivery. John Dixon has used this database to offer rankings of 172 benefit systems, based on five main criteria suggested by the International Labour Organization: universality, adequacy, a minimal set of restrictions on eligibility, security of income and not basing entitlement solely on past earnings. For elderly people, Finland, Sweden and Denmark emerge most favourably; the US is ranked as 22nd, below Brazil and Belgium, and the UK comes in at 33, below Colombia and Bolivia.[11] Programmes for disability are headed by Australia, with Sweden 6th, Belgium at 25, Germany at 51, the UK at 72 and the US at 76.[12] For unemployed people, Finland, Australia and Ukraine lead the rankings, with Germany and Sweden coming 10th, the UK and France at 30 and 31, and the US at 43.[13] Overall, he finds that 'Australia has the best-designed social security system in the world',[14] despite its heavy reliance on income testing. It is followed by Sweden, France, Denmark and New Zealand.

---

[9]   For example, P Kaim-Caudle (1973) *Comparative social policy and social security*, London: Martin Robertson; M Gordon (1988) *Social security policies in industrial countries*, Cambridge: Cambridge University Press.

[10]  US Social Security Administration, *Social security programs throughout the world* (www. ssa.gov/policy/docs/progdesc/ssptw/)

[11]  J Dixon (2000) 'A global perspective on social security programs for the aged', *Journal of Aging and Social Policy*, vol 11, no 1, pp 39-66.

[12]  J Dixon and M Hyde (2000) 'A global perspective on social security programmes for the disabled', *Disability and Society*, vol 15, no 5, pp 709-30.

[13]  J Dixon (2001) 'A global perspective on social security programs for the unemployed', *International Social Work*, vol 44, no 4, pp 405-22.

[14]  J Dixon (1999) *Social security in global perspective*, Westport, CT: Praeger, p 217.

Britain comes in 37th, equal to Brazil but below a clutch of countries including Israel, Japan, Albania, Turkmenistan or Uruguay. If it is any consolation, Canada comes 46th and the US comes 62nd, below Iran and Turkey.

It is possible to draw some general lessons: that neither a high national income nor political posturing guarantees a commitment to welfare, and that standards which apply in one field of action do not necessarily apply in others. However, it would be unwise to put too much weight on this approach, and that is not just because people may reasonably disagree about the criteria. What appears to be true on paper may not reflect the situation in practice; problems of take-up, administration and delivery can mar the performance of any scheme. Benefits cannot be understood in isolation – what matters for people who are unemployed, disabled or retired is not just what the rules are for particular benefits, but how it all stacks up.

The main alternative approach to comparison was developed as part of the Luxembourg Income Study, a multinational project based on data from a range of developed countries. The analysis was based around the idea of the 'income package'.[15] The precise mechanisms and structures of benefits were less important, they argued, than what the benefits systems actually did. By this argument, the proper comparison between pensioners in Britain and pensioners in other countries is not whether the benefit is insurance based, or means tested, or work related, or even what the level of benefit is; it is how much a pensioner ends up with, when money from all sources is taken into account. In the same way, the impact of social security systems has to be understood in terms of what they actually deliver.

In the course of this Part, I have considered three issues which lend themselves to comparison: the level of expenditure, the impact on inequality and the impact on poverty. Table 27.1 shows some of the headline data from the OECD.[16]

All the countries listed begin by being more unequal, and taxes and transfers make them less unequal. It is noticeable, however, that the western European countries in Table 27.1 generally do more to reduce inequality than the English-speaking countries. Before transfers, the most unequal countries are France, Belgium, Germany and Italy; after transfers, two of those countries are among the most equal. The same pattern emerges in the figures for poverty reduction (predictably, because the measurement of poverty in terms of 'economic distance' is also basically a measurement of inequality). The countries that reduce poverty most effectively through taxes and transfers are Sweden, France and the Netherlands – all countries that rely heavily on earnings-related insurance benefits, supplemented by social assistance where appropriate. The UK follows close behind. It should be recognised, however, that using percentage points

---

[15]  L Rainwater, M Rein and J Schwartz (1986) *Income packaging in the welfare state*, Oxford: Oxford University Press.

[16]  Source: OECD, at http://stats.oecd.org/

**Table 27.1: The impact of taxes and transfers on poverty and inequality, mid-2000s**

| | Public social expenditure (minus health care) as a % of GDP (2005) | Inequality before tax and transfers (Gini coefficient) | Inequality before tax and transfers (Gini coefficient) | Poverty before tax and transfers (60% of median income) | Poverty after tax and transfers (60% of median income) |
|---|---|---|---|---|---|
| Australia | 11.2% | 0.46 | 0.3 | 32.6% | 20.3% |
| Belgium | 19.1% | 0.49 | 0.27 | 34.9% | 16.2% |
| Canada | 9.7% | 0.44 | 0.32 | na | 19% |
| France | 21.4% | 0.48 | 0.28 | 34.1% | 14.1% |
| Germany | 19.0% | 0.51 | 0.3 | 36.4% | 17.2% |
| Italy | 18.2% | 0.56 | 0.35 | 37.6% | 19.1% |
| Netherlands | 14.9% | 0.42 | 0.27 | 28.6% | 14.4% |
| New Zealand | 11.6% | 0.47 | 0.34 | 29.8% | 14.4% |
| Sweden | 13.5% | 0.43 | 0.23 | 29.8% | 11.4% |
| UK | 14.3% | 0.46 | 0.34 | 29.8% | 15.5% |
| US | 8.9% | 0.46 | 0.38 | 31% | 23.9% |

can be misleading – it also matters what the distribution of income is, what categories of people are poor and how great the gap is that has to be filled. Table 27.1 does not include expenditure on health care, but the impact of health care is worth a further note. In some countries, expenditure has to include payments that are unnecessary in others – for example, reimbursement for the payment of health care. By the same token, the cost of public health insurance does not feature in the UK accounts. The NHS is not just worth what people receive from it directly; it has a financial value equivalent to the cost of health insurance. Attributing an equivalent notional income to all households would have a substantial effect on many of the figures; it is likely that international comparisons consequently underestimate the extent of redistribution and poverty alleviation in the UK.

I have counselled caution about many of the figures used in the UK, and the same reservations apply even more strongly to generalisations that are made across different systems. Despite the considerable efforts made by the Luxembourg Income Study and other statisticians to ensure a basic comparability of data, there are always problems about interpretation, the accuracy of figures, the time frames they relate to and their significance in context. There is obviously a problem with the first column in the table, 'public social expenditure': what seems to get spent depends on how the accounts are kept. For example, the UK spends more on housing benefits than any other OECD country, which reflects a policy of increasing rents to a so-called market value where the 'market' is actually the product of the benefit rates.

## Policy transfer

There are good practical reasons for trying to compare welfare systems. Politicians and decision makers often compare their approaches to other countries, and try to draw lessons and models from them. Sometimes those lessons have been salutary: the confidence of British politicians in the Beveridge system was shaken by the realisation that the occupationally based, earnings-related systems used in continental Europe were more generous and more securely founded than pensions in Britain. There is often a suspicion, however, that the lessons that are being drawn are not well chosen. British politicians, decision makers and researchers tend by default to get evidence from other English-speaking countries before they look at the experience of their European partners.[17] Dolowitz's study of the foundation of the Child Support Agency explains that its origins 'are to be found in policy transfer from the United States and, to a lesser extent, Australia; and that inappropriate transfer from the US led to important implementation problems'.[18] The influence of the US is particularly marked: further examples include the Earned Income Tax Credit, which is the model for Tax Credits in the UK, and Workfare, which influenced 'welfare to work' policies.

By contrast, the influence of the more developed and sophisticated European systems seems to be less direct. The UK joined the European Union in 1972, and it might reasonably have been expected that the EU would have done much to shape the structure of benefits in Britain. It is debatable whether the influence has been stronger than that of the US. The strongest example of European influence has been the application of rules on gender equality – many of the legal cases have started in Britain. The British government successfully argued that the rules about gender equality should not apply to social security,[19] but it lost the same argument in relation to free prescriptions,[20] and eventually the government conceded that the only practical way forward was going to be to equalise pension

---

[17] See, for example, R Crisp and D Fletcher (2008) *A comparative review of workfare programmes in the United States, Canada and Australia,* London: Department for Work and Pensions; A Rangarajan, D Wittenburg, T Honeycutt and D Brucker (2008) *Programmes to promote employment for disabled people: Lessons from the United States,* London: Department for Work and Pensions; D Armstrong, Y Byrne, L Patton and S Horack (2009) *Welfare to work in the United States: New York's experience of the prime provider model,* London: Department for Work and Pensions.

[18] D Dolowitz (2000) *Policy transfer and British social policy: Learning from the USA?,* Buckingham: Open University Press, p 39.

[19] Case C-9/91, *R v Secretary of State for Social Security ex parte Equal Opportunities Commission* [1992] ECR I-4927, [1992] 3 CMLR 233.

[20] Case C-137/94, *R v Secretary of State for Health, ex parte Richardson* [1995] ECR I-3407 [1995] 3 CMLR 376.

ages.[21] Similarly, the rules for Invalid Care Allowance initially discriminated against married women, but the European Court forced the government to change the approach.[22] At the same time, this is a principle that also carries considerable weight in British society; EU rules have helped campaigners, but it is difficult to say that progress would not have been made without them.

The development of European Union policy in social security, as in most issues in social policy, has been strongly resisted by successive UK governments. For much of the 1980s and 1990s, the emphasis was on either on 'harmonisation', largely understood in terms consistent or common rules,[23] or 'convergence', which was taken to mean the acceptance of minimum standards. The EU recommended Europe-wide standards in its *Recommendation on common criteria concerning sufficient resources and social assistance in social protection systems*[24] and the *Recommendation on convergence of social protection objectives and policies*.[25] The UK government argued strongly for the recommendations to be watered down, and qualifications were added throughout to allow governments to take into account economic and social circumstances, or the needs of industry. The changes did not really make much difference, because the UK largely complied with the standards being laid out anyway.

The expansion of the EU and the use of a less structured (and largely ineffectual) approach, the 'Open Method of Coordination', means that the EU has done less in recent years to extend its influence on social security policy. Two key principles have gained ground. One is the idea of activation, developed in Denmark and extended to a range of countries including Germany, Poland, Ireland and the UK.[26] Activation, referred to in Chapter 20, combines a stress on improving labour market participation and entry with a degree of conditionality in the receipt of benefits for unemployed people. Unemployment insurance becomes

---

21 Department of Social Security (1991) *Options for equality in state pension age*, Cm 1723, London: HMSO.

22 Case 150/85, *Jacqueline Drake v Chief Adjudication Officer* [1986] ECR 1995, [1986] 3 CMLR 43.

23 P J Slot (1996) 'Harmonisation', *European Law Review*, vol 21, no 5, pp 378-97.

24 Council of the European Communities (1992) *Recommendation on common criteria concerning sufficient resources and social assistance in social protection systems*, OJ L 245/46, 26 August.

25 Council of the European Communities (1992) *Council recommendation on the convergence of social protection objectives and policies*, OJ L 245/49, 26 August.

26 N Gilbert and R van Voorhuis (eds) (2001) *Activating the unemployed*, New Brunswick, NJ: Transaction; S Wright (2002) 'Activating the unemployed: the street-level implementation of UK policy', in J Clasen (ed) *What future for social security?*, Bristol: The Policy Press.

less a matter of social protection or income smoothing, and more a means of promoting engagement in the labour market.[27]

The other is the principle of inclusion, derived from the French discourse on solidarity and exclusion. That principle, though considered in Chapter 21, has been only dimly reflected in UK policy, where the problem of exclusion has either been identified with the existence of an underclass in long-term poverty or, in Scotland, with urban regeneration. The idea of inclusion is not just something that is done to deviants; it is about extending networks of solidarity and support to those who otherwise would be left out. This takes in the development of opportunities to work, education, social facilities and participation in social life. The EU has now moved formally towards the promotion of 'active inclusion', a combination of the two principles. Active inclusion has three planks: adequate income support while unemployed, inclusive labour markets offering quality jobs and access to high-quality, 'comprehensive and coordinated' services.[28] It seems likely, as with previous recommendations, that the UK will agree the sentiments in principle, but that this will be deemed to have no practical implications for policy.

While it is important to be aware of developments in other countries, and open to new ideas, policies that are imitated from abroad are unlikely to have the same meaning, or to work the same way, as they do in another administration. It follows that the scope for transferring policies is modest – at least, if the policies are going to be appropriate in the situation where they are applied. If any policies are directly transferable, it is most likely to be seen in the specific rules applied in relation to particular kinds of benefit. I have referred to a few examples in passing, such as the possibility of assessing contributions on a quarterly rather than an annual basis, crediting benefits to children rather than to their parents, the creation of bank accounts to pay claimants or the payment and calculation of benefits on a monthly basis, slowing down both the frequency with which assessments have to be made and the rate of fluctuation in people's incomes. These approaches show that schemes can be delivered effectively in alternative ways, and that if there seem to be administrative problems, they can be overcome.

## QUESTIONS FOR DISCUSSION

What kind of welfare state is the UK?
Should policy in Britain follow policy in the United States?

---

[27] J Clasen and D Clegg (2006) 'Beyond activation', *European Societies*, vol 8, no 4, pp 527-53.

[28] European Commission (2008) *Commission recommendation of 3 October 2008 on the active inclusion of people excluded from the labour market (2008/867/EC)*, OJ L307/11, 18 November.

# Social security: a programme for reform

We do not need more 'vision'. Some of the worst mistakes in social security policy have been made because reforming governments had an idealised view of how things could be done, disregarded the practical constraints and steamed ahead even after the problems started to show. Examples include:

- the development of independent pensions schemes without arrangements for solidaristic protection (Chapter 15);
- the withdrawal of general housing subsidies in favour of Housing Benefit (Chapter 9);
- the management of Tax Credits on the basis of the tax year (Chapter 9);
- the individualisation of responses to unemployment (Chapter 20); and
- the importation of inappropriate models from abroad, such as Child Support (Chapter 27).

Many current proposals for welfare reform seem to me equally to misunderstand what social security benefits do and how they do it. This applies, for example, to:

- the supposition that the primary purpose of benefits is to promote work (Chapter 20) – or indeed, the assumption that benefits have any 'primary' purpose at all (Chapter 1);
- the belief that means testing is efficient (Chapters 8, 23);
- the assumption that testing needs rather than means avoids the problems of selectivity (Chapter 10);
- the hope that a unified system of taxes and benefits can resolve the administrative problems (Chapter 12);
- the misconception that lumping benefits or programmes together means that the system will be less complex (Chapter 6);
- the idea of 'personalising' benefits (Chapter 5); or
- proposals for a single working age benefit (Chapter 6) or Universal Credit (Chapter 12).

The arguments in this book point to a different kind of approach. There is considerable scope for practical reform, based on incremental improvements rather than a root and branch structural redesign.

*Reducing insecurity* The belief that benefits are capable of responding rapidly and precisely to changing circumstances for millions of people is misguided.

It underestimates the importance of unpredictable and insecure income to claimants, and the problems it causes for budgeting, transitions in and out of work and day-to-day living. Insecurity cannot be prevented altogether, because much of it is generated by conditions beyond the reach of social security, but it can be reduced by:

- extending the scope and value of less conditional benefits, like Child Benefit, which also help to stabilise the income of people during transitions (Chapter 12);
- slowing the rate of adjustment, standardising periods for payment and clarifying the relationship between benefits, by moving to monthly benefit payments (Chapter 14); and
- fixing benefit entitlements for six months or more, without requiring repayments when circumstances change (Chapter 9).

These prescriptions are precisely the opposite of what the government proposes to do in the design of Universal Credit.[1]

*Reducing complexity, error and administrative confusion* The room for manoeuvre is limited because the only way truly to simplify benefits without hurting recipients is to increase benefit rates to the point where fine adjustments no longer matter. The problems can at least be reduced by the measures above, and by:

- replacing some claims with automatic payments (Chapter 13);
- making the calculation of benefits independent from others (Chapter 14);
- seeking ways to establish benefits paid without reassessment over the long term (currently, this mainly applies to pensions); or
- ending transitional payments, by buying out rights (Chapter 14).

*Developing responses that relate better to people's experience* The income package, rather than the name on the benefit, is what matters most, but unless benefits are reasonably adapted to common contingencies, it is rarely clear why or on what terms people in different circumstances are likely to receive them. People with particular needs, stemming from circumstances like divorce, a return to education or a need for supported accommodation, cannot necessarily claim benefits specifically intended for their circumstances, so they have to claim something else. The effect is that benefits like Incapacity Benefit, Jobseeker's Allowance or Housing Benefit invariably finish by paying for an unexpectedly wide range of conditions, often stretching the role of the benefit to breaking point. It is not possible to specify every circumstance, but four are so common that it would make sense to redefine benefits to deal with them deliberately, instead of haphazardly. They are:

---

[1]    Cm 7913 (2010) *21st century welfare*, London: DWP; Cm 7957 (2010) *Universal Credit: Welfare that works*, London: DWP.

- long-term disability — a role not adequately met by incapacity benefits or Disability Living Allowance (Chapter 16);
- early retirement (Chapter 17);
- further and higher education; and
- social inclusion (Chapter 21).

*Building on successful administration*  The bane of social security policy has been the repeated attempts to replace systems that work with new approaches that may or may not deliver. The effect is visible in the transfer of Housing Benefit to local authorities (Chapter 9), the over-ambitious computerisation of the 1990s (Chapter 6), the imposition of inappropriate restraints on the staff of the Department for Work and Pensions (Chapter 13) or the inept privatisation of employability support (Chapter 20). We should value the competence and skill of DWP staff, and develop a professional structure for them.

There are, of course, many other ways that benefits could be improved. In a better world, benefits might be more generous — replacing most of a claimant's previous income, as they do in several European countries. They could be supplemented by a range of public services, for example in health, education, housing and social care, that could make some benefits unnecessary. If governments were committed to full employment, instead of leaving it to unemployed people to sort it out, many people who are currently claiming would have the opportunity of work instead. In the current climate, sadly, that is howling at the moon.

# Appendix

# Social security: sources of data

It has always been difficult to keep track of sources in social security, because the speed at which rules and structures change makes it difficult for conventional books (like this one) to keep up with the data. The statistical data on social security benefits tend to refer to a previous financial year (in 2011, that will usually be the year 2009-10); most books take nearly a year from final draft to publication, which means that any book will be two years behind, and by the time many readers see the book, three or four years will have passed. The position has been aggravated in recent years by two trends. One is the split between the Department for Work and Pensions and Her Majesty's Revenue and Customs – it is sometimes difficult to find figures on Tax Credits. The other is the retrospective rewriting of data by governments who are preparing new policies. In anticipation of the introduction of the Employment and Support Allowance, the figures for Incapacity Benefit have been reworked to present claims for Income Support, Severe Disablement Allowance and Incapacity Benefit together – that is why some sources talk about one and a half million claimants, while others talk about two and a half million.

## The rules relating to benefits

The best guide to specific rules is the long-running manual produced by the Child Poverty Action Group, the *Welfare benefits and tax credits handbook*. CPAG also produces a range of specific guides, including handbooks on:

- child support
- debt
- students
- young persons
- fuel rights
- personal finance
- Housing Benefit and Council Tax Benefit
- migration
- welfare to work.

In relation to disability, there is the Disability Alliance's *Disability rights handbook*. Sweet and Maxwell also publish a series of guides to the law under the name *Social security legislation*.

## Updating

CPAG produces a *Welfare rights bulletin*. Citizens' Advice produces *The adviser*, a relatively accessible publication covering benefits, consumer affairs, housing, debt and employment issues. There are online services for several of the CPAG publications, including child support, Housing Benefits and migrants. Newcastle Welfare Rights Service also hosts an invaluable service listing recent and forthcoming changes in benefit rules, at:

www.newcastle.gov.uk/core.nsf/a/wr_nav2_bennews?opendocument

## International information

Details of the pattern of social security provision in different countries is available from the website of the US Social Security Administration. They publish *Social security programs throughout the world* online at:

www.ssa.gov/policy/docs/progdesc/ssptw/

The International Social Security Association's Observatory, which prepares this information, has a searchable database at:

www.issa.int/Observatory/

## Sources of data

Most data are now available directly on the internet. The place to begin is not, unusually, the Office for National Statistics, but the Analytical Services Division of the DWP. They have an index of 'Benefit statistics A-Z' at:

http://statistics.dwp.gov.uk/asd/index.php?page=statistics_a_to_z

At the time of writing this site linked to nearly 70 specific sources on different benefits. Probably the best single source of material is the ONS's NOMIS system, which is not arrived at from the ONS site but at:

http://nomisweb.co.uk

This is presented as being about 'official labour market statistics'. An 'advanced query', however, gives access to a wide range of statistics about specific benefits.

## Summaries of data

The *Annual abstract of statistics* has a long-running series of tables covering key information, and the *Benefit expenditure tables* prepared by the Analytical Services Division offer useful numerical summaries over time. Despite the names, neither *Work and pensions statistics* (discontinued after 2004) nor *Statistical summaries* offers a basic summary of benefits.

## Labour market statistics

Statistics on the labour market are distinct from statistics on benefits, but they include much information that is relevant, as well as information about economic inactivity and coverage of several population groups. The NOMIS site has already been mentioned. There is a guide to labour market statistics on the Office for National Statistics site at:

www.ons.gov.uk/about-statistics/user-guidance/lm-guide/index.html

## HM Revenue & Customs data

This information is not as accessibly indexed as the Department for Work and Pensions material, and the HMRC website suffers from the common vice of frequently changing the location of files without redirecting users to the material they were looking for. *Child and Working Tax Credit statistics* should be available at:

www.hmrc.gov.uk/stats/personal-tax-credits/cwtc-quarterly-stats.htm

Child Benefit statistics have been a problem. After HMRC lost its Child Benefit data, the quarterly statistical series was suspended. At the time of writing, the last figures relate to 2007. They have promised to resume the sequence, and will catch up with figures for 2008 and 2009 in due course. However, some aggregate statistics, including the numbers of families and children claiming, are available along with the geographical distributions at:

www.hmrc.gov.uk/stats/child_benefit/geographical.htm

## Local data

The *Benefit expenditure tables* are broken down to local authority level, and NOMIS data go down to ward level. Other detailed, up-to-date information is available at local level through Neighbourhood Statistics:

www.neighbourhood.statistics.gov.uk/

and Scottish Neighbourhood Statistics:

www.sns.gov.uk

These sites are particularly helpful for local groups looking for indicators.

## COMPANION WEBSITE

A companion website, accessible via www.policypress.co.uk, provides regular updates to the material in this book and is suitable for lecturers and students.

# Index